SARAGOSA

The Town
Killed By A Tornado

Derwood Lane

EAKIN PRESS Fort Worth, Texas
www.EakinPress.com

Published By Eakin Press
An Imprint of Wild Horse Media Group
P.O. Box 331779
Fort Worth, Texas 76163
1-817-344-7036
www.EakinPress.com

Paperback ISBN 978-1-68179-397-9
Hardback ISBN 978-1-68179-398-6
eBook ISBN 978-1-68179-399-3

Cover photograph by Larry Jackson and courtesy *The Pecos Enterprise.*

Last night I had a dream. It was about my mom. I dreamed that I was at my home, and I was watching TV. My mom was in the kitchen making supper for me. I asked her what was for supper, and she said, "You will see when you start eating."

I asked my mom later, when I finished eating, "Are you going to go walking today?"

She answered, "Yes, and I want you to go with me, Jacob."

But I didn't want to go, and I told her so. She made me go with her anyway, and that was the end of my dream of my mom.

I think now about the times when I didn't want to go walking with my mom, who will never go walking anymore, and I say to myself, "What a fool I was!"

Jacob Sanchez, tornado victim,
From his student journal, September 22, 1987

Contents

Dedication and Acknowledgments

To the bewildered and grief-stricken people of Saragosa and Balmorhea who took us into their homes, their hearts, and their confidences, where we all stood as one upon the holy ground of their own painful and sacred memories . . .

To the hallowed memory of all our loved ones — the injured, the deceased, and the dispossessed — without whose incalculable losses and suffering there would never have been such a story . . .

To the nameless and numberless multitudes of caregivers, both nearby and far away, who were not disposed simply to hand over to God's mercy the problems at Saragosa, while they themselves offered no mercy of their own, but who felt the woe of their fellow man and rushed in to rescue him and to bear his burden, wearing the true badge of nobility . . .

To my wife Raquel, without whose tireless help in transversing language barriers, assisting in interviews, encouraging me on during numberless late-night vigils and in remembering names and details with a mind and heart that must surmount the memory bank of the finest computer; to her, without whose genius and caring this book would have assumed the stature of a task far too large for me ever to have completed alone . . .

To Miss Delilah Alvarez, a loyal friend who sacrificially devoted untold hours of her time to typing this manuscript, which must be saturated with distressing memories for her — in fact, typed on the very typewriter her beloved sister left behind when she and her husband lost their lives at Saragosa . . .

To these all — with so many faltering words, the small-change, the fallout, if you will, of a wealth of feeling, as well as an express train of thought forged in the fires of unexpected and challenging associations — this book, since it had to be written, is humbly and lovingly dedicated.

Preface

Here is a tragic story written for numerous reasons, and for each of those reasons, I had to write it. It is written for the millions of you who cared when stark tragedy struck and wiped out a tiny community of which most of you probably had never heard. But you demonstrated your human concerns when, in a horrendous moment of time, fellow human beings were mutilated either physically or emotionally, while countless others were left destitute and desolated with anguish. That beautiful empathy you evidenced with your prayers, with letters and telephone calls, with your selfless sacrifices of unbelievable amounts of donations of food, clothing, shelter, water, volunteer work, and funds beyond the reasonable call of duty — that interest assuredly entitles you to a complete and factual account of the Saragosa story.

As a disaster volunteer worker, I assisted others in receiving, sorting, and distributing some of those gifts of love from you wonderful people, far and wide. Since the news reports only partially enabled you to see what some of us saw, this story is one man's attempt to enable you to see more, to meet your beneficiaries, and to hear their stories. It is my conviction that you are entitled to that. When, on certain occasions, the media was restricted in their efforts to bring you the whole story, I experienced no small degree of indignation that there was no central coordinating authority to appoint responsible people to help handle matters so that everybody concerned could have come out a winner.

It was incumbent upon me, therefore, to write this story. I submit it as a record of remembrance of those who perished and for those who survived and suffered, whether maimed or heartbroken at the loss of loved ones, family, and friends. One family, close friends of mine, lost six close family members; others lost parents, children, brothers, sisters, cousins, aunts, uncles, grandparents.

The heartrending list is endless everywhere one turns for visits and interviews. This story, at best, can but poorly summarize the tragic story of the trauma suffered by so many.

Finally, I *needed* to write this account, which is a piece of me personally. Writing is great therapy. I have used it in counseling troubled students, and I employ a total writing approach to the teaching of English and literature. I believe in the message of one of my classroom posters: "No experience that you have is ever truly complete until you write about it."

So, I have written about it, and in the writing, learned some stern lessons of life — lessons that remain as enduring concerns. The ashes of one and a half million Polish Jews and other people lie in the site of the infamous concentration camp Midanek, in Poland. Above their remains is an inscription: "May our loss be a warning to you." It is with something of the same sense of loss that I felt constrained to urge our collective horror as a warning to a carefree population that tends to count disaster with indifference, skepticism, and ignorance. Out of our tragedy untold lives have been drawn together, knitted closer in the warm fabric of human love, understanding, tolerance for each other in our differences and in our mistakes, and made truly kindred in our mutual concern that each other succeeds, that every soul among us is a winner in life. That means happiness — true, unvarnished, unpretended happiness.

In one of Zane Grey's novels, a tough character who had experienced a great change of heart said, "If I had my life to live over, I would begin at once to find my joy in other people's happiness." We must not lose the closeness that has grown between us here. If anything good has resulted from this colossal tragedy, it has been the general growth in mutual love and caring in our communities.

What is more worthwhile? And yet, must it be so fragile that it so readily erodes away with time and distance and with our selfish preoccupation with temporal things? "What is essential is invisible to the eye," wrote Antoine de Saint Exupery. Material things canker and corrode, and set men at each other's throats, whereas unadulterated love edifies both the person who loves and all those upon whom he bestows it. In all of its expressions, genuine human love always remains fresh and young, though it matures and grows ever more beautiful with the swift passage of time.

Introduction:
A Lingering Need

Behind the scenes of the Saragosa, Texas, tornado disaster, and behind the faces of those unfortunate people victimized by it, there is a maze of frantic human concerns, of fervent human lives disrupted, and of broken hearts refusing to be rehabilitated. Each and every family has its story of stark tragedy, or of grim adventure, or both. As time goes by, the keen recollection of details will tend to fade, and will be all but wholly lost in another generation or so when the death of Saragosa becomes a half-forgotten fragment of history. The lessons and warnings of this devastation should never be lost upon society.

Who of us today remembers the explosion of the New London, Texas, school that wiped out 387 students and school personnel in 1937? Who still recalls the horrendous Texas City disaster of April 16 and 17, 1947, when a staggering 567 people died, along with a toll of 3,000 injured and 2,500 left destitute and homeless? Who, other than a relative few, even cares anymore?

One of my concerns has been to chronicle the vivid details of the various misadventures of the people who were there, of some who were near, and of a representative number of those who responded to human disaster and came to lend a helping hand. This has not been an easy task. A great number of personal interviews with victims and their families required incessant travel, but more difficult than that, the opening up of painfully sensitive wounds in order to gather the actual facts in each person's story. Without a single exception, those interviewed have been cooperative and helpful in the extreme, and without their kind assistance this narrative could never have been written with the volume of details and the depth of pathos that it bears.

The story proved to be a gigantic jigsaw puzzle, a complicated mosaic of many separate and complex parts. My goal has been, first, to mull through and sort out the relevant pieces of the complex riddle, then to mesh them together into an accurately integrated gestalt whose whole is greater than the sum of all its separate parts. Each chapter is a complete episode within itself, yet the sum of them all forms the total diamond, composed of many facets, each replete with its own unity, wholeness, and integrity.

A few ambiguities, seeming inconsistencies, have puzzled us, but what has amazed me is that there have not been outright contradictory stories. When apparent inconsistencies have occurred, they have withered away under the searchlight of dogged perseverance. Once all the information was compiled, there was always something there that served to harmonize such seeming conflicts.

This pursuit of accuracy in reporting has been rewarding. If any later documentation exposes the slightest error or fault in my recounting of this grim and tragic story, the error will be sincerely and appreciatively acknowledged. Reports have been made in all honesty, but there stands the ever-present possibility of human error, especially under the stresses that commonly surround disaster climates.

The separate segments of this story grew and came together, each one another treasured bead added to the growing string making up our narrative. Scores of beautiful people became far more than faceless names. They became, through our close association, warm, fellow human beings needing encouragement, companionship, understanding, and desperately needing human love.

My wife and I count it all joy to have been blessed with the opportunity, in some small way, to have cared and shared as we did, in our hearts, right along with the many, many others who did the same. We have seen human need for love, expressed in compassion, empathy, and caring, met in countless beautiful and effective ways.

This need lingers, not alone in Saragosa, Texas, today, but with all people in every place throughout the world. Why must it take a cruel disaster to waken us to such ever-present and universal needs of our fellow men? And why must we forget so soon — or ever?

PART I
The Storm

[1]

"Tommy, You've Gotta See This!"

TORNADO! SARAGOSA DESTROYED! Those were the headlines following the May 22, 1987, storm that wiped a small West Texas town off the map. Thirty lives were lost, and one hundred twenty-one injured survivors were hospitalized. Those people were student friends of mine, members of their families, and other citizens of the community of Saragosa and her sister community, Balmorhea, Texas.

I teach high school English and art in Balmorhea, which is located a mere eight miles southwest of Saragosa. Students of Saragosa attend the Balmorhea school where I teach. The two towns are as one family, almost everyone in both towns being related either by birth or marriage. Thus it was that students, their families, and others of my friends were directly affected by the storm, and I, by them.

An excerpt from my journal, under date of June 6, begins as follows: "The events of the past week and a half have paralyzed thousands of hearts in horror and shock, and have left scores of us numb with fatigue. The whole country has been in a state of shock while rallying beautifully to the aid of the grieving and destitute survivors of one of the worst tornadoes in Texas history."

It all began for me on that Friday afternoon at 3:30 P.M. when the last bell rang, dismissing the final classes of that day and of the thirty-fifth week of the school year. One week of the school year was left to go. The next week would wrap it all up with final exams for most students.

Students in my high school English classes had been assigned two dozen or more biographical summaries of the lives of our great authors. These resumes of the lives of notable writers were to have been written as entries in their journals and were to serve as their semester exams. These journals were due that Friday so that I might read and grade them over the coming weekend.

The students' journals had piled up before me during the day as classes came and went. A few students, having not quite finished their work, asked if they might bring their assignments in at the end of the day, or on the weekend. I had acceded to their requests.

About a year and a half before, Simone Contreras, our head custodian at school and a close friend of mine, had died one day at school from a heart attack. Mrs. Olivia Contreras, his wife, left without any means of financial support, had been given a custodial job at our elementary school. She, like her gracious husband, had endeared herself to the hearts of all the personnel at our school.

Balmorhea, Texas, is a very small town with no banking facility. Most of the townspeople do their banking in Pecos, which is thirty-seven miles to the north. Mrs. Olivia Contreras almost always drove into Pecos after school on Fridays to do grocery shopping at the supermarkets for her family. On payday Fridays, she also went to the First National Bank to deposit her paycheck. It had been her custom for months to do me the favor of taking my salary check along and depositing it for me while she was in the bank.

When the 3:30 P.M. bell rang at school that afternoon, I walked down the long hallway to the opposite end of the buildings complex, where I could see Olivia Contreras, my friend, putting the final touches to her work for the day. "I have my check here, all ready for you to deposit for me at the bank, if you don't mind," I said as I approached her.

Olivia Contreras was a lovely lady, the living essence of courtesy and Christian grace. "Oh, Mr. Lane, I am so very sorry, but I won't be going into Pecos this evening. You see, I plan to attend the graduation program in Saragosa tonight."

"Graduation? I didn't know about a graduation . . ." I began.

"It's the little kids, sir . . . you know, the Head Start program. They are having their graduation, and my sister has two children in the program. She asked me to go, and so I am. That's why I won't be going to Pecos. I'm so sorry, Mr. Lane."

I thanked her, wished her a pleasant weekend, and expressed hope that she might enjoy the graduation program. Less than five hours later, this sweet lady would be dead.

Upon returning to my classroom, I noticed that on the top of a stack of spiral notebooks a note was taped. While I was seeing Olivia Contreras, a tenth-grade student, Kathy Escovedo, had come to my room with her journal. Finding me gone, she had taken a sheet from my "Period Absentees" report pad and on the back of it penned a note: "Here is my assignment. Love Ya — Kathy."

That was in all probability the last thing this adorable sophomore girl ever wrote in this world. In less than five hours she would pass from this life into eternity. I would look upon her lifeless body in that dark sea of rubble left in the black wake of the Saragosa tornado that night.

I was extremely tired that Friday afternoon, and, instead of staying at school to work on my mountain of compositions, as was my custom, I walked to my house, less than a half-block from my classroom. My wife Raquel had gone to Fort Stockton with a teacher friend, Betty Hopper; they left right after school on some matters of business. I settled down on our divan, anticipating an evening of pleasant solitude and relaxation. It had been a long, fatiguing school year, and there remained only one week to go. Perhaps I would turn in early and enjoy some much-needed sleep. What an idle dream that would prove to be!

I ate a light snack and then reclined again on the living room divan, switched to the television news channel, and promptly fell asleep. While I reclined there, deeply and blissfully adrift in the evanescent sea of the subconscious, a dim, distant jangling pierced my ear. Involuntarily I sprang up and was halfway to the phone when my feet found the floor, bent on throttling the jarring jangle of the telephone. I glanced up at the clock, making a mental note of the hour. It was 6:00.

In response to my sleepy "Hello," I heard a cheery, "Mr. Lane . . . this is Tommy! Would you like to come over and eat with Ike and me? I'm fixin' fried chicken, potatoes 'n gravy, green beans, and —"

"Tommy, you're a pal," I interrupted, "and I appreciate this, but I ate a snack earlier, and I'm really not hungry."

"That's okay. Come on anyway. Surely you can eat a piece of chicken and have some tea with us," Tommy Ward insisted. He was a great giant of a man, warm of heart, generous to a fault, and a good friend. He and his brother Ike Ward had lived alone in a rambling rock house on the east edge of town since the vicissitudes of life and the erosion of time had, in part, disintegrated and scattered his family after his mother's death seven years ago. Tommy Ward had learned some fine culinary arts out of the need to survive, and had become an accomplished cook in the process. My mind wheeled back to numerous well-remembered repasts we had shared before.

"What time, Tommy?" I wondered, torn between the urge to return to my nap and to go for a second supper.

"Oh, about seven. I'll expect you . . ."

I went, eager to be out of the empty house now that I was fully awake, always glad to enjoy the companionship of my friend, another school custodian of whom my fondness had grown over the eight years I had taught at Balmorhea.

When I arrived at the Ward home just minutes after 7:00 P.M., two things commanded my attention. There was a tremendous dark cloud lying to the north and east of us. It seemed alive, restless, ominous and threatening, although it was some distance away. The other matter that captured my interest and aroused my curiosity was the news bulletin that was being aired on Channel 9 television from Midland/Odessa.

"A very large and potentially dangerous thunderstorm is now centered about fifteen miles south of Pecos," the voice went on, edged with a suggestion of danger. "Thunderstorm Warning" showed across the lower part of the screen. Thunder rumbled in the distance as infrequent flashes of lightning made themselves known.

"Tommy, don't you think we ought to disconnect the TV set, what with all this storm brewing?" I asked. He agreed, and I pulled the plugs. I glanced at the clock on the wall nearby: 7:10 P.M.

I had been reared in Central Texas, which is in tornado country. I had watched them form and pass on several occasions before. All nature had long been my love, my interest, my companion, and weather had long been my fascination. "I'm going outside to watch this cloud," I tossed at Tommy as I marched through the kitchen where he was at work.

The cloud was oriented in a great circular mass. Its southwest-most periphery was directly above my head. The circulation of the cloud was a negative one — counterclockwise. "Tommy," I called, awed little boy that I was, "come and have a look!"

He left his dinner preparations for a momentary glance upward and a passing comment. Within this huge house of flesh lives a genial, often boisterous, man who would prefer tending his dinner than cloud-gazing, and so he hastily returned to his chicken-frying inside. For him, happiness was born a twin, its simplest joys to be shared. His joy that night was in preparing and sharing his delicious fried chicken, cooked to a golden brown perfection. The child in me likewise regarded happiness as a twin that must be shared, but the joy in which I now exulted (with perhaps a tinge of fear) lay in that frowning cloud gathering strength resolutely and majestically before me. To share my awesome cloud, I called to Tommy and Ike several times during the next twenty minutes or so, urging them to come outside and take a look.

As my eyes roved the heavens, I noted several remarkable phenomena consorting together to set the stage for coming events. The gigantic, circular cloud was a large wagon wheel rotating from north to south and bending to the southeast as it passed overhead, making its great, gentle turn. According to the television report, we were about twenty miles from its center, giving the cloud about a forty-mile diameter if its circle was not a distorted one. That ominous negative flow meant to me an intense localized low-pressure cell.

While far from being a meteorologist, I possessed some knowledge of weather phenomena gleaned from experience and observation. Knowledge means awareness to me, and there are many paths that lead to it. Some are paved with formal education, some are not. Some may even defy logic. At times a sensitive person may be guided by sheer intuition. Was I being led to a strange, sinister awareness by something felt in the wind, something out of the wastelands of my experience and subconscious self that remembered? What grim drama was about to be staged in that cloud colossus towering above me, dwarfing the land?

The sky had been, and still was, fair off to the west toward the Davis Mountains, where sunshine still lay along their slopes. The air was clear, and the day had gone by like the silent, purposeful drifting clouds until I had scarcely noticed its passing. I am one to listen, learn, and say nothing, but as I thrilled in the presence of that grim, towering thing, I had to say something. I could not hold my peace.

"Tommy, you've gotta come out here and see this," I kept telling him. Each time he glanced out and went back to his cooking, leaving me alone before the dark-visaged, threatening sky.

Outside this vast wheel of storm there were fingers of scud rushing headlong from all points of the compass toward the center of that great cloud. It was building, growing, sucking up all the atmospheric forces of a wide region into its vortex. Being an artist, I am accustomed to seeing "everything." The multiphasic weather phenomenon of that great cloud held me spellbound, thrilled — but concerned.

During the next few minutes, I observed to the north, just beyond Toya Creek, a strangely behaving appendage to my weather wheel. The wild wall cloud, extending like a finger, or with more the aspect of a gigantic saw blade, being jagged at the bottom and thrusting very rapidly out from the edge of the circulating cloud wheel, was moving fast and forcibly toward me. It was strung out westwardly along the creek and moving rapidly my way. Other cloud fragments were boiling furiously, like a handful of leaves tossed into a cauldron of vigorously boiling water. All the cloud elements were growing more feverously agitated by the second. The shredded cloud fragments tore at each other like a pen full of cocks in a pitched fight, feathers flying in all directions.

The great flywheel, circulating remorselessly on, brought with it the wild appendage, careening and bearing down like a great flock of birds wheeling in a tight turn, hurtling at me until I had the distinct frightening feeling of being engulfed. Rain spattered down, and I backed through the screen door, my eyes glued upon the now advancing ripsaw about to strike. Hail chattered on the roof, then commenced thudding down, a scattering of the hailstones the size of golf balls, or larger. The capricious onslought was brief, gone in a minute or two.

Fascinated by the scattered hunks of hail out in the yard, I ran out and scooped up a few to show to my friend, who, by now, was taking dinner from the stove. We remarked on their outlandish size and novelty, and I suggested we toss them into the deepfreeze so that we might preserve them.

After another five minutes or so, I saw what appeared to be even larger hailstones farther out from the house. I ran out and gathered a handful of real "prize-winners" in size, and glanced up for a moment, then stared in utter amazement.

Either the wild cloud formation had gathered fanatical fury or it had passed from view, but there was now a cloud wilder in appearance than the former, about a mile to the east of where I watched. Once again, I called to my poor friend, Tommy Ward, who was trying desperately to complete dinner despite all of my interruptions. "Hey, Tom, you've gotta see this!" I shouted.

Just about a mile to the east of us was the wildest cloud I had ever witnessed in my life. What a magnificent but frightening sight it became as its shredded elements wheeled loosely but angrily this way and that. A wild, cyclonic disturbance was already taking place as it circulated with the main traffic flow of the greater cloud pinwheeling toward the southeast. That terrible assemblage of cloud tatters was being drawn more tightly into the greater mass, tightening the turn of circulation. It appeared to be hang-gliding about a mile to the east of Balmorhea, somewhere near and to the south of the Carrasco Mercantile store, out toward the interstate.

As Tommy and I watched, we saw one dark shred of cloud, shaped roughly like a man's pocket comb, shooting vertically, straight up into the dark evening sky much like a rocket ship launching into broken clouds at Cape Canaveral. This wild thing appeared to be climbing at the rate of a hundred miles per hour. Other such cloud shreds were racing in eccentric, and even opposing, movements of circulation, much as the leaves of October cascading in a golden storm, swirling and boiling downward.

"Mark my word, Tommy, that cloud is spawning a tornado!" I announced with conviction and feeling, continuing, "We will hear from this one!"

The curtain of mist and rain began to dim our view of the highly agitated cloud phenomenon as it plowed deeper into the mass of the parent cloud, penetrated the gigantic wheel, and moved eastwardly toward the interstate highway. Tommy insisted that we'd better go inside and eat. We did.

Moments later I heard a distant rumble and went outside once more. The phone had but moments earlier rung, and Ike Ward left without eating.

I yelled excitedly to Tommy to join me outside. "Listen to that!" I practically shouted, excitement tinged with fright in my voice. "Hear that sound . . . like a train roaring through the dusk? That's a tornado as sure as anything! I know that sound, Tommy, and there are no railroads around here. That's a tornado — a big one for sure!" I felt drained, exhausted, helpless with a forboding of disaster. The sound seemed to us to be traveling northward — it was.

We had just begun to eat when the lights winked out everywhere. Tommy and I sat in the growing dusk. Then he arose and lighted a candle in the center of the dining table. The time was frozen on the wall clock's face at 8:20 P.M. We commented facetiously then about our candlelight dinner. The roaring of that "train" had stopped now, and in another moment a siren wailed. A high-speed emergency vehicle of some sort was roaring through town on Highway 290, a mere hundred yards away. Another roared past. Then another. We looked at each other with wonder and worry then went on with our meal, scarcely reassured or tasting what we ate.

"Where did Ike go?" I asked Tommy.

"With the storm brewing, I guess he went to blow the siren down at city hall," he replied.

I quipped, "He will have a hard time doing that with all the electricity shut down." We laughed a bit nervously at that.

Moments later, a neighbor youth, Jason Jones, appeared at the door, eyes wide with excitement and possibly a trace of terror. "We just got the word: Saragosa has just been hit by a tornado. It struck the Community Center where the Head Start program was being held. There are lots of casualties. They are calling for help . . . volunteers, vehicles, blankets . . ."

"Let's go, Tommy," I grated, as the names and faces of people I knew and loved flashed across my mind. "Oh, God, how horrible!"

Then our nightmare really began, a nightmare that will go on for a long, long time. We scarcely dreamed of the devastation we soon would see — a town leveled, friends victimized by the scores, some dead, others dying, many injured. I remember mumbling hopes that the strike was a minor one, and that people escaped with nothing more than fright and a few scratches and bruises. I was in for a rude awakening.

In moments my car was racing out of town on old U.S. 290 and mounting a ramp onto Interstate 10. Four miles to the east we glided off onto the State Highway 17 exit. We observed in our passing that a huge highway marker was down, snapped off of its supporting steel posts. There were some trees dismembered too. My mind told me that the funnel must have made its initial contact with the ground at this place. Foliage pointed to the north, toward Saragosa, three miles away in the impenetrable blackness of the night.

As we left the interstate, we began seeing winking lights like happy fireflies far away, flitting about in the murk of a black night. Emergency vehicles ahead . . . at Saragosa. Astounding! How did they converge on the town so quickly? We wondered, amazed.

About a mile and a half from the site of the devastation we began to see downed power lines on our left along the roadway. Unroofed buildings were barely discernible, silhouetted in the dark to our right. Traffic already had backed up for over a mile. That was too far for us to walk or to run in the darkness where debris was strewn everywhere.

"Let's go back to the farm-to-market road, Tom, and go into Saragosa by the back way," I suggested as I swung the car around, threading between already stopped and arriving automobiles. In less than five minutes we found ourselves approaching the lightless town from the southwest.

Things looked all right at first. A row of houses was situated on the left of the road, lined up like soldiers for inspection. They looked perfectly normal to me, ignoring the fact that no lights burned within any of them. I was beginning to breathe a small sigh of relief, but in moments we rounded a curve where the roadway bends eastward toward Highway 17 and threads through the main part of town. The night was impenetrable but for the vague clumps of trees here and there. We had now come about two blocks, and suddenly there were no houses anymore — besides the wrecked mobile home which lay directly in our path, across the road. There could be no further traveling except on foot. The street was completely blocked by the mobile home. Two or three automobiles had already arrived ahead of us and parked off the pavement on the soggy shoulders of the roadway. The body of an elderly lady lay wrapped in a blanket beside the wreckage of her mobile home.

From that point onward, we saw nothing but sheer and complete devastation which prevailed upon all sides. The tornado had leveled the entire town except for those few houses lined up in the darkness behind us. Mr. Ward and I made our tedious way on foot, crawling under or climbing over debris and cables swinging or stretched across the vaguely visible roadway. In a very short distance we met and recognized two of my student friends from Balmorhea.

Adrienne Chance, a junior, recognizing me, blurted out, "Oh, Mr. Lane, it's awful! Kathy is dead, so is Brenda, and —"

"Oh, my God!" I breathed, interrupting her, and hurried on, not waiting or daring to hear any more.

At the intersection of the main highway and the road we had traveled, there was a beehive of activity under a hastily erected cluster of emergency lights glaring defiantly into the encroaching obscurity of nightfall. This was the site of the now-demolished old Roman Catholic Church building, which had, in recent years, been used as the Saragosa Community Center. The roof and walls had fallen in on the crowd gathered for the Head Start program, and there, prostrate before us, was a scene of devastation and death that defied description and comprehension. A penumbra of horror lay about us, stark testimony of the devastation of a storm possessing the power of a cataclysm.

So many people were working in that wasteland of rubble, searching for bodies, that my friend and I at once knew the futility of our joining them. We could do nothing but stand in the way of effective progress, and so it was that we took our stance where a growing crowd of anxious people stood. We watched that army of rescue workers as they seemed to sink, one here, one there, like sea divers going down into the depths of their uncertain element. Here and there one would surface with a misshapen mass of mortar, or a human body as misshapen, which would be brought grimly but triumphantly out.

Looking about and searching the taut, eager faces of my students, I made cautious inquiries. Almost all of them were in a state of near shock, answering my questions absent-mindedly, or not at all, looking at or through me, some seemingly not seeing at all. Words cannot express how utterly helpless I felt during this nightmare of anxiety and horror. I found myself consumed with the hope that I might be of some comfort to somebody, although I doubted the possibility of such a thing happening that night.

And so we stood, and watched, and waited, huddled there. The vast reserve of surrounding darkness extended like a tight noose about us on all sides, and stretched out from there to eternity. Most of all, I guess, we hoped — hoped as desperate men at one time or another have been forced to do. As we hoped, we lived through an eon of expectancy. I doubt not that all of those shattered souls huddled here and there, numbly and anxiously watching the rescue operations, sensed with me that we were already sitting up with the dead.

Suddenly, a man, grave of face, eyes portraying intense concern, stood beside us as if he had suddenly materialized out of thin air. He kept peering at the tangled mound of masonry that had, until tonight, been the Community Center, but now grimly entombed scores of dead, dying, and living, but trapped, victims. He followed with anxious eyes the stout-hearted men and women as they scurried here and there under the glare of harsh lights. As I watched this man and the workers, it was as if we had crossed together some strange border of the familiar world of reality into an uncertain and forbidden world from which it would likely be infinitely difficult, if not absolutely impossible, to return.

As we watched, men went right on probing for bodies, listening for cries somewhere beneath their feet, cries covered and muffled under tons of collapsed rubble. As moans were pinpointed, mass efforts were made to reach them. Some people were brought to the surface, critically injured; others had only minor injuries, saved by the heroic dead, who, in their final acts of dying, flung their bodies as shields upon the others, enduring themselves the fatal blows, giving their own lives sacrificially in a split-second impulse of love, to the noble impulse that someone else might live. I think of the words of Epicurus: "The art of living well and of dying well are one."

I turned to Javier Lozano, the man beside me, and asked him whether he had been in the storm.

He tore his eyes from the stony tablelands where determined men drove themselves in a fever of desperation. "I saw it coming, and I drove as fast as I could to this building. My boy was in the graduation program, and my wife was there too. I raced into the building with the funnel not far behind me. I ran down to the front and grabbed my boy under my arm, and then raced for the front door. All the time I was yelling, 'Tornado! A tornado is coming!' Everybody in that place panicked. They all went wild. I did not see my wife, and there was no time to hunt for her. I ran with my boy to my car and raced away just before it hit. He's okay, but my wife . . . I haven't seen her yet, and I don't know how she is. There is her car," he pointed at one of the smashed automobiles in the parking lot thirty feet away, "all demolished. I don't know anything about her! I just came back from racing from that storm."

I expressed to him my gratitude to God that he was able to rescue his son, but how does one comfort a neighbor in such an uncertain and agonizing hour? I later learned that Mrs. Lozano survived the horror of the storm and the collapse of that structure that had killed and injured so many people only a few minutes before.

Law officers were everywhere, directing, helping, or watching. Several were in the Community Center rubble, sweating beside a complete cross-section of community members from Pecos, Balmorhea, and other nearby villages and towns. Under the glare of portable lights rigged above vehicles, volunteer rescue workers dug out fifteen bodies, along with a growing number of injured, from the rubble during the first hours of the feverish search. High-lift jacks, picks, backhoes, a front-end loader, and bare human hands probed through the debris right on through the night. Midst the incessant clatter of mounds of broken masonry being moved by a front-end loader, my ears were hearing the sounds of crashing brittle pottery or pavement. While I watched, the intrepid army of rescuers, with the obstinancy of an army of ants, dug on.

As I waited near a group of high school students huddled and watching, the justice of the peace, Rosendo Carrasco, came stumbling out of the rubble. He grasped his son Sammy, a high school senior, by the shoulders, and looked him straight in the eyes. "Sammy," he began slowly, tenderly, "it is official . . . Kathy is dead!" Arturo, Kathy Escovedo's brother, standing there, broke down. Then everyone else seemed to burst into tears simultaneously. Students fell into each other's arms in a brief burst of emotion, as if the lives of each of them, in that moment of mass trauma, sank into quicksand together.

Kathy Escovedo had for years been Sammy Carrasco's girlfriend. She was one of my dearest friends, and one of my most dedicated students. She had come to my room that afternoon to leave her assignment, and had missed me by a minute or so. She was a lovely young lady and a beautiful person, a kid sister to me. I had known her for eight of her sixteen years. As a daily routine, Kathy would come to my classroom and hug me before our class began. For years I have taught my students the great human need we all share for loving, caring, sharing, and expressing that love with positive strokes. I have long drilled into them that "love unexpressed is love unknown." Kathy Escovedo had learned her lessons of love very well. Not only did she love people — all people, it seemed —

but she held communion with tranquil pastures, with birds, flowers, and butterflies, with trees and fallen leaves. Kathy loved all nature. She had practiced the art of expressing love in the most beautiful and artful ways. There was no doubt that she loved God above, and now she had gone to Him, gathered up into His loving and eternal arms.

I had taught in her class a course in writing poetry only a short time before her tragic death. Kathy wrote a beautiful poem in memory of Robert Frost, whom she loved and admired, especially for his poems depicting nature. I hadn't the faintest dream that I would shortly be writing a poem in memory of her. This is her memorial to her beloved Robert Frost:

Thank You Note
To Robert Frost

My dear, dear friend, Poet Robert Frost,
Thank you for all you wrote . . .
For all the beauty shared with me,
I pen this Thank You note.

Thank you for all the autumn leaves
From a new point of view:
I see them in a different way
With gratitude to you.

And now a question comes to mind;
I wonder, since you went away,
If you are busy writing still
Such poetry in heaven today.

Kathy Escovedo
10th English
April 8, 1987

[2]

The Unidentified Girl

After some time several officers came running down the highway from the direction of the north part of town. At first I heard shouts, then saw waving flashlights as they emerged from the curtain of darkness into the area of uncertain light cast by the emergency lights nearby. The officers called for help, for volunteers to fan out and search the demolished town for others out there who might be dead or dying. Survivors themselves had initially located a few bodies, had covered them and left them to be carried out later. Since there was no helping them now, all efforts had been directed at the demolished Community Center in order to rescue the injured there. A more systematic search was now about to be launched.

Impulsively, I ran after those waving flashlights. Near the north side of town we broke into several groups of four or five, each led by an officer armed with a flashlight. As we fanned out in our search, I found myself following Floyd Estrada, our local deputy sheriff.

We soon found the necessity of moving most cautiously. Shredded lumber with dangerous nails was scattered everywhere. Automobiles were battered, bashed, and thrown in heaps here and there. Debris of every conceivable description — sharp, pointed, jagged, and frightfully dangerous — was encountered every way one turned. On several occasions I was forced to call to Mr. Estrada to point his light my way so that I might see how to extricate myself from the horns of some implacable dilemma.

We crept cautiously onward in the obscurity of that weird wasteland. One had to force his mind to concentrate upon the grim task at hand. If "fear has the largest eyes of all," as Boris Pasternak once wrote, then we must have picked and probed our way with eyes wide that night. Ours were not so wide from fear of any harm to ourselves as for dread of what or who we might find. We stopped at every rubble heap that had once been somebody's home, and we stood in mute silence there, looking and listening. I suppose that one question burned into every brain among us: "Is there somebody trapped under this mound of wreckage?" We listened with intent, straining ears at each devastated homesite, but we heard nothing. One was torn between being thankful that there was no sound indicating another injured, and being fearful that we could not hear the cry of some unfortunate victim. We moved quietly and expectantly.

The uncertain bleating of a bewildered goat once drew us aside to investigate, and having made our find, to pass on, dark silhouettes in the murky night.

There was a commotion just ahead of me in the blackness. Floyd was thirty or more paces ahead, and I was struggling against an amorphous mountain of debris in the darkness. I recognized the deputy's voice and struggled toward it. Suddenly, I saw the reflection of his flashlight showing indistinctly beyond the wrecked building before me.

"Floyd, what is it?" I called as I finally approached within conversational range.

"Erica," he grated out with tense resignation.

I caught a glimpse of the face of a young girl as the flashlight wavered, swinging about. Stunned, I hurried to his side. "Erica? Floyd, are you sure?"

He turned the light upon her fair face then, and whipped some sort of clean cloth covering from her recumbent form. "It's Erica, all right!" he affirmed with some finality.

I bent closely, my face but a foot or so from hers; then I straightened and took in her entire form from head to foot. I shook my head and my voice could not bring itself to affirm his identification. She wore a beautiful, very feminine dress, edged in lace and ruffles. Strangely, the dress was fresh and clean. She was a very pretty girl, indeed, but not one whom I could with certainty recognize. I was convinced that she was not Erica Lopez, Floyd's niece. If anyone should know, however, he should, and I did not think it appropriate to argue the girl's identity.

With uncertainty in my heart, I said to him as I held my gaze, steady upon that sweet, damaged face, "Floyd, I don't know who she is, but she surely doesn't look like Erica to me."

The body structure was more that of Erica's older sister Elizabeth, a high school senior. Both girls were students in my classes at Balmorhea High School, and neither seemed to be this girl.

"It's Erica," he persisted, penetrating my uncertain musings. He covered her once again, and we moved off into the darkness, leaving her there alone.

"Where are we, Floyd?" I asked him.

"We're at the site where the Lopez home stood," he declared. He had led us to the wrecked home of his wife's brother's family. That made sense. Floyd would, of course, want to make a personal search, and it was natural that he would think the dead girl was one of the Lopez sisters. They were a large and lovely family of four daughters and one son. The son, Raul Lopez, just home from Texas State Technical Institute (TSTI) in Sweetwater, Texas, had already been removed to a hospital earlier that night, a fact I didn't know at that time.

A few yards away from the house site, Floyd announced in the darkness ahead of me, "Here's Raul's red Camaro—what's left of it!"

I rushed over, and we surrounded the upside-down squashed automobile, which I recognized. I had helped Raul to obtain admission and a grant to TSTI and had seen him in that red Camaro just before he left for school the previous fall. Eyes now intent upon every detail, I spotted a light down deep somewhere inside the smashed auto. "Hey, there's a light burning down in there!" I exclaimed, and the other fellows gathered in a cluster to have a look.

Floyd came around and peered down into the bowels of the wreckage. "Sure is," he agreed. "It's possible somebody is in there." My heart skipped a beat as I realized I might be standing upon the threshold of some grim discovery.

We grouped on one side of the overturned auto and lifted, but we could not budge it. A piece of metal was found and used to pry open one of the upside-down doors. A quick glance revealed to us that the Camaro was empty. We moved on, relieved. But I wondered about Raul, the driver. What had happened? Where was he now? I was destined to hear much in answer to those questions before the complete story of the tornado was told to me in coming weeks.

Our search was soon augmented by a group of Balmorhea firemen and their firetruck. James Garlick was there, and I joined him on the truck as it picked its meticulous way forward, slow as a turtle.

We found no more bodies, and in time reached the westmost edge of the settlement. Whimpers of injured dogs were heard coming from one badly wrecked house to our left. The pets were victimized by the tornado as were their unknown and absent owners, because our search turned up nobody in the almost totally dismantled house. Someone asked what should be done about the animals in agony, and we all agreed that they should be put out of their misery. Several gunshots shattered the quiet of the late hour, ending the whimpers and moans of the piteous animals.

"Where are we?" someone asked.

I looked carefully about, studying the land features, noting the driveway in particular. Suddenly, recognition dawned. "This is the Ramirez residence, the home of Frank and Natividad Ramirez. Three of their children, Alex, Regina, and Rene have been in my classes, and I visited here before." The family also included two younger children, Ramiro, who had been taught by Raquel, my wife; then there was the youngest of all, sweet little Rose Ann. I kept wondering where they all were. Had they escaped the storm, or . . .? I refused to make any further conjecture. A specter of horror intimidated my mind, pondering the alternatives, and so it turned to other matters.

As if reading my thoughts, someone nearby in the darkness observed, "Their house sure got smashed up; perhaps they were away . . ."

That gaping wreck that had been the Ramirez family's home concerned me but little now. It was beyond human helping. My hopes for the well-being of these dear people, whom I long had known and loved, possessed my heart as we turned our backs on the wreckage of their home and moved out into the darkness once more.

We were at the back side of a devastated town, killed by a malevolent tornado. There was no need to hurry now, and so we rested like troops on bivouac at the end of a long, exhausting march. Silence reigned all about in the wake of the thunderous rumble of the storm now gone. That dead silence was broken now and then by a scraping boot or shoe as a body shifted its weight, and by occasional muffled words cloaked in a spell of concentrated tenseness.

The indistinct silhouettes of two or three houses back along the creek presented themselves to our eyes after a bit. We made a short search, found them abandoned, and took our leave. Then we picked our way cautiously along an indistinct street littered with the artifacts of a destroyed community, and after a short series of adventures, found ourselves once again at the center of activity, the demolished Community Center, where most of Saragosa had gone ahead of the arrival of the storm.

As best I could ascertain, Tommy Ward had not gone with us to form the search parties. Since he had come to Saragosa with me, I felt the necessity of finding him and taking him back to Balmorhea. Officers were now hustling the thinning crowd of people away from the scene. The hour was very late, and it was their plan to seal off the town for the night. While drifting toward the exit ropes that blocked off the highway, I kept looking for Tommy's face in the compliant mobile crowd. Peter and Paul Matta walked along with me for a short distance. No, they had not seen Tommy; had I seen Jesus, their brother? We saw neither of these men.

As we exited the roped-off area, I bade the Matta brothers goodnight and plodded wearily back to my car. Inquiries at the area of the continuing rescue operations having been of no avail, I had an idea that my friend had become tired and decided to wait for me in the car.

I hiked that three-quarters of a mile almost groping my way along in the blackness. Arriving at my car at long last, I found nobody there. I simply couldn't leave without my passenger, so I forged my way back toward the highway intersection once again. The distance grew longer as I grew more tired, and the debris seemed to grow thicker and harder to see and dodge. The body of a dead horse lay in a ditch on the right side of the road, dimly outlined by the distant cluster of emergency lights toward which I plodded wearily. A young colt, confused, or so it seemed, shuffled about uncertainly some forty or more paces beyond the dead horse. I wondered whether the dead horse was the mother of the colt, then moved on.

Suddenly, without warning, I crashed headlong, making a desperate effort to control my fall. I was shocked almost senseless by my tumble. My left leg suddenly and painfully gave way under me. The muscle in the calf of my leg felt as if it had been torn apart. I had caught my shoe under a downed power line cable and had lunged heavily forward, tensing that leg, snapping something. The pain was excrutiating, and I sensed that I was in trouble.

I stopped momentarily to take stock of the situation. Could I walk? I had a long way to go under the circumstances, and there was absolutely nobody anywhere near to give any assistance. I was all alone out on a lonely abandoned road and now crippled. My car was several hundred yards from the center of activity, where I felt I must inquire about my friend, Tommy Ward. On the other hand, I felt that I might need to give up and return to my car, conserving every ounce of strength and mobility I could muster to do so and, hopefully, to be able to drive home somehow.

I pondered the alternatives but a moment. Leaving my friend was out of the question, and so I went on to search for him. The hike was agony. I dragged my leg, hopped on one foot, and tried every conceivable shuffle in my efforts to reach the highway ahead.

When I made it I found quite a scattering of people still inside the police barrier. I told my story to an officer and thus gained permission to penetrate the barrier and make inquiries. Finally, someone came up and told me that he had seen Tommy leave on the school bus with the driver, Charles Towry. Tommy had been summoned back to Balmorhea to open our high school gym as a shelter for homeless tornado victims.

Relieved to know Tommy's whereabouts, I turned my attention once more to the momentous problem of making my painful way back to my car in the Stygian darkness. The agitation of that group of disaster workers and their living tumult soon faded from my immediate awareness as I made my uncertain way through the night. The remoteness I felt in that wretched shuffle, with a leg so painful and useless that it may as well have been broken, must have been, I realized, nothing compared to the unimaginable desperation of some of those trapped victims beneath the rubble behind me. I suddenly felt shame that I expended so much concern for myself and the slight inconvenience that had claimed all of me in that hour. Nothing is more deadly than a concern when it is the only concern we have, and when it is for our own pains.

I soon found my car and discovered that I could drive it in spite of my near-useless left leg. Soon I was parking before my house in Balmorhea.

The place was dark. I wondered about Raquel. The possibility that she and Betty Hopper might have collided with some part of that horrible storm had nagged at the edge of my mind several times during the evening. The storm had gone east, and they would be coming in from Fort Stockton, which lay some fifty-two miles to the east.

It was obvious that she was not at home; the door was locked, and nobody responded to my knock. Equally as obvious was the fact that she had been there, because the door was locked, and I had not locked it when I left. I seldom ever do.

The school where we teach was only a frisbee toss away from our home, and with the town blacked out, nothing stirred except around the front entrance over there. Someone had rigged up some emergency lighting in the front hallway, and a few people came and went. A Red Cross vehicle was parked at the curb out front.

I hobbled through the entrance and met the surprise of my life. People came hurrying to me, some exclaiming, "Mr. Lane! Mr. Lane! He's here! What happened? Were you in the tornado? Here, sit down; get off that leg . . ."

My wife was there, curious, concerned, questions written all over her face. And while I was the center of attention for a few moments, I did not hold that attention for long. A crew of newsmen came trooping in right behind me and began asking questions.

Raquel was at my side and with her the Woods family, close friends of ours. Beary and Mary Sue Woods, as well as their older son, Morris, all appeared as if they had been run over by a Mack truck and wrung out with the wash. Morris stood by smiling in obvious; relief at seeing me alive. He was a graduating senior and salutatorian of the graduating class.

A newsman asked, loud enough to be heard all around the hallway where the small crowd stood, "Were any of you people in the tornado?"

Morris Woods, chubby, imposing, and of ready wit, was standing nearby. He replied, seriously, "I was, sir."

With that the newsman looked as pleased as a man who had caught his first-prize catch of the season. "Where were you?" he inquired.

With all the candor and simplicity in the world, Morris answered, "In Gallegos's Bar."

The tension-charged audience found its sense of humor, and much to the chagrin and confusion of the unwary reporter, burst into peals of laughter. Robert Clanton, the superintendent of schools, joined in the release of laughter. Some of us laughed, I suspect, at the confusion evidenced by the reporter as much as at the double entendre in Morris's answer.

Not being one to keep my big mouth shut sometimes, I added more fuel to the flames with: "His mom and dad were in that bar with him when the tornado hit!" I had just been briefed with the facts of their having taken refuge in the bar at the last minute before the funnel cloud smashed into Saragosa. The reporter was unaware of this fact, and my statement triggered laughter all over again.

Laughing was needed relief for us all, a safety valve for pent-up emotions. There were hundreds, even thousands, for whom there would be no laughter at all that night, a night far from being over for people with missing family members, people overwhelmed in their loss or anxiety, anxious loved ones far away who could not communicate or learn any information. Not only were our electric lines out of commission, but our telephone links with the outside world were severed as well.

News cameras whirred and interviews were recorded by news-gathering crews of the national networks and of independent stations and newspapers, far and near. All of us had first-hand experiences to share with a world beyond our borders — a world torn with anxiety and concern.

Beary Woods was one of the first to relate his story to the media, a story of how he and his family, who did not even live in Saragosa, were caught in the storm. They had driven to Pecos in their Bronco after school that afternoon. While en route home, driving south toward Saragosa, they kept anxious eyes on a developing and dangerous-appearing cloud "back toward Balmorhea" and southwest of Saragosa.

"We saw a patch of clear sky ahead of us and supposed we could go through ahead of the rapidly gathering storm," Mr. Woods, a tall, lanky rancher, explained. "But just before we reached the outskirts of town, a small funnel dropped out of that cloud for just a few seconds. I watched it closely, and felt just a bit relieved when it was drawn back up into the cloud. When it disappeared into the cloud, however," he went on, his voice growing husky with the fear he was remembering, "suddenly, without any warning, a great wide funnel, like a very dark wall a half-mile across, dropped to the ground and came at us head-on!

"It was too late to turn and run! We were crossing the Toya Creek Bridge approaching the Gallegos Bar, now, and that awesome thing was right on us! I braked the Bronco in front of the bar, and we all scrambled out and into the bar for cover. The storm was starting to strike the building just as we dived headlong under a pinball machine table and braced for the big blow. Some of the walls gave way, and the roof beams boomed down. The table above us took the brunt of the blows of the falling timbers, but the legs on one end gave way under the torture, and Morris and I had to brace up under the table to hold it from collapsing and crushing us."

"Were any of you injured?" a newsman asked.

"Not really. Just a lot of bruises and a lot of fright!" Woods related that his Bronco was flipped upside down, and the hundred dollars' worth of groceries they had bought in Pecos were gone. "We're blessed — just happy to be among the fortunate ones who are alive, you know," he said.

Woods's parents, living on a ranch near Van Horn, had not heard of the tornado but caught the late evening telecast, and saw their son and family, somewhat disheveled, telling their story for the first time. They later commented with a smile that people who go before TV cameras should at least straighten up their hair and wear fresh clothes.

A temporary Red Cross emergency station was hastily set up in the high school lobby, and presumably I was their first tornado-related patient to receive medical attention there. The gymnasium had been thrown open and pallets placed in orderly fashion over the entire floor area. The only occupants were two small children — little girls named Maria Baldera, age five, and Amparo Baldera, age four.

"They lost their mother in the storm tonight," Raquel whispered to me, adding, "and they have not been told yet; so be careful what you say." My cautious, thoughtful wife — always considerate and caring, and possessing an information bank of everybody's name.

The little Baldera girls had been pulled, unharmed, from the demolished Community Center by Elie Estrada, wife of Floyd Estrada. They had been brought to the shelter at the gym, and were now bedded down on the floor near the spot where the Red Cross had placed me, leg raised and encased in packs of ice. The hour was 3:00 A.M., and I, who had come home exhausted at the end of the school day last evening, didn't even feel tired or sleepy now.

Raquel sat lovingly watching over me after two aspirin cut the pain and allowed me to sleep. She later told of groups of my students who each crept in on little mouse feet and regarded me with worlds of loving concern as the wee hours wore on. What beautiful, loving people they are!

I slept for only two of those small hours that wore on. My wife was there when I awakened, watching over me like a loving mother sitting out the long, tedious hours of the night with a sick child.

"What time is it, dear?" I wanted to know.

"Five o'clock," she replied.

I lay inert for a few more minutes, my mind steeped in deep reflection upon the catastrophe that had engulfed our two tiny towns. More than anything I wished to return to Saragosa and help out, but then I shifted my ice-numbed leg and winced. I realized that I could not return to the scene of the devastation. "Let's go to the house," I said decisively. "A lot of people may be pouring in here for shelter in a little while, and I don't need to be here taking up space."

I hobbled out of the gym, Raquel supporting me. The Red Cross nurse spotted me and insisted that I take a pair of crutches, go home, and "Stay off that leg!"

Clumsily, at first, I ambulated with the crutches, making my slow, tedious way across the hundred yards to our residence, Raquel at my side.

I awakened from a deep, peaceful sleep around 8:00 A.M. There could be no lying around the house for me, and I was soon mounted upon my crutches and thumping my way back to school once more.

My spirits were renewed, and one would wonder *how*. Perhaps I had acquired something of the secret of the ninety-seven-year-old man who, when asked of his undiminished youthfulness, replied, "I make the most of life as it comes, and the least of life as it goes." My formula is to dwell wholly in the here and now, to regard each arriving new moment of life as unique, different, all mine. Hats off to that insightful, unknown author who began his little poem "Today" with these lines:

> With every rising of the sun
> Think of your life as just begun.
> The past has canceled and buried deep
> All yesterdays. There let them sleep . . .

What could such one as I do, crippled and on crutches, in such a place and time as this? I had an answer ready in my mind for that negative gig as I went on toward the high school building. I doubted not that numberless friends — students and their families

— would be coming and going. There would be many in need of comfort, encouragement, hugs — caring in any form or fashion. I had much of that to offer, and I only wished for the opportunity to be there should I be needed.

And I wanted news — updated news of the deceased, of the injured, of the surviving. There would be no television news, for we were still at the mercy of the electrical blackout.

I found my way over to the school fairly well on my crutches, unaccustomed though I was to them. I stood around and waited, soon to be rewarded. After a little while, in shuffled Elizabeth and Brenda Lopez, two of my students.

Brenda! Was this her ghost? I'd been told she . . . I couldn't think it; I had grieved much for her and Erica, her sister, whom Floyd insisted we found last night. I hugged Brenda, emerging from the forlorn madness of my sea of bad dreams. Suddenly, there was Erica! Oh, thank God! Floyd had been mistaken last night. Oh, sweet little impish Erica, *alive!* And beautiful, dear angel Brenda! The two of them, understood to be lost, were here with "Lisa," another of my favorites. I was so overjoyed at seeing these darling Lopez girls in the flesh that I must have impressed them as one gone groggy or insane. Well, I was, without a doubt, virtually insane with joy and relief.

They moved on with other matters calling to them, and there I stood with my thoughts, holding a mystery in my mind: who was that dear girl we had found last night? I puzzled over that for two days. Then, on Monday night, Floyd came by the high school wing of our school plant where Raquel and I were working as disaster volunteers with the Salvation Army team. The hour was very late, and we were keeping the building open deep into the night due to some administrative problems that had come up.

Estada strode in and had scarcely greeted us when I turned a level gaze at him and began, "Floyd, that girl we found out there at the Lopez place Friday night . . . we now know she wasn't Erica, as you then thought. Who *was* she?"

"Kathy," he said simply. "She was Kathy."

I was stunned by a fact I had secretly suspected but could not bring myself to believe. "Oh, my God," I breathed, as softly as the footfalls of a timid breeze. "I *did* get to see her one last time, and didn't even recognize her! Oh, darling little Kathy . . ."

[3]

Observers of Disaster

Ike is Tommy Ward's brother. He works for the City of Balmorhea and is a member of the Balmorhea Fire Department, a volunteer group. Ike is a trained and certified paramedic and drives the ambulance for the town.

When I was at the Ward brothers' home, as the storm was gathering strength just before its onslought upon Saragosa, the phone rang and Ike answered it. Then, without a word, he was gone. Tommy and I had wondered what was going on. Later, I asked Ike for his account of the events of that fateful evening following his brief telephone conversation and departure.

Reliving the horror of his adventure in Saragosa, Ike Ward displayed with his face and eyes a tense, grave, and somber internal souvenir of the storm.

> **Ike Ward:** Crennie Crenshaw called and asked if I was watching the storm. I told him I was, and took another look. I called him back, and we decided we'd better get down to the fire station right away — in case a tornado hit somewhere.
>
> After I arrived at the station, Billy Lozano drove up, asking for an ambulance and all the firemen, saying they were all needed at Saragosa because a tornado had hit the town. All the lights in Balmorhea had gone out by then.
>
> The rest of the firemen — James Garlick, Craig Huelster, C. T. Gray, Q. A. (Crennie) Crenshaw, Larry Turnbough — and

Cliff Ward, a male nurse, all took off for Saragosa, sirens wailing. I drove the ambulance, and Rita Lozano, another paramedic, was with me. All the others were in the firetruck except for C. T. Gray; he drove the second ambulance.

When we arrived, we began taking out bodies from the old wrecked church. They were underneath walls and pinned underneath tables. Some were dead, some alive . . . more were dead at first. Some you thought would live, but they died. Corina Brijalba, I remember, was underneath a table — injured bad. Pat, her husband, was too. Lucas Carrillo, about twenty-six years old, was underneath the wall that fell on him. He was Mrs. Brijalba's son. He was killed instantly right there.

We all worked right there in the wrecked Community Center . . . We worked all night . . . until about six o'clock in the morning. When we finished searching in the rubble of that demolished building, Cliff and I were put in charge of doing a thorough house-to-house search for bodies in the town. We didn't find any. A lot of people had gotten out ahead of the funnel.

Following our search we checked back in at the Community Center to learn if there were any more bodies found there. Then we checked the Candelas place; after that, we went across the highway and checked for dead and injured over there. We walked out the entire storm-hit area quite thoroughly.

Then we returned to Balmorhea — all of us, ready for some rest. My feelings had been drained during that tour of duty out there that night. All of that crying, yelling, moaning, and screaming coming out of the rubble of that wrecked Community Center had about done me in. I had been glad when they assigned me and Cliff to search elsewhere. My ears were ringing from all the human noise down in there below our feet! It was almost more than a man could take . . .

* * *

Ted Woodruff is a science teacher and assistant football coach at Balmorhea High School. He is a lanky, genial, and fun-loving graduate of the University of Texas at Austin. Ted is one of my close neighbors and has been a professional friend for several years. Against the sage advice of Thomas Fuller, I have the habit of inquiring as to what boils in other men's pots, and so one day I asked Ted whether he had been involved in any way in the Saragosa storm and how it had affected him. His story gave me some new information about Ramon Meneses, a former student in our classes. Ramon, better known as "Kiki," had been critically injured in the storm. Ted warmed to his story, though giving evidence that the recollection was painful indeed, and in the extreme.

Ted Woodruff: Coach Rivera [Eddie Rivera] and I were out riding around and watching the weather in the late afternoon. It looked pretty bad, especially the spiraling cloud system right over Balmorhea. We drove out to the lake and back, then over to the highway underpass near Carrasco's. The large hailstones fascinated us, and we busied ourselves collecting the largest ones to put into the freezer for use the next week in our science class — you know, saw them in half and study the formation rings inside them — only there wouldn't be any *next week* of science classes, but we didn't know that then.

Anyway, we came under the low underpass and found Dora Valerio and her family sitting under there, waiting out the hail and wind. We joked a bit with them, then drove on to Victor Hernandez's Chevron. While there, we watched a strange man brake to a stop, and then were shocked at the story he had to tell. He informed us that he had just come through Saragosa and that a bad tornado had hit out there and done a lot of wreckage.

Eddie and I took off over there, arriving fairly soon after some of the first ones already there.

I was stunned. The devastation was absolutely incredible. We got busy trying to help in the downed Community Center, and shortly there were so many people in there, we were stumbling over each other. Without heavy equipment, which hadn't come yet, we were licked and felt helplessly impotent. People were all in a state of shock, I suppose, and there was a lot of confusion and disorganization. I couldn't even get others to help me remove a telephone pole that had blown into the wreckage!

I got out of there and started to go out into the wreckage of the town. I soon teamed up with Coach Barrandy [Head Coach Michael Barrandy] somewhere, and we made our way through tangled piles of cars and blasted homes.

It was incredible: the old people we found, their homes partially wrecked, were themselves all right! This was truly amazing!

Then we found Kiki. He was in bad — I mean *bad* — shape. He was way over to the west of Gallegos's Bar — two or three blocks behind the bar. That would place him quite some distance from his home, where he reportedly had just driven and parked his car. I never saw his car at all, and he evidently had been hurled all that distance by the force of the wind.

As I said, he was in bad shape. We got him out of there and eventually he was put on an ambulance and taken to Odessa.

I saw other people down. Looking closer, I'd suddenly realize they were gone—dead! I'd shudder as I moved on in our grim search. We could not help them. We were looking for people we could help. It was a terrible thing—just simply incredible.

* * *

Joel Muniz and Martin Garcia have been students in my English classes at the Balmorhea Public Schools now and then in past years. Last year, Joel was a member of the junior class, the class of which I have been the faculty sponsor for several years. He is a quiet, unassuming youth of slight build who minds his own business and is a good citizen in our school and community. Martin is tall, humorous, well-mannered, and pleasant. Both boys lived in Saragosa.

Addressing Joel, I asked where he was during the tornado, and both he and Martin, taking turns, readily volunteered the following account:

Joel: I saw the storm coming, and I ran into the house as it approached. Martin here was in his yard next door, and had been watching it too . . . Before we ran inside, I saw a gray, very smooth cloud formed back in the direction of Balmorhea. That was sort of southwest of our place. A second smooth cloud — it was dark, black-looking in appearance — had formed straight south of us . . .

Martin: Just like Joel said . . . two clouds — both smooth, one very dark and the other very light . . . They moved together . . . like two rams running head-on and smashing their heads. They just raced toward each other and collided!

Joel: As they collided, they began spinning, like a Spanish girl doing a wild dance. They kept gaining velocity up in the air, then they just moved downward . . .

It just spread out then, grew in size . . . and moved straight toward us. Out in the pasture to the south of town the tornado moved north a bit, then seemed to change direction as it swept into Saragosa; then it seemed to make a U-turn right over town.

Martin: It sure did . . . made a U-turn all right! It was black and awful, with sheet iron flying everywhere!

After the storm was gone, I went out looking for my relatives . . . you know, the Melendez family. I had seen them start to go into their house when the house rose about ten feet into the air! At this moment they turned, and with a lot of confusion, they climbed into their car. That car was really dancing about, but their weight seemed to have partly stabilized it.

They are a very large family, and even after they filled up the car completely, I could see it still shuffling sideways, threatening to go on over . . . or away . . . any second! It was scary!

But they came through the tornado all right—just shook up, and the mother had a minor scalp wound. That was all. Thank God that was all!

* * *

Leonardo Melendez told me and Diana Castillo, a ninth-grade neighbor, how he and his family were saved from the Saragosa tornado. The ten-year-old is a bright fourth-grade student who attends Pecos Elementary School. His father, Jesus Melendez, is deceased, and his stepfather is Carlos Esparza, his mother Juana Esparza.

Leonardo, understandably wide-eyed as he remembered and related the shockingly realistic ordeal he experienced with his family, was, at the same time, somewhat philosophical for a child, amazing us all with his account that portrayed both the frivolity and the fury of the tornado.

Leonardo Melendez: The tornado was about to strike. We were all outside in our yard, and we saw it coming, getting very close. We tried to run into our house . . . but we couldn't make it to our house in time. Besides, it was about to go!

So, we all piled into our car. It was in the yard close to us, and we hurried and got into it . . . That wasn't easy, because we were ten people! Ten people getting into one car made it very crowded for us in there, but we didn't mind. We were all afraid of the storm funnel that was coming straight toward us.

Ours is a large family. Only one of the ten was somebody else. Her name is Lorena Garcia. She was a neighbor girl who was visiting at our house. We all crammed in there together, Lorena and all the rest of us . . . Some of us were on the bottom, and others were above. It did not matter where we were just as long as we were saved. My parents pressed us down and lay on top of us, and we were okay . . .

While we were in our car together, a window of the car was broken, and the storm just blew it away. The air was full of things blowing and banging against our car. The sound was awful! Our car was all banged up, and it was dancing around, trying to take off into the air. But I guess our weight helped to keep it down. It did move a little, but it did not go. We sure thought it would, and we were really scared.

Then a big piece of lumber slammed in. It came right into our car through the broken-out window. It made a cut in my mother's head . . . on the back of her head, you know. That was because she was bending over us, face down, as low as she could, over all of us. She took that blow, but it wasn't too bad a cut, and she did not mind it very much. She was just glad we were all saved when the storm blew over and went on.

Mom is okay now. I guess we all got off easy when you think of what happened to others in our town. We were lucky . . . or blessed . . .

* * *

Mrs. Anna Contreras, a woman of remarkably short stature, is the wife of Richard Contreras, who works as a custodian for the Balmorhea School District. Anna is the daughter of Pat Brijalba, Sr., a tornado victim. She is an eternally smiling, joyous mother of five bright-eyed children. Richard and Anna are our friends, and we were relieved beyond words when we learned that their "near miss" was yet a safe one, and that they are still around to relate their story.

Richard was away from home the evening Raquel and I visited the Contreras home and heard Anna's story of their brush with death in the Saragosa tornado. Richard added some comments later.

Anna Contreras: We had gone to Pecos that afternoon, and it was uncanny how many unexplainable delays we encountered there. Richard was in a great hurry to go home. Everywhere that we would stop he would keep insisting that we hurry. I couldn't understand his urge to rush off home, but he kept making an issue of getting on the road right away.

At the same time that Richard was insisting that we hurry things along, there was something else going on just as unexplainable to me. In fact, it was downright weird! In spite of all my efforts to hurry, there was a series of uncanny delays!

First, I met Mrs. Marge Timmerman at the Safeway store. We met near the meat department, and we talked and talked and talked. I simply couldn't seem to get away from her, and I was aware that Richard was on needles and pins to be gone.

Later, I met Mrs. Timmerman again where we were checking out. We visited and talked like crazy once more. Poor Richard was out there stewing in the car, anxious, for some reason I could not comprehend, to get going home to Balmorhea. He hadn't been feeling well; perhaps that was it. I wondered.

After finally getting away from Mrs. Timmerman the second time, I met Mrs. Woods [Mary Sue Woods of Balmorhea]. We talked and talked. It was all so odd that I couldn't bring the conversation to a close, while here I was supposed to be hurrying — for Richard.

We drove to the Furr's Supermarket for some more things, and you won't believe this, but who had trailed us there? Right . . . Mrs. Timmerman again! More talk! It was becoming ridiculous, uncanny!

Finally, we headed for home. As we traveled south going out of Pecos, I saw this dark, dark cloud before us. It was the blackest cloud I had ever seen. Before we were out of town, the rain set in, really coming down!

We have one window in our car that won't close . . . and the rain was blowing in. When we reached the Interstate 20 overpass, we stopped under it and stuffed something into the open window to keep out the slashing rain. Another delay!

We then drove through the heavy downpour to Verhalen. The rain was coming down in torrents, blinding us at times. Driving was hazardous in the extreme. Hail was beginning to smash into the car, too, and our girls were frightened and crying. So, once again we stopped, this time at Verhalen, for a little bit to get them quieted down. Another delay!

A little further on, down the highway just a few miles, we saw a stalled ambulance sitting beside the road, its colored lights winking in the blackness. Another ambulance seemed to be taking on the load from it as we passed by. We had no idea then that this had something to do with a tornado down the road, or that someone we knew, Lisa Carrillo, was the victim out there.

As we drove on a little further, not far south of Verhalen, we met an extremely heavy downpour of hail. It was smacking down in huge hunks. We stopped the car — more delay! — and when the hail let up, we drove on. Still a bit further on, the hail was thick on the road. Do you remember the green house by the highway? The hail was piled up there in banks like snow. We couldn't believe our eyes!

As we drove on, the dark clouds were swirling above us, and we noticed as we passed the Curly house that all the windows were broken out. I kept experiencing this very strong sensation . . . something weird. There seemed to be something strange going on! I felt an uncanny fear. Richard kind of kidded me about that, saying I was just seeing things.

When we reached that first sign that says "Saragosa," up where the "new" Saragosa used to be, we saw this weird, frightening cloud above us and slightly to the south and left of the road. It was a churning mass, very dark — with swirling, ragged, and torn murkiness in its heart. It looked awesome. As we watched, it appeared to be drilling its way from near the earth ahead right on up into the greater bulk of clouds above it. I suppose that we were seeing the remnants of the tornado as it finally left the ground to the northeast of town and swept back up into the cloudbank.

Richard Contreras: It was unbelievable the many frustrating delays we suffered in Pecos. While I was waiting with the children in the car, and trying to be patient, I heard on the Pecos radio station that there was a tornado only ten miles south of town . . . I suppose I really did not pay much attention to it; maybe it just half registered with me, because I was fretting about Anna's taking so long. Anyway, I should have waited, but didn't. As it was, we had our delays that may have saved us our lives, for had we gone on home on "schedule," we would have tangled with that tornado for sure!

You know, we had seen the Woods family, and they left before we did — not long, but a little bit. We had our little delay later at Furr's, and one or two brief ones on the road, else we would have been immediately behind them! They had a close call and lost their car and groceries. We might have been a quarter of a mile back and couldn't have made it to the safety of Gallegos's Bar as they did. We very probably would have run smack into that thing!

Anna: (continuing) In a minute we were stopped. I think the man was a truck driver. He was stopping traffic, telling people they could not get through because a tornado had just hit Saragosa! I looked around, then, and we noticed that the Lucas Carrillo mobile home was gone — vanished! We were opposite the location where it had always been. Lucas's pickup was parked in its usual place, but there was no mobile home anywhere! It was gone! We were really shocked. Now, things really did seem weird, very frightening as well.

I told Richard, "Let's go and look for Rosie Carrillo and the kids," but he said, "No, let's go on and get out of here!"

Since we couldn't get through on the highway, we took a backroad detour all the way out by the Balmorhea Feeders. Those backroads were a real mess — water everywhere! In some places the road was under water, and we had to risk it and drive slowly through the high water out there. It was very dark and scary, believe me! The trip seemed so long and tiring, but we did keep going until we finally reached Balmorhea and found the whole town blacked out. After some driving around, and being a bit bewildered and confused, we drove to Richard's father's house, and there we were told how bad it all really was . . .

I knew then . . . that we had been Providentially delayed. God had timed it, I suppose, so that we had to put up with one delay after another. I feel certain in my own heart that the series of delays we put up with in Pecos and afterward saved our lives, our family. God had a hand in preserving all of us. He had a hand in it, and He had a purpose. I told Richard, "Let's don't waste it! We're closer to Him now than we've ever been before!"

* * *

Lee Renz is a local rancher, who, with his wife Darla, also teaches in the elementary school in Balmorhea. They are staunch friends of ours. He is not an import like we but is a native of the Balmorhea Basin. He is ranch-wise, weather-wise, people-wise, and Indian artifact-wise. Thus he and I share a common interest in the archeological relics left behind by primitive peoples who roamed this region in ancient times. We have both long cherished our collections of artifacts gleaned painstakingly over a period of many years.

I asked Lee if he and Darla were involved in the tornado episode. The cowboy-teacher chuckled and gave a wry grin. "I guess Darla and I were the last people in the United States to learn about the tornado," he drawled.

It was not necessary for me to ask why. Lee was sensitive and responded by warming to his subject. He chuckled now and then in his warm, musical manner, in a sort of self-conscious way — almost as if he felt some vague sense of guilt, as a sentry caught by himself sleeping at his post, unperturbed by great problems. Had he not been made the butt of a colossal joke by the vast tribunal of a tempestuous sky?

Lee Renz: Darla and I had been to Pecos to do our grocery buying that Friday afternoon after school. We must have come through Saragosa around seven o'clock, about an hour or a little better before the storm hit over there. We drove on out to our place in the country, where we were in the process of moving to another house.

I had some hay down, and I wanted to get it baled before it rained. The weather looked pretty much like rain to me. In fact, it had showered a little on my hay, and I went out to examine it.

There was just enough moisture in the hay to toughen it, making it just right to bale. So, I cranked up my rig and bailed hay for about an hour.

When it started to rain, I came in and sat watching the weather. Since our weather generally comes from the direction of the mountains to our west, I never even looked toward Balmorhea and Saragosa. I did see a strange, wild cloud to the north a little ways where a piece of ragged cloud would shoot first this way and then that. There was this one torn, ragged strip of cloud that was very dark and moving fast, parallel to the ground. It raced to the west at a great speed, then other patches of cloud ripped across it . . . This was the same wall cloud you said you observed sweeping in low over Toya Creek and over Balmorhea. It was on an ever-circling pattern, wheeling counterclockwise over Balmorhea and on to Saragosa.

Not long afterward, the lights went out all over. Darla and I hadn't eaten supper yet, and so we ate in the twilight and turned in early. We then simply slept through it all!

The next morning I went up to town — Balmorhea — and met Mrs. Hopper [Betty Hopper]. When she saw me, she said that some of Darla's folks were trying to reach her by phone. She said Darla should call them, because *they were frantic!* I suppose she thought I knew about the disaster, and for that reason, she never made any explanation. I thanked her and left.

Mystified and still in complete ignorance of the terrible thing that had happened, I drove back out to our place in the country and told Darla that her family wanted her to call them . . . We had been moving and did not have our phone service in our new place, and they couldn't call us. So, I told her she'd better call her folks back, but I didn't tell her about their being frantic. That part didn't make any sense to me at all.

Well, we drove into Balmorhea, and Darla used the pay phone by the drugstore. I waited in the pickup parked at the curb. That's when I noticed something strange about the personality of the town. There seemed to be a lot of excitement; everybody was hurrying here and there. Red Cross vehicles, rarely seen in a little burg like Balmorhea, were coming and going, and other cars seemed to be hurrying as if their drivers were under the pressure of some great event and preoccupied with desperation. It was strange, very strange to me, so unlike easy-going Balmorhea.

Then along came Helen Humphries, the mayor, and I asked her what all the commotion was about.

She eyed me narrowly for some time as if trying to figure me out. I guess she finally decided I wasn't joking. That's when she exclaimed, "You mean you don't know?" Then she told me about Saragosa blowing away the evening before. I was totally dumbfounded. Here we were, living so close by, yet had been so far away, ignorant of all that had gone on!

Like I said before, I guess I was the last person in the whole United States to know anything about it!

* * *

Tall, rangy farmer-rancher Larry Turnbough, with his father, Rick Turnbough, operates one of their several farms where the gigantic tornado dipped down from a boiling cloud mass and lunged at the throat of Saragosa. After James Garlick called Gina, his wife, to report his spotting of the gigantic funnel near the interstate, Gina called Melanie Turnbough with the news. Larry shrugged the report aside, saying, "Aw, I wonder if they even know what a funnel cloud looks like." Larry later told me, "Well, I'll never say 'never' again! Not after what happened out there!"

A man of long experience living close to the land and the sky, Larry related his account of the storm and its wake of wreckage.

Larry Turnbough: I have been out on my farms in that area, and I guess from the signs, it started pretty close to here — to Balmorhea. The first major damage shows up where Toya Creek flows under the interstate. Some trees were damaged pretty badly right there. Then, there is a couple of big cottonwoods knocked down in that line of trees behind Jimmy Carrasco's house. Then, behind Herman Tarin's home, there is a small, portable building tipped upside down. Juan Armendariz told me that he was outside his mobile home — out in a little house behind his trailer. He described an almost perfect silence and a very warm atmosphere which would suddenly be followed by a tremendous suction pulling on him. I suppose this was due to the differences in pressure, a very weird sensation he described as coming and going two or three times.

Then, there was a sign and a tree knocked down by the old experiment station. There were other interesting evidences to be seen out in those fields on the north side of the interstate where it finally all came down . . .

As you know, from four to six smaller funnels were variously reported. What I saw was doubtless the evidence of their several activities in those separate localities.

When it all came together and fell out upon those fields, it remained constant right on the ground until it struck the jugular vein of Saragosa itself.

The Big One started off in a perfect northeasterly direction, which is how tornados usually behave. It angled across, and was wide enough to extend across Highway 17. There it mowed down power lines and caught that barn of Dale Toones', while, at the same time, it spread across those fields of ours and hit our barn. Veering from its northeasterly path, the huge twister then drove straight northward toward town . . . six-tenths of a mile wide — and wiped out Saragosa. Actually, the western fringe of that funnel was away over near that Cuban house. It had crossed between there and our barn, and it hit pretty hard. That is close to the place where Craig Huelster was hiding in that big irrigation ditch — he and his wife and daughter. They all made a dash from their pickup to that big ditch.

A guy who works for me was driving a dusky green pickup over near our barn when a two-by-four came hurtling through the air and smashed into the windshield. When it did, he ducked and swerved, going off into the roadside ditch.

He left the pickup. In fact — well, I'm not sure — I heard that he did that after the tornado. He turned and ran off from there in complete panic. He was an illegal alien. Whatever he did, he did not get hurt, and he ended up in the school shelter for a couple of nights.

One highly interesting result of that storm was the great number of people with eye injuries. They did not lose their eyesight; they just suffered blurred vision for weeks and even months afterward.

In part, one might account for that as caused by blowing dust, but that does not satisfy me and explain the evidence. That high-velocity wind with dust in the atmosphere was as abrasive as sandpaper. Even without the dust, that wind had a polishing or honing effect. You know, there were few, if any, gushing types of blood injuries. All of the wounds that I saw seemed to be seared over, almost as if cauterized. Those wounds, while fresh, appeared to be three or four days old! They were not bleeding! Nor were they blood matted with dirt as one might surmise. It was something like a burn . . . like a rope burn, or like you'd taken sandpaper and rubbed someone's arm vigorously until the blood came, until it got hot and sort of seared the flesh.

There was Fernando Balderas with cuts, and later, with stitches in his back. Yet when I looked at his cuts, they appeared to have been inflicted two or three days earlier. There was little or no outward show of blood! The cut he sustained seemed seared and sealed over against bleeding!

So, I think that a lot of the eye injuries, such as those of Pat Brijalba, are just improving all the time. The vision was badly blurred in so many cases, and I think it was the violent wind itself, with degrees of dirt and mud in it that inflicted these unusual injuries. That tornado was a gigantic sand-blasting machine that both destroyed life and eyesight, and yet prevented total blindness and bleeding to death at the same time!

The weird power of that tornado was unimaginable! Billy Gallegos's pickup was hurled down Toya Creek a hundred yards or so. Joe Gallegos's pickup was out there, too, in that creek, a distance from the highway. The hood off of Billy's was wrapped around a telephone pole about a half a mile away over by the Seventh Day Adventist bakery, just about one half a mile due north. Fernando Balderas told me that, while he was hiding in the pickup there by the Community Center, he saw automobiles and pickups pin-wheeling through the air above him, sailing like frisbees above the tops of the electric highline poles out there along Highway 17!

* * *

"Incredible as it must have been frightening," I mused upon the completion of Larry's story. One would have thought that Joseph Conrad had been there just before he wrote, "The Westerly Wind asserting his sway from the southwest quarter is often like a monarch gone mad, driving forth with wild imprecations the most faithful of his courtiers to shipwreck, disaster, and death." *(The Mirror of the Sea* (1906), 28)

[4]

Memories Etched into Journals

I taught Aidee Muniz for six years in the Balmorhea Public Schools. In all that time I never had a moment's problem with her. She is a positive person, in love with school and with life. That meant love of nature, love of God, and love of man. Aidee is a hard worker, a diligent and friendly girl whom I have long loved as a friend and student, a most wonderful privilege for me.

Aidee shares my belief that people can all be winners in this world if they but truly care for one another and feel genuine concern for the problems of others. We share the concept that genuine love in the heart expresses itself in the decision to make another person's problem our problem.

She graduated this year, and I felt honored that she and her classmates chose to invite me to speak at their graduation program. I am further honored that these students call me up from time to time, or else come by, to share things they have written in their journals. This has happened on repeated occasions since their school careers ended here this spring.

Aidee Muniz is one of the most beautiful people I have ever known: sweet of nature, uncompromising of values, warm of heart, and loving of God. Can one say more than that? Hers has not been a life of affluence at home, and she has grown up with the necessity of overcoming cruel obstacles that have loomed large in her pathway of life. The recent tragedy that smote her little town called for the greatest latent capacity of her people there, a people who now have the ultimate sorrow.

In her modesty and dignity, Aidee has written things in her journal that reveal an exalted purpose, a deep humility, and an unshakable faith.

A Tornado Struck Our Town and Our Hearts

Aidee Muniz

On Friday, May 22, 1987, a killer tornado struck the small town of Saragosa, Texas, where I live. It left many people injured and dead, and many others numb with trauma beyond pain. We, the people of Saragosa, never expected a thing like this ever to happen to our small town.

That day was just an ordinary day for everyone I knew. Coming home from school that afternoon, I remember clearly that Noemi Garcia and Elvira Casias sat right across the aisle from me on the bus. Elvira was telling me about a problem she had, and I was always giving her my sage advice . . . As on other days I told her not to listen to what people said when they gossiped about her, to ignore them and to leave them alone. The last thing I ever told her was, "I'll see you Monday . . ." Little did I suspect that I would never see Elvira Casias alive again.

That day I remember clearly that the weather was great. The day had been rather warm, with just a slight breeze blowing. Upon arriving home, I visited Jose and Melissa Muniz, his kid sister, next door for a while. When I went back over to my house, my father and my uncle were packing up some equipment to take over to our little ranch near Candelaria, down near the Mexican border. By the time my dad left, the wind was already blowing strongly, but we thought nothing of that. We are used to strong winds out here. As my dad was leaving, my mom jokingly said to him, "If you leave us, you're never going to see us again!" She was only kidding, of course, but her teasing very nearly proved prophetic!

I remember sitting in the dining room listening to my jam box when I learned that a tornado was coming. My mom, brother, and my sisters were sitting in the living room watching TV. In just a short time we found out that the report was true, that a tornado was actually near! The confirmation came from Joel Rodriguez, my cousin. He came running to our house as fast as his legs could carry him . . . By then the appearance to the sky was heavy gray clouds and rain, but we didn't see any funnel.

Mom glanced out the window, looking for one, and urged me to watch for it too. I remember laughing at her and teasing her about imagining things from listening to other people.

She seemed suddenly stern with me, and said, "I'm not kidding; look out the window!" I looked and saw this huge funnel already formed! It was only a few hundred yards from our house!

It was panic time for me, especially when my mom screamed, "Quick! Take cover!" Other family members were running to different rooms, but I dashed next door to Jose's home, this time to warn him and his family of the tornado.

The Muniz family was panic-stricken, too, and Jose disappeared into a closet momentarily . . . Jose Rodriquez, the father of Joel, appeared in the yard with his family in their car. My mom was there then, shouting, "Hurry! Get into the car!"

I told her to go with them, that I would stay. Jose Muniz, followed by his family, suddenly burst out of their house and piled into their car. I changed my mind about staying, and in my sudden spurt of energy, I slipped and fell on the porch, taking a hard fall on the cement. In a frenzy of desperation, I bounced up and somehow scrambled over to my uncle's car, already packed with fourteen people! I somehow wiggled in there where we were piled on top of each other.

My uncle took off in desperation, driving as fast as he could, while Jose and his family followed us. We stopped two or three times to look back and determine whether the tornado was still coming. It was! And just as we reached the stop sign at the highway there before the Community Center building, we saw a number of people out front, standing there looking confused, almost motionless, as if unsure of what to do. Many of them would die just moments later! . . .

We made our escape from the grim hand of the tornado by only a few minutes as we drove toward a farm road that branched off the highway and led to my aunt's ranch. How my uncle drove us safely out that escape route, I will never understand, because it was pouring buckets of water, and golf-ball-sized hail was slamming into the car which was overloaded with people overwhelmed with terror. I remember glancing back to see whether Jose was behind us, and he was . . .

Another thing that I remember of those moments was my aunt telling my mom, "Let's go back to the church; we'll be safe there," but my uncle refused to hear of such a thing. He said, "No! We don't turn back! We have to keep running away from it. Everything is now in God's hands and will."

Finally, after what seemed an eternity, we felt the threat of danger was past, and we turned back toward Saragosa. We were hoping against hope and praying fervently that nothing disastrous had happened to Saragosa. It proved a vain hope.

When we were about a mile or so from our little town, we noticed that Lucas Carrillo's trailer was gone. Then, all along the road, telephone and electric poles were a shambles with wires and cables and everything imaginable strewn about. Then the stark horror of the destruction left by the tornado hit me, numbing my senses. All I could do then was to cry, and I was to do plenty of that before this night was over . . .

As we crept along, dodging debris, I saw survivors of the storm running about feverishly. Soon I recognized Angelica Casias as she stood screaming for help. I remember wanting to go to her and help her, but I was in no condition for that, lost and panicky and troubled as I was at that moment . . .

Then all the cars and ambulances were coming. People lay out there buried under houses while many others were blown away. The rest of them were out there trying to be helpful, all of them running scared, I supposed . . .

I remember that, as we threaded our way on to our house, how I feared as we went that the tornado had demolished *all* of the town, taking our home away with the rest. We arrived there at length, and were relieved but appalled at what greeted our eyes. Though the house was intact structurally, all the doors and windows had been blown out! For some reason, I was afraid to go inside. The dreadful unknown was lurking in there for me, and fear clutched with a strangling death grasp at my throat.

Not having had the time to get into my shoes when we left, I was still barefooted. We didn't go inside then; instead, we went with my uncle and his family to their home. It, too, had suffered some damage from the storm that had swiped at it along its very edge in passing . . .

We returned to the location where the bodies of the dead were still being carried out of the ruins of the Community Center. It was an unbelievably busy place with people running back and forth in an agitated frenzy.

Thinking rationally was not our greatest accomplishment that night. After having had a good look there, we drove to Balmorhea, where all phones were dead, for the purpose of making a phone call at a friend's home. Following that futile try, we returned to Saragosa, concerned, with my uncle, about the members of his family. They were in that destroyed building somewhere . . . so far as we knew. Ambulances were coming and going still. My uncle made inquiries, but could obtain no satisfactory information at the Center . . .

Finally, we decided to drive to Pecos to discover who might be in the hospital there . . . The hospital was packed with people — policemen, TV news people, and everyone else imaginable. Like us, many of those people had come there hoping and praying that their family members and friends would be all right. For many, it seemed that their prayers had helped, but for others they obviously had not.

I remember standing at the hospital door while the staff came and went, announcing the names of the dead and really seriously wounded. The announcement that hit me especially hard was that of the death of two of my dearest friends, Kathy and Elvira. At the moment I couldn't move a muscle, and felt as if I was going to faint. In my anguish and weakness I cried and cried, joining with my other friends and family members. After a time, my head hurt me so badly I began feeling quite ill. My back and hip hurt, too, from the fall I had taken earlier that evening. But all of this, along with a scraped and bloody knee, was as nothing as I concerned myself with what was happening in the lives of countless others. Although I felt all lost, lonely, and afraid, I felt a certain security and comfort in knowing that my family and friends were there to support me . . .

At length we left, not wanting to stay and see any more. Some of us simply could not handle it, for, as time passed, the shock and sadness became harder and harder to endure.

When we arrived at the outskirts of Saragosa that night, there was a road block, forcing us to detour around on a farm road to my uncle's house.

Sleep would not come for me that night, because we were all afraid of new developments and the news we dreaded to hear about friends and families from whom there had been no news. They had been scattered, and each had, so far as we knew, been somewhere in the path of that killer tornado, but in what house? In what building? Where were they now? What had happened to them?

About six in the morning my dad and his brother arrived from the ranch, both anxious and praying for the best. Were we all okay? News had somehow gotten to them about the tornado . . .

Still in a state of shock and dread, we feared the arrival of any added news of who else had died. But we had to know. The morning inched by like an eternity . . . People visited briefly and went on to hunt around the ruins of their houses for the remains of their personal belongings . . .

Then came the saddest day of all . . . that following week . . .

when we all went to the Balmorhea School. There we crept from room to room to view the bodies of our loved ones in open caskets. The hardest thing I faced that day was viewing the body of Elvira. I couldn't believe that all of this was happening. Hadn't I just talked with her . . . and now she was gone? My dear, my good little friend . . . I found myself asking over and over again, "Why, of all people, her? *Why?*" I still ask myself this question, because it is impossible to forget and as difficult to understand.

It continues to be my painful lot to keep thinking about this incredible tragedy every day, and at night I cry myself to sleep . . . almost two months after the storm came and struck mortal blows to both our towns and to all our hearts. It continues being something scary . . . something that must go on . . . life, you know, with all its pain from the past and risks that lie ahead to be encountered in the future . . .

My birthday came on May 25 . . . just three days after the horrendous catastrophe, and I was at the funeral services weeping. Every birthday I may ever have in the future will be the reopening of memories that will pain old wounds.

Our graduation was first cancelled, then postponed, and we had it a few weeks later, but it was all too sad . . .

These days I find myself emotionally locked in a new conflict. I am fighting an anger that rises inside me and is directed against those who had the time to take pictures of the on-rushing tornado, placing that concern against sounding warnings and directing people needing to escape. Another object of my anger is those who have been saying, "I wouldn't rebuild at all if I were you." Well, they're all wrong, so lacking in understanding. We are a family out here, and have been for such a long, long time. We may be a tiny, insignificant little town a long way from anywhere, but we possess strong, loving, and caring hearts. We proved that by being there to support and succor each other. That's why we all hurt so much, so deeply, because we were so close . . . one big happy family with profound feelings for each other.

I know that God will give us the strength we need to carry on, to keep on going. It rejoices my heart to know that my two very special friends are in the Kingdom of God, along with members of their families and their friends. One day, I, too, will join them, for I have a living faith that I am a child in God's Kingdom . . .

I press on, giving thanks to God that we are alive, and I thank Him for everything He has done for us to enable us to endure our trauma. He has given us unbelievable help, love, and support through people all over the world. Most importantly are the prayers that they have sent up for all of us here, and by the grace of God, we are getting by one day at a time.

Worlds of people never knew before where Saragosa was, or, that it even existed. They all know now! But what a way of finding out!

For the few whom I have known who made slight remarks, saying, "Oh, it was nothing much," I have something much to say! You are so very wrong: it was something, and it was a colossal tragedy that lives on and on, still haunting some of its victims, if not all of them. Most of the homes we lost may have been poor men's shanties, but they were the only homes that we had. The little personal effects that vanished might not mean much to a man or woman of affluence . . . but they were the collections and mementos of a lifetime . . .

For those who have taken our tragedy lightly, I only hope and pray that nothing approaching this catastrophe may ever descend upon them . . . People cannot feel what we feel, because they have not seen what we saw. That tornado not only touched our homes and our properties, but it touched something even more dear . . . our hearts, and left them broken and bleeding . . .

Only by strong faith and determination have we survived, but we still have that strong faith and determination, and by that, with God's help, we will move on into the future, living in peace, conquering the fear that grips us still, but that, in time, we trust, will largely fade away.

July 15, 1987

* * *

Jose Muniz attended my English classes at the Balmorhea Public Schools for six years. Our relationship was superb, partly because I do not reckon myself a teacher, but as the eternal student. With my students I am engaged in the eternal quest for fascinating insights into life. The credit for my close and rewarding relationships in and out of the classroom is due, in large measure, to such remarkable students as Jose Muniz, who almost run ahead of me in their eagerness to know, to learn, to explore.

Many a heart-gripping paper have I been privileged to read from Jose Muniz and his delightful classmates. Jose, while small of stature and slight of build, is immense of mind and generous of heart. He is serious, intense, beautiful from the inside out, delightful to know. We have shared much in conference and in what we both have written, but more delightful even than this is our tried and true friendship and unqualified positive regard for each other.

He wrote about Saragosa in his journal this summer. Then he brought it over to "help me with my book" if I could use it. I find it gripping reading, and feel that other readers will appreciate it as I have.

So Many Came As Strangers
and Left As Friends
Jose Muniz

Losing loved ones is terrible. Most of us can deal with the pain if we lose someone we love, but when we lose about thirty friends and relatives at one time, then dealing with the pain assumes catastrophic dimensions.

This past summer I experienced this horror in my hometown of Saragosa, Texas. The tornado that hit Saragosa was a shocking surprise to all of us here, and was a tragedy that bewildered people in almost every part of the world. People came from many faraway places to view the shambles of my death-stricken town. These people helped us through the worst crisis at Saragosa by stopping and rendering aid to an insignificant little town I never thought of as very important. On May 22, 1987, however, my perception of my hometown was proven to me to be wrong, and it reversed itself by one-hundred-eighty degrees.

It was about 7:45 at night and thoughts of the final days of my public school career were coming and going through my mind. I was thinking that next Friday would be the Big Day for me and my classmates. That would be the Friday of May 29, 1987, and we would be graduating from Balmorhea High School. I was also recalling my past experiences from elementary school on through high school. It was hard for me to realize I was one week from leaving that dear old familiar place in my life, leaving it forever behind. Internally, I cried.

During this time we had the TV tuned to the KOSA Channel Seven in Odessa. The weatherman announced a tornado warning for Southwest Reeves County, but I wasn't worried. He also advised the people in this area to take cover, but I didn't think much of that, either. About a minute later my sister Irma called from Alpine to see if we knew that there was a tornado warning for our area. I told her not to worry, because in the past we had had so many of these warnings that we weren't bothered by them. My mother then turned the channel to watch her favorite night-time soap opera. It came on at eight o'clock.

We had only gotten about five minutes into her soap when my cousins, Aidee and Hector Muniz and their mom ran to our doorstep. Their faces were white with horror and fright. A friend of mine, Joel Rodriguez, had just come to warn them that a tornado had touched down to the south of us and was coming directly toward our houses that were rowed up near a creek at the southwestern corner of Saragosa. We all agreed in short order that we would flee in our cars.

My mother, my sister Melissa, and my little niece Jamie, and I followed Joel's dad out of the town. We soon passed the Community Hall, at which time the road we drove was barely visible. Water was pouring in torrents. We saw through the deluge that people were still inside the hall where the children's graduation was taking place. Something from within me, a nameless instinct, told me not to stop . . . told me to get out of town with all possible speed. All I wanted to do was to save my mom, my little sister, and Jamie.

As our little rain-drenched caravan drove north out of town along State Highway 17, we decided to change routes. We took the branching farm road that led north and west toward a large cattle feedlot a few miles further on. Out there under a driving curtain of rain, both our cars began to be wrenched from side to side by both the strong winds and the baseball-sized hail that pounded down on our cars. A couple of minutes later the storm seemed to have stopped, or else we had outdistanced its forward edge. After a short time we stopped, too, and after taking stock of conditions, we returned to Saragosa to learn whether everything was in order in the town. What incredible and astounding surprises were awaiting us there!

The spectacle that we encountered was not a pretty or a welcome one . . . I felt utterly helpless as I confronted the devastation in all directions. In a little while, I was told of people whom I had known all my life . . . dead! I was too numb to react to their words, because I could not accept the farfetched fact that they were dead. Even after I attended their funerals, the reality of this disaster and its personal consequences for me had not hit me full force. My mind could not capture the magnitude of the horror. My soul could not identify with it and achieve any satisfactory congruity within. I wonder whether it ever can.

Three months have passed now, and I know that what happened on that nameless night of May 22 was more than a passing, torturous nightmare. It was real alright! People so dear, so loved, have actually gone. Their souls took flight, went away with the wild, swirling winds that night. I have vivid memories of them all, of the blessed times we shared. There was Kathy Escovedo, who was only sixteen, like a sweet little sister. I remember how she always welcomed my jokes with a sweet, cheerful smile. That smile somehow hangs around in my memory, and won't go away. And dear, quiet, warm-hearted little Elvira Casias . . . such a friend . . . It could have easily been me who met death that fateful night instead of them . . .

As I reflect now, I can honestly vow that during that time when I felt that the monster tornado might, at any moment, suck away the car we were in, that I was not afraid to die. I knew that if my time had come, well, so be it! I wasn't going to fight it. I felt safe . . . I still feel the same way about it, and I feel this is well.

The hardest part for me was to make myself actually realize that those people on the death list of the *Dallas Morning News* were no longer among us, the living. I always ask myself, "Why them and why not me?" . . .

After a few days . . . perhaps weeks . . . of puzzling over such questions as these, I found my answer. The Lord of Glory didn't need me in heaven yet. He still wanted me down here on earth, to live and to serve Him here. I am eternally thankful for that. I know that there is not a thing I can do about the past, and I should not dwell on it, nor allow it, with its mistakes, to haunt and crucify me now. I shall look forward to the future with confidence and with a great deal more understanding of how . . . precious life really is.

I am deeply grateful for the generosity and loving nature of people throughout the United States. Because of their help manifested in multitudes of ways, Saragosa is now on the threshold of being rebuilt. So many of the people from far and near have come to Saragosa as strangers to lend a hand, and they have left as friends. As I mentioned before, I never perceived Saragosa as being very important in the world's scheme of things, but I was all wrong. When it came down to it, Saragosa was just as important as New York or L.A., because part of humanity is here, too, and is filled with the same feelings, aspirations, and concerns in life. When Saragosa bled, the whole nation bled as well, and that proves its importance as a piece of humanity as a whole!

PART II
The Victims

[5]

Victims in the Community Center

She has four children and nightmare memories of a terrible tornado. Now she will live forever in an emotional world of insecurity. Her name is Norma Rodriguez, a youthful mother now, a girl grown up who was reared in Saragosa, Texas. There she worked as a Head Start teacher aid to Lisa Carrillo. Norma drove the Head Start van, hauling the five-year-olds to and from their first school. In the storm that zeroed in on the Head Start graduation ceremonies of May 22, 1987, Norma lost six very close relatives, all of them perishing within but a few feet of her and her girls.

On that fatal day, Norma left the school in Saragosa at 1:00 P.M., her delivery van loaded with children. She stopped long enough at every home in the Balmorhea area to urge each mother to give her child a nap during the afternoon. After all, children should not become sleepy during their graduation ceremonies!

Norma drove on to her residence in Balmorhea. There she prepared a mountain of refreshments she had agreed to donate for the children and guests at the ceremonies that evening.

At 5:00 she supervised her daughters as they dressed for the program. That done, Norma made herself ready, and they all left home at 5:30. She and her girls were the first to arrive at the Community Center. They would be among the last to leave.

Norma Rodriguez shuddered now and then as her memory emerged and her story unfolded, and we found ourselves shuddering too.

Norma Rodriguez: I opened the building and unloaded the refreshments, then later helped decorate the tables. We soon encountered our first of many problems of the evening, though it was but a minor one. The fresh breeze kept blowing the name cards of some of the children off onto the floor. In time I turned up some Scotch tape and fastened the names in their places . . .

Mary Jane Ontiveras arrived with her little niece, and she assisted me with the decorations. A party atmosphere was building as more and more people arrived and lent a hand in all the preparations. Lisa Carrillo and her little Rachel stopped and chatted a minute before she busied herself with other concerns. Soon the parents and kids were multiplying everywhere, and we began to line up the children in alphabetical order.

At this point we discovered that Billy Lozano, Javier and Linda's little boy, was missing. When Linda finally arrived with Billy, we were ready to get the program under way. Although the director and some of the teachers from Pecos were running late, we decided to begin without them.

Joey Herrera began with a prayer. Then the children said a poem, titled "A Rose." As I thought back later, their poems all seemed a bit grimly prophetic. There was symbolism in them — a rose — *red.* There was another one, "Traffic Light." Then "My Family" was recited, followed by others. After a lot more songs, the children sang the "Goodbye" song. Before long, there would be flashing *red* emergency lights, *traffic lights, families* disrupted forever, and a lot of sad and permanent *goodbyes!*

I had to coax timid little Lorinda Carrillo to allow me to assist her in putting on her gown during the gowning of the girls. It was at about that moment that more strange things began to happen. Javier Lozano rushed down to the side where Lisa Carrillo was busy directing the program, and his wife dashed down to the side where I was busily engaged.

I heard somebody say he hollered something about a tornado, but the commotion had Lisa distracted, and I don't believe she ever understood. She just stood and stared at me, confusion written on her face. Linda told me. "A tornado is coming!" I asked, "Where?" She replied, "Outside the front door!"

Sudden chaos overtook us all. While running toward the door herself, my sister, Irma Garza, was sending my three girls back to me. On the run they came, fright masking their faces. Joey Herrera and his wife Elsa stood uncertainly with surprised looks shadowing their faces. I assumed it was an ordinary storm, never dreaming that a tornado was sweeping down upon us. It really was not clear in my thoughts even as the building came apart minutes later. Had I known what was coming, I never would have stayed in there! That old building always seemed weak and dilapidated to me, and I would have gotten out had I only known . . .

A struggling, frantic crowd of people was now at the door while a growing number was shuffling chairs and tables to the sides of the auditorium. Over by one wall I saw some people scrambling awkwardly under them.

Turning suddenly, I saw Joey and Elsa Herrera standing still, looking confused. She held Jonathan, her baby, in her arms. I stepped over and shook hands with them both. Impulsively, Joey announced, "I'll go to the door and check the tornado report." That's when Elsa went and sat down near Amelia Carrillo, Corina Brijalba's mother. I realized I'd better do something myself, and I went to the middle of the building and flung myself onto the floor. My girls were with me, and except for them, I was all alone there. They lay beside me, only we had nothing to put over us for protection as so many others had.

I noticed my aunts, Amelia Carrillo and Nora Brijalba, standing by the wall. Nora yelled to me and to Lucas to come over and stand with them so we could all hold hands. On an impulse, I ran over with my girls and joined them. As I went, I saw my sisters, Olivia Contreras and Irma Garza, running to the restroom with their kids.

I raced after them and plead with them not to stay in there. Following me out, they hurried over to a corner to a little serving table, and with their kids, somehow got under it.

Once more I got my kids with me down on the floor. I had two of them on top of me — one on my legs, and one over my neck. But Bianca was missing! I had no idea where she had gone in all the confusion. I glanced frantically about, then I saw her feet! That's all I could see of her, but I could recognize her by her sandals . . .

All was quiet . . . then came a downpour of heavy rain. My awareness of that rain was brief, because the windows suddenly began crashing and falling in onto the floor! Then some huge cement chunks came down with grinding thuds. They were large — like a half a wall in size, and they were connected by steel bars that prevented their breaking completely apart. Some of those wall sections fell in such a manner as to form a sort of triangle that helped to protect several of us — my friends and others near me — from instant death!

Now big sections of broken light poles were smashing in, hurled by the wind, slamming down all around us. Some were splinters split off those utility poles as they rained down and hurtled to resting places here and there around us. I lay there in pure terror, my mind a storm itself.

Lisa Carrillo, on top of the stage, was higher than the rest of us. The wall near us fell in while the one near Lisa fell *out*. When it went, she was sucked out after it. Lisa was on top of Rachel, her little girl. Both of them went . . . just vanished into the unknown on a horrendous draft!

After a brief eternity, the storm was gone, and I crawled out with two of my daughters. There stood Floyd Estrada's patrol car near where we emerged. Wonderful, welcomed sight! I settled my girls and myself inside and tried to breathe easy at last. But at that moment I saw a lady coming by, and I cried out to her, "Please help me find my Bianca . . ."

She was Libaria Lopez, Mary Jane's mother. She went with me around the wreckage of the building, and that's when we found Lisa, down outside, and with her, little Rachel. I must have been the first person to her. She looked up at me, her dark eyes pleading, and she told me, "Pick me up, pick me up!" Mrs. Lopez told her to wait a minute. "The ambulance is here, and they will pick you up," she told Lisa, who looked a fright and was obviously in great agony.

Her lip looked like shredded meat, and her right eye was big, swollen. Pieces of something — stickers, or hangers — were protruding from her face. I could see that the back of her head was smashed. Someone brought a blanket then and covered her.

Distressed and hurting for her, we turned away, concern suddenly returning . . . for Bianca. We still had not found Bianca! So it was that we left Lisa Carrillo to search for my child once more. I climbed up on top of a big window frame where I could look down inside the tangled wreckage. That's when I spotted my two sisters — just their backs. The cement slab was over them, and a long timber had their heads pushed down — *far* down.

Gerald, Olivia's younger boy, was holding Irma's head with his hand . . . Big spike nails from the lumber had gone into her skull, killing her, and had pinned Gerald's hand to her skull . . . He was unhurt otherwise.

Olivia had her head bent way down. Her teeth were knocked out. There they lay, white and scattered nearby. But she lived! She was even then calling for Gerald . . . dying herself, Olivia's first concerns lay with her boy . . .

My boyfriend, Julian Fuentes, was there, and he wouldn't let me watch any more. He and somebody helped me to Mr. Rhyne's Blazer, and I sat there about two hours until the rescue workers got the rest of my family members out. It was dark, and I had no idea that the town was wiped out until later. I saw some close-by damage, but had no idea the town was gone until next morning.

In time they found my brother-in-law, Lionel Garza, who was trapped under the debris in there. I had his two girls [Joanna, three, and Abigail, four] in the Blazer with me. I also had Armando Morales in the car. It was some while before Lionel had been freed. At the time, my girls Bianca and Tammy were still trapped underneath the rubble.

Sometime later, I was transferred to the Pecos sheriff's car. Someone tried to take me to the shelter in the Balmorhea school building, but there were so many wires down at the time that we could not go over there.

When that failed to pan out, the deputy dropped me off at Eddie Mondragon's house just east of the Community Center wreckage. I spent the night there, almost in shock . . . I kept remembering small episodes, like Jacob Sanchez running around right after the storm, peering into holes, looking for his parents, I suppose, both of whom were dead. Stunned by the horror of it all, I could not sleep . . . I still was deeply concerned and uncertain as to the whereabouts and condition of my two sisters.

It was about 7:00 the next morning when Lionel Garza came in from Pecos. He had been slightly hurt, treated, and released. He asked about his wife, Irma, my sister. Olivia's boys were in there, and Lionel did not want them to hear what he had to tell me. He had news that their mother was dead, and so he called me to the next room.

"Olivia is dead," he almost whispered to me once we were in there. I couldn't bring myself to tell him that his wife Irma was also dead — both my sisters gone! I pretended ignorance and let him think she was probably somewhere injured and in a hospital.

It was early that morning that my brother, Jose Rodriguez, came over to take me to his home. I found my sister-in-law, Maria Rodriguez, and the rest of the family all bothered about those who were missing and unaccounted for. That's when I called Maria aside and informed her that Irma was dead.

Olga Contreras, Olivia's daughter, had been in Pecos that morning, looking for her mother and for others. Somebody came over from Fort Stockton and informed Olga that her mother was over there — dead.

Maria told Lionel that his wife had been killed, and he went outside in a terrible daze . . .

As for my girls, they all turned up in time, all right but for minor cuts, bruises, and scratches. We went to Alpine and had them all checked over. One reason I was so concerned about my children was that an unidentified man fell on top of Tammy. I tried to pull her out, but I just couldn't. I could see her, and I lifted the man's arm. I said to him, "Please let Tammy out." He didn't answer me. Then I released his arm, and it fell, limp and lifeless. I was talking to a dead man. But he had taken the blows that my little girl would have received . . .

I subsequently learned that Bianca was still trapped. The men used hydraulic jacks and finally freed her. She was unharmed, but she was trapped in that cement tomb down in there for quite a long time . . . a lot of anxious hours for me!

It was a life-scarring time for my children too. Bianca was eight, Tammy, seven, Amanda, six, and then Jacob, my son who lived with Olivia, my sister, was eleven at the time.

As for myself, I had a lot of splinters — big ones — in my hair. During the storm, once I turned myself and moved my arm, and the wind tore my ring right off my finger! That ring barely fit me, you know — very tight — but that thieving wind took it off and away. It also stripped my shoes off my feet and made away with them as well!

[She formed a shape with her hands, like an A-frame, as she voiced her final sentence.] I was protected by a folded cement wall, held together with strong steel bars . . .

* * *

A very attractive young woman, dressed daily in her crisp white, works as a serious-minded member of the crew at the Balmorhea school cafeteria. She is Elda Montes, as dedicated and dependable as she is neat and wholesome. She is a 1979 graduate of Balmorhea High School, where she was, understandably, nominated the "Best Natured" member of her senior class.

Her husband, Ricky, works for the Balmorhea Housing Authority. Their two sons, J. R. (Jerediah) and Kevin, were six and five years old when the tornado tore into Saragosa to interrupt young Kevin's Head Start graduation ceremony there.

The little family had gone together, along with Elda's parents. They had arrived a little late, their hair tangled by the briskly blowing wind . . .

Elda Montes: After the program finally got under way, and the first part was over, then Javier warned us of the tornado. He suddenly ran in and grabbed his little boy and left. My first thought was to get Kevin out of there quickly. I grabbed him and ran to the front door, but it was already too late! There was the funnel right in front of me! It was *big* . . . right there, close by . . . too late!

I scrambled with Mom and J. R. underneath a table. We had barely gotten under it when everything came down. We were under the right side of the building, and when the thing hit, it was like a cannon shell smashing right into the front door . . .

The wall fell on the table where we cowered. Where was Ricky? I never saw him after we scrambled under there. He and Dad had simply vanished. Ricky was yelling like crazy for me, but I never heard him in that din. He told me later about his yelling, and of how, in the confusion, he and Dad were separated. Dad died, Ricky didn't. Dad was under a log . . . He was among the last to be taken out.

Mom and Dad — both of their faces were beautiful. Neither of them was marred like so many other people were.

As for me, I couldn't get air. We were suffocating under there where we were buried. It was so dark down under all that crumbled masonry and other debris that you could not see. There was no circulation of air, making it virtually impossible to breathe. We were trapped in that pit of horrors until about 9:30 that night.

Ricky was one of the first ones out, and he was going crazy looking and yelling for me. I could hear his voice off in a vague distance somewhere. J. R.'s whole body was stuck. He was on top of my mom, and all he could move was his two hands — his wrists. That eight-inch-thick wall on top of us was awfully heavy. My boy had bruises on his head, and kept pleading, "Mom, I want to go to sleep, I want to go to sleep."

After everyone was taken out, we all went to the hospital, were checked over and released . . . so that people far worse off than we, the really unfortunate ones, could be kept there. My husband had a big hole in the back of his wrist, mashed there by the wall that fell over him. Slashes on his back and shoulders have left a lot of scars — these from things driven into him by the vicious winds . . .

We had unbelievable amounts of mud and dirt on our bodies and in our clothes. I put my dress and the kids' clothes in the closet there. All of that clothing was brand new, but I haven't the heart to launder them.

Ricky was one of the first to get out, and he saw so much horror . . . he wouldn't talk for two weeks.

At the hospital in Pecos, my sister came and asked about our parents . . . I had a feeling my dad and my mom were dead, but I kept hoping, hoping my mom was only sick or hurt. About my dad, I wasn't sure at all, but, as it turned out, we lost them both.

* * *

Elodia Garcia was one of Saragosa's fortunate few on the night of May 22. A young housewife and mother, Mrs. Garcia took Amy, her five-year-old, and accompanied her parents, Virginia and Tommy Martinez, to the Head Start graduation at the Community Center. Armando Garcia stayed with their baby daughter Angelina at the Martinez home.

Elodia's eyes told of the horror as she remembered masonry wall sections falling at such angles above them that they were trapped and injured — but their lives spared.

Elodia Garcia: The base of the fallen wall supported the roof as it wavered and fell. As we went down, I grabbed a small folding table and pulled it to my side. That table caught and supported the wall section, saving us from instant death as it slumped to the floor at an angle above us.

I flung my right arm outward as I went down. The irregular bottom edge of the fallen wall caught it and pinned me there. It did not sever my arm, although it cut it deeply. It was close to two hours that we all lay pinned down and helpless in that death trap. Breathing was difficult, and none of us could possibly move our bodies in our cramped cavern where we were confined.

Rescue crews attacked the mountain of rubble above our heads. With a high-lift jack and a heavy chain, they slowly eased a huge block of masonry that rested above, so protecting us that we never even realized that it had rained and hailed while we were trapped below.

Meanwhile, my husband Armando, keeping our baby at my parents' home, went through horror and a miraculous escape himself. When the big blow began, he pushed our baby and her crib to the bedroom floor. Then he flung himself over her just as the tornado smashed the house down on top of them. As this happened, the dresser, shoved by the blast, blew against the bed, right where they lay on the floor. They found themselves inside a "v" formed by the two pieces of furniture. The bedroom door smashed in and down over them, coming to rest on the dresser and bed. This sheltered them in that split second, just as walls and wind-driven debris crashed down.

Armando suffered only a minor leg injury and bruises . . . He managed to free himself . . . and we were all reunited in the midst of the ruins of our town.

* * *

Lisa Williams — pleasant, outgoing, beautiful — grew up in Marfa, Texas, a desert town in far West Texas. It was in her hometown that Lisa met Tony Carrillo of Balmorhea in 1973. They were married the following year, and now have two lovely children, Richard, eleven, and Rachel, nine. Before the tornado, Lisa worked as a Head Start teacher at Saragosa. Tony is a maintenance supervisor at the Law Enforcement Center near Pecos.

Lisa spoke of her work as a Head Start teacher, her beautiful brown eyes smiling through the pain and discomfort of her bandages and splints. Having sustained severe occipital head injuries, Lisa Carrillo has problems now in recall and in phrasing her thoughts. Reflection seems painful, too, but her efforts are heroic and cheerful.

> **Lisa Carrillo:** I was directing the program. The children were singing their "Goodbye" song . . . just finishing it when everything was disrupted. We hadn't given out the diplomas yet, and we never would. In the storm that followed moments later, they perished . . .
>
> While the kids were still singing, my little Rachel came up on the stage and kept trying to tell me she was afraid. I partly ignored her, because I was busy watching and directing the children involved in the program. But she was trembling, really frightened . . . I turned to see what might be wrong, and as I did, my eye caught sight of something swirling, dark and ominous beyond the window. It was bearing down upon us!
>
> Suddenly, the terrifying truth hit me . . . a tornado! . . . I became aware that people were dashing up and snatching their children right off the stage . . . others were still sitting as if uncomprehending or unaware. I told the children then to go quickly to their parents. One little boy just sat there crying as death and destruction bore down upon us all . . .
>
> I later learned that Mr. Lozano . . . shouted a warning . . . I have no memory of any of that. Perhaps I never was aware of it.
>
> [Lisa's daughter spoke up] **Rachel:** I heard him hollering at the door, "There's going to be a tornado!" That's when I became frightened and went to my mother.
>
> **Lisa:** I never did see him grab his child. I was very confused at the time . . . you know, with growing irritation that the program for which I was responsible was being totally disrupted. The children were attempting to sing while a lot of noise and dis-

tractions were going on, and I was concentrating with some difficulty on the program we were struggling to give . . .

I remember . . . that I threw Rachel down on the floor of the stage . . . and I fell on top of her. Suddenly, there was a loud sucking sound like a very powerful vacuum cleaner — you know how the nozzle sounds when it pulls hard on the carpet . . . My memory is so faulty. I do recall being outside. I think the wind *sucked* me out of that building and threw me down outside somewhere!

I remember a lot of water . . . like a lot of water running . . . I can't feel any rain. One tornado rule is to get into a canal . . . But I'm in all this water. "We'll all drown in all this water . . ." I said that, and that's the last I remember.

[According to Jacob Sanchez, who witnessed this terrible episode, Lisa's face was whipped up and down by the wind into a puddle.]

I had both body and head injuries. There was a deep incision under my chin. I had a broken right arm. A stick, or shaft of wood of some kind, went through my left leg. There was a very deep cut in my right leg as well. It left a hole where the flesh was literally scooped out. There were multiple scratches, cuts, and bruises all over my body. My right hand had multiple cuts forming a zig-zag pattern across my fingers . . .

I am blind in my right eye — the one that was my good eye before. You see, I had poor vision in the other eye all along. Now, it's the only vision I have left. I had this terrible blow on the back of my head, which, the doctor said, resulted in extreme damage to my right eye.

Rachel: I had a cut on my arm . . . and there was one on my left thigh. There was glass . . . in my lower leg . . . My left ear, not the ear, but right over it . . . had a cut, and there were splinters of wood in me. I was knocked unconscious, and then I remember getting up outside the building. I remember running to some men and begging them to come and help my mom who was lying out there bleeding badly. They didn't believe me. Then a man put me into Floyd's car. I stayed in there about two minutes, and then I saw some men putting my mom into an ambulance, taking her away.

Mr. Rhyne was there, and I told him that my arm was hurting a lot . . . Mr. Rhyne stopped the ambulance that my mother was in, and he put me in there too. I remember seeing my daddy somewhere later, but it is all mixed up in my mind. Some of it is just too hard for me to remember.

Tony: Our part started at home. I had come in and taken a nap. While I slept, it rained . . . really rained. Richard came to me and wakened me and told me to look. I peered out, and the world looked as if another deluge had come down. Water was over some of the roadway, and I thought of the dips and low crossings on the back way between here and Saragosa. Lisa might come in that way after the program, and she would never be able to make it home if she did . . .

I decided I had better go to a telephone and call her not to come home by the back roadway. Richard and I took off for the Tumbleweed Inn, a bar over on the main highway, to call Lisa from there and warn her of the high water.

At the bar some men told me that a tornado had hit Saragosa. All of a sudden, I forgot all about making that phone call! Instead, I took off down the highway south for Saragosa. We drove like mad for about three miles, and suddenly I saw an ambulance parked on the side of the road. Apparently it was having trouble, or was broke down. I saw yet another vehicle there near the ambulance. It was Marcos Contreras's station wagon. He is the assistant director at the prison where I work, and he had stopped to help. I also stopped to render aid, being an EMT (Emergency Medical Technician) myself. We were working to remove the gurney from the ambulance, and I was yelling, "Hurry up!" to the driver, Isaac Martinez. Rita Lozano, his assistant [Tony's cousin], was behind me, and she tapped me on the shoulder and ordered sternly, "You get out of this, Tony. *I'll* handle *this!*"

That astonished me, because I am an EMT myself. Just who did she think she was? I hadn't noticed who the passenger in the ambulance was . . . not just yet . . . I looked closer. I did not know this lady, could not make out the face. It was an unspeakable sight . . . swollen, puffed up like a balloon until I could scarcely distinguish the nose. Unrecognizable . . . except . . . *suddenly, it hit me like a blow!* I was suddenly sick — weak, dizzy, and dumbfounded. That lady . . . was *Lisa! My wife!* I snarled at Rita, "You get the hell out of this! I'm handling her from now on!"

Lisa: When they were putting me into the ambulance, there came a flash of consciousness. People milling around me were talking about the tornado. Somebody kept saying he was sorry to hurt me. I didn't know what that individual meant. I do remember mumbling something to myself — something like, "They're crazy; I can't hurt any more than I'm hurting now!" Something utterly devastating happened then . . . Just a man's voice droned, "It's going to hurt a lot, but it *has* to come out!" There was a sudden shocking, blinding, wrenching stab of pain unlike anything I had ever known! I didn't know who had done what to my leg, but it was the total, the ultimate essence of unendurable agony!

Darrel Rhyne had decided that the shaft of wood that was all the way through my leg had to come out, and with all his strength, he yanked it free.

[Lisa had brief moments at the hospital when she emerged from long periods of unconsciousness and moaned, "I'm a reject!" Tony would lean over her and ask, "What?" By then, however, she had lapsed into unconsciousness once more. When Tony asked her why she had said that, she didn't remember saying it — at first.]

Finally, I remembered: when the tornado hit, and we were all so frantic, I remember giving myself completely to the Lord in a renewal of my commitment to Him. Then I asked Him not to take my girl — to take me instead of her. When I was not taken, and I realized that when I first regained consciousness for a brief moment, I remember the fleeting thought flashing through my mind and exploding in my awareness: "He didn't *want* me! I'm a reject! I'm a reject!" I guess that thought kept emerging from my subconscious mind, and I kept repeating it to myself . . .

This young couple had been hit hard, with Tony off his job and devoting all of his time to caring for Lisa for two months, and with the family not eligible for disaster services since their mobile home was not located in Saragosa and was not destroyed. The Head Start school carried no insurance to cover Lisa's injuries. But with love and encouragement, the best of all therapy, and with what help their true, caring friends can offer, they could recover. No person deserves happiness more than one who patiently endures that which cannot be changed.

* * *

Maribel Ortega, a native of Saragosa, attended high school in Pecos until her marriage to Gilbert Ortega in 1981. Maribel, in her early twenties, is attractive, vivacious, and very level-headed, as her account reveals. Gilbert is a highly respected young man who works as a school custodian at the Balmorhea schools. He spoke with quiet dignity in response to my indulgence in asking questions.

"I did not think it was wise for Maribel to go off that afternoon, because the clouds forming up looked dangerous to me. She decided to go anyway, and I didn't even know of the tragedy at Saragosa until it was all over," he said.

Gilbert did not elaborate upon his being the first to arrive from the outside world after the disaster struck. He and his brother, Joe Ortega, had been forced to stop and wait to keep from overtaking the twister. Both of them were effective in early rescue operations, as is related in his younger brother's account in Part III.

The succinct revelations in this account by Maribel Ortega are shocking, leaving one to feel something of the magnitude of her loss.

Maribel Ortega: Armando Morales, my nephew, was in the Head Start graduation, and that is why I went. Both Anastacio Morales, my brother, and Corina, his wife, were killed there. She was the mother of little Armando, and was seven months pregnant. Their one-year-old son Andres died with them.

A big wall fell on top of my brother. They were not together in the building, and they found her somewhere else.

The weather was pretty when I arrived at the Center. No one could have guessed the horrors to overtake us in a little while.

The program was late in starting, but things went smoothly until Javier ran in — Javier Lozano. He just ran in yelling that a tornado was coming, grabbed his kid, and rushed out again.

I did not stay after that. I dashed out the door and took off in my car as fast as I could. My brother and his wife ran out too. They were already in their car, ready to go, but their boy wasn't there. They ran back inside to get him. I told my sister-in-law to let me go in and get their kids . . . Armando and Andrew . . . but she frantically screamed, "No! I'll get them!" So, I took off . . .

They ran back for the boys and were killed . . . Andrew too. Norma Mendosa took Armando and some other kids to a corner of the room. My mother said that when the wall near my brother started to fall in, he and another man, Lucas Carrillo, were struggling to hold it back . . . but it overcame them and came down. They scrambled to dodge it, but it fell on them, crushing them instantly.

In the meantime, I drove like crazy to my mother's house, which was out in the country on the road going directly east from the site of the Community Center — it's about five miles.

I kept my eye on the rearview mirror as I sped to outdistance the storm. I watched it as I went. My dad was in the yard watching it when I dashed up. There were two barns about a quarter of a mile along that road. They're not there anymore!

I lost other relatives back at the Center. Corina Morales, my sister-in-law, had a sister named Leticia Martinez. She was injured, but her husband, Jorge Martinez, was killed, and so was Roxanne, their daughter, who was only eight months of age . . . Corina's brother, Socorro Rodriguez, also of Kermit, was there and died that night. It was only a year ago that Corina and Anastacio Morales moved to Balmorhea . . . All six of them were taken to Kermit for burial.

My husband here, Gilbert, was at home that fateful afternoon. He tried to talk me out of going to that graduation program, and now I wish he had succeeded!

* * *

Friendly as a pair of Texas mockingbirds, Pat and Corina Brijalba live just a stone's throw from town, across Toya Creek, north of Balmorhea toward the interstate highway. Corina is a cousin of Maggie and Victor Hernandez, two close friends of mine who told us of having lost six relatives at Saragosa. Those relatives were related to the Brijalbas as well.

Deceased family members were Corina's mother, Mrs. Amelia Carrillo, Nora Brijalba, an aunt, along with Lucas Carrillo, Corina's son. In addition, Olivia Contreras and Irma Garza perished at the Center. Mrs. Garza likewise lost her one-year-old son, Jose Lionel Garza. Anita Brijalba, Pat's aunt, lost her life in the wreckage of her mobile home, the floor and running gear of which were blown across the farm-to-market road leading into town on the southwest side.

The most fortunate of all, Pat and Corina survived, although they suffered extensive injuries.

The Brijalbas were at the Community Center attending the Head Start graduation of their granddaughter, Lorinda Carrillo, Lucas Carrillo's little girl. How they admired the little beauty when Norma Mendosa marched her out onto the stage!

They sat near the stage, behind Olivia Contreras and Irma Garza, her sister. When Corina went outside to smoke a cigarette, she saw the approaching tornado, ran inside, and reported it to the speaker, Tony Martinez.

By this time people were fighting in a frenzy to find the door, but it was impossible to fight their way out. Pat saw the mighty funnel a mere 200 yards away and coming fast. They took up a position to the side of the door below a window, pulling little Lorinda down between them as the monster poised to smash the building to shreds.

As the mighty blow slammed into the building, they saw windows popping out. Situated at the entrance end and to the side of a large old window, they all went down, throwing their bodies upon that of Lorinda. The masonry walls collapsed about their heads.

Pat Brijalba: We were by this big old window, an old window long since plastered over with thin plaster which wasn't strong. It being thin and weak, the whole window was blasted out, smashing into the room. A split-second later the wall came down, and the ceiling collapsed. I went through the hole in the falling wall where the window had been. When we were freed later, we came out through the window opening in the wall. Had that hole been solid wall I would have been crushed to death!

Corina: I was knocked out cold. When I came to, I asked my husband, "Where *are* we?"

He answered with one word, "Saragosa."

"Well, what are we doing in this place?" I demanded, still not "with it" yet. Then Pat explained that we had come for Lorinda's graduation. He was patient and understanding, and I appreciated that as I took it all in with a sweep of my eye. All I could see was walls down all around me.

Pat: My little granddaughter said to me, "Are you all right, Paw-Paw?" and I told her that I was.

"But you have blood . . ." she insisted. I had a gash on the left side of my head above the ear.

"Only a little cut on my scalp; I'll be all right, baby," I explained, seeking to soothe her in that frightful moment of our helplessness.

We weren't really all right, but compared to all those dead people under all that concrete rubble, we were. We were trapped in there for about three hours.

Corina: The wall section came down on me but missed me because of the window opening. It pinned my legs, and there was no way to move, and I was injured all over. Pat was also pinned down but not wedged in as I was. We waited under there, and minutes crept along slowly, stretching into three hours. I was conscious at first, but in time I passed out.

Pat: My son, Pat, Jr., arrived then. He gave me a cloth and told me to hold it to my head where blood was flowing. Corina was out of her mind and kept wanting to know, "What are we doing in this place?"

During the tornado strike we could actually see chunks of concrete, driven by the wind, flying through that old building. As it was subsiding, I took the mask of dirt off my eyes and peeped around. Stuff was flying like cannon balls and shrapnel . . . everywhere! Then it was over, and I pushed our granddaughter upward, and somebody reached for her. I never knew who it was up above us there, and so very soon after the funnel had passed.

I turned and looked at my wife lying there pinned down, helpless and hurting, and out of her head. There was a steel rod sticking out of a huge hunk of concrete, and that thing was pointing at my temple, inches from my face! I grabbed it and tried to pull myself out of the little cavern where I was trapped, but I couldn't budge my body an inch . . .

Corina: James Garlick came later, and eventually pulled me out, helped by the crew. Working in stages, he'd inch me up just a bit while other men jacked up the wall a little, a little more, and a little more, easing the wall up . . . by the big jacks. On and on it went until I was out and in an ambulance headed for Fort Stockton.

I knew there was another woman in the ambulance [Mrs. Contreras], but my right eye was blinded, and she lay to the right of me, so I never could figure out who she was. Later, a nurse, Kay Magee, checked to find out where Pat had gone and told me . . . that he was in a hospital in Pecos.

Pat: At Pecos, the doctor checked me over, X-rayed me, and informed me that, other than scratches and bruises, I was okay. But I hurt for three weeks . . . couldn't move, lie down, or sleep. I had to sit up in a chair at night for all that time. After three weeks of that torture, I decided something had to be done and went to the hospital in Fort Stockton. Dr. Lancaster there found three broken ribs! Would you believe? He treated them, and I improved at once.

Corina: Most of my injuries were on my left side. Tons of concrete fell and horribly depressed my upper left thigh. It cut and bruised and gouged out tissue, making a depression where there was massive tissue damage. The tissue of my stomach wall, also crushed, still shows it like this. I was black and blue all over, had collapsed lungs, a skull fracture, and a broken toe on my left foot. A large sliver of wood about five or six inches long was embedded in my right temple. Actually, they dug out three such slivers; one or more of them damaged the optic nerve of my right eye, almost totally blinding it.

I feel confident that I will see with it some day. I sense some small improvement some days. I see a little, but that eye is not lined up with the other, and toward the end of the day, the little vision I have from it causes me to see double . . . you know, when I am tired.

I lost my purse and glasses out there, but they were found and I recovered them. In spite of some reported looting right after the storm, my purse was not rifled. [There had been reports of looting by credible witnesses who named scoundrels. Rings were seen being removed from fingers, purses emptied.] People who would do such things are pretty low down. I had almost a hundred and fifty dollars in my purse along with credit cards, and none of it was missing . . . except my checkbook, which was never found. Strange . . . the wind lifted my checkbook and took it away, leaving everything else. My glasses were not even broken during that wild episode.

Pat: Everybody, just about, lost their glasses, either knocked off or blown from their faces. Corina was one of the fortunate ones who retrieved hers.

You know, Lucas Carrillo, my stepson, didn't have a single body injury — no broken bones, no cuts, no bruises, nothing! He was trapped under the rubble, and as best we could figure, he simply suffocated down under there. People squatted down, and the closeness must have shut out the air; they couldn't breathe, and that did them in.

* * *

Only the scales of a tragic, broken heart can weigh a great personal tragedy. On May 22, 1987, a door leading to an unbelievable world of terror and heartache opened for Nancy Prieto Matta, and it will never close.

She is the wife of David Matta, a popular and outstanding student in the Balmorhea High School who graduated in May 1984. After Nancy graduated from the eighth grade, David coaxed her into leaving school and becoming Mrs. Nancy Matta, a marriage that proved a happy one for them. Nancy is a quiet pool where waters run deeply and beautifully. She is warm and personable, and sits, demure and quiet, allowing David to do most of the talking.

On the evening of May 22, David was installing an airconditioning unit in their mobile home in Balmorhea. Earlier, Nancy had expressed the desire to attend the Head Start program with her sister, Linda Lozano. Nancy invited David to go, but he preferred to stay at home and finish installing the cooler. Nancy and Linda, along with their mother, Matilde Prieto, Nancy's two-year-old son Jourmain, and Nancy's baby brother Joe, went to Saragosa for the graduation.

After David Matta finished installing the cooling unit at home, he drove to Saragosa. Upon leaving the interstate out by Gallegos's Chevron station, he noticed a number of automobiles parked up on top of the overpass. On turning north he noticed what he thought might be a tornado. The cloud, big, grayish-white, and just a little to the northwest of him, was all in a whirl. Seemingly it had hit the ground, but the funnel was so wide, so large, he could not be sure. It was an ominous curtain hanging out of the cloud, and it bore the appearance of smoke or dust, stirring up a lot of dirt on the ground.

David Matta: There was too much dust for me to see. Then came the rain and hail. I really could not see Saragosa from my place below the overpass. Since it was hailing pretty hard, I stayed under there for protection. In just a bit, Floyd, our deputy sheriff, came through real fast, his lights flashing. Very shortly after he went by, I pulled out and followed him on into Saragosa. There I saw all this wreckage. What a horrible, frightful place of complete desolation it was! And right there, as if waiting for me to come, was a woman and a child standing among those uninhabited ruins. It was Nancy! And with her was Jourmain, our little boy!

Nancy: Floyd was the first to arrive after the storm; then David came next, right after he arrived.

When the warning was sounded by Javier Lozano, my brother-in-law, most everybody scrambled toward the front door. There was a big crush of people there, and it was generally decided that we couldn't get out and make good our escape. A few did, but I knew I could never make it, because the funnel was near and closing in fast. Running toward the east wall, I pulled Jourmain under a large table with me and held him in my arms as it hit, slamming down the wall onto the table above our heads. We suddenly found ourselves in a low hollow formed by that tilted wall. Our protecting table was gone, pushed out beyond our reach, but still holding the wall at a narrow angle, forming a safe pocket under there. Strangely, my boy who had been in my arms in front of me when the tornado struck, was behind me when it went!

Mother was about five feet from me and under the wall . . . dead. What caused death we do not know, as there were no marks on her except a minor cut on one hand. She had high blood pressure, and we think she suffered a heart attack which killed her. We just don't know. Beside my mom, clinging to her body and hugging her, was my little brother Joe. He was okay.

When we all dived for cover, Linda Lozano, my sister, was shoving people left and right under tables, especially the children. Our table was crowded, and my mom was only partially sheltered under her table. My sister Emma was all right, and she and I went to the hospital late that night to see Mother.

David: When they finally got [Nancy's mother] out, they put her into Mrs. Donna Davis's van and took her body with some others on to the hospital. One of the others was Mrs. Eva Meras, Elda Montes's mother. Mrs. Nita Rhyne rode with us, and we delivered the bodies to Pecos, then made a run to the Correctional Unit and picked up about 125 blankets for Saragosa disaster needs.

> **Nancy:** Officer Kelly Davis put a child into Nita Rhyne's arms and told her to deliver it to the hospital. That was Armando Garcia's baby girl, who was at home with her father when the storm hit. Armando rode out the tornado at his wife's parents' place, caring for Angelina. They came out all right, dashed over to the Center looking for his wife, and somehow the child was sent to Pecos with us. Everybody who weathered the storm was, as a practice, sent in to be checked out for injuries. She was all right.
>
> My sister Emma has a daughter named Myra, a third-grader. When the tornado struck the Center down, Myra was in another part of the building. She later told us that she was with Jacob and Orlando Sanchez. She reported that they put their legs over her to protect her, and she feels that this act of caring on their part probably saved her life.

Nancy Prieto Matta smiled beautifully as she related details of the tragic loss of her mother, of how Rogelio Vasquez, her brother-in-law, identified her mother, of the funerals and empty hearts and the vacant place left in their home. But that smile bore its touch of sadness. The door to her heartache is still open, and we counted ourselves greatly privileged to be welcomed within, to stand with her and David on the sacred ground of their grief.

* * *

Jacob Sanchez was a seventh-grade English student in one of my English as a Second Language classes last year. Students in these special classes have some deficiency in the use of English as their second language, their major language being, in this case, Spanish. Jacob, a conscientious student, had worked diligently to overcome his language handicap.

My heart went out to this lad when I learned of the tragic loss of his parents in the Saragosa storm. For weeks I had not been able to see Jacob until one day I spotted him relaxing by the canal in downtown Balmorhea. After visiting a few minutes, he began to give details of his experience.

He told of being at the graduation program, of sitting near the stage where the little kids were, to watch and admire his little sister, Deborah, who was in the program. He felt very proud of her. Then, when the tornado hit the Community Center, his mother shouted for him to get Deborah and bring her to her mother.

An apparent contradiction surfaced here. His aunt Delilah Alvarez said that his mother ran down to the front for Deborah. I checked this out with Jacob and found both accounts to be true. It seems Jacob jumped onto the stage, grabbed Deborah, whirled about, and there came Sylvestra, running forward. She had not waited. Jacob handed the child to his mother, and they all ran for the door.

He recalls that all of his family made it outside, where his parents made a quick assessment of the tornado. With them were, in addition to Jacob, his two sisters, Alexa, a sixth-grader, and Deborah, in Head Start; Delilah Alvarez, the children's aunt, was also there.

A little argument passed between his parents, his dad wanting to go, his mom wanting to stay. She prevailed, and they rushed back inside at a moment when the funnel was only about 200 yards away and moving in fast.

Back inside, Jacob's mother, with little Deborah, crawled under a table as his dad ran over and lay by the wall. People were scrambling this way and that in the lightless gloom of the old building. Certain details were unclear, and mistaken identities came easily. Minor inconsistencies, therefore, in Jacob's and Delilah's accounts are understandable.

At first, Jacob reclined with his mother. When a window burst, he shouted, "Look, Mom! The window is breaking!" She ordered him to keep his head down. But he couldn't position himself completely under the table with his mother. Suddenly, seeing his uncle, Orlando Sanchez, shoving benches over by the wall, he rushed over there to assist him.

When Jacob sprinted across the room to help him, the windows really began shattering, glass flying everywhere. As Jacob ran, he had to cover his face and brave the missiles of glass slicing through the air.

His uncle and his family scrambled under a table, urging Jacob to get under there with them. In the process, however, Jacob saw a little girl who was crying. He grabbed her and took her with him under the table. She was Myra Dominguez, eight or nine years old, the daughter of Jimmy and Emma Dominguez of Balmorhea. Jacob held his arms around Myra as they cowered in desperate fear under the table.

> **Jacob Sanchez:** All of a sudden I could hear a loud noise coming from the direction of the door . . . everything started to cave in! I felt the wall beside me *rising!* Then everything just came down. I could feel all this wood and masonry getting heavier and heavier on top of me. The table over me had collapsed under all that weight. Then . . . *I could look outside!*

When the wall rose and fell, a big metal tank just appeared there — suddenly — out of nowhere, and the wall partly came down on it. That's probably what saved my uncle's family and me . . . and the girl.

Anyway, I could look out from under the wall past that metal tank. Everything was going 'round — swirling in a circle like a gigantic whirlwind. Suddenly, I saw a body flying around in it just outside the walls! It was a lady! I turned my head away . . . it was awful! Then I looked up again. I saw her on the ground. She was about fifty feet from me. The tornado was just throwing her all over the place! I was horrified . . .

That lady's little girl suddenly appeared out of nowhere. She ran, driven by the wind, and fell on top of her mother. It was wild — the wind just knocking her around . . . Then the little girl, Rachel, was just lying over her . . . hugging her . . . crying piteously. The lady was Lisa Carrillo . . .

As the tornado was passing, it started to hail. Some of it was the size of a golf ball. Then my uncle got out . . . and started to help that lady . . .

In the storm my foot was stuck in some boards . . . boards on top of my foot. I was able to get loose, and then I went outside to go look for my parents. The rescue people hadn't yet arrived; so me and my uncle were some of the first people that started helping other people . . .

The first thing we did was to go and start looking for my parents . . . and when we went where they were, my uncle got my dad out. I helped him take my dad out, for he was halfway under the wall.

Desperately, my uncle started giving my dad mouth-to-mouth . . . but he wouldn't breathe, or nothing. We tried everything we could to get him to breathe again, but we didn't make it. I was scared. I knew that my dad was already dead.

Then I went to look for my mom to help her. By now the emergency crews had come, and they were trying to lift the wall with a huge jack. As they lifted it, I recognized my mom by her shoes . . . because her head was in there first . . . out of sight. Then I took one of her arms to try and pull her out. She wouldn't move or nothing. When I would let go of her arm, it just fell . . . limp . . . I knew she was already dead.

. . . And then I began to look for my little sister. Deborah was by, or fairly near, my mom. She was okay, and they took her out. And then they started to take Delilah out — my aunt. She was just screaming and crying. Delilah was under her . . . my mom threw her body over Delilah and saved her life.

Then they took out my older sister Alexa. She was okay too.

But by that time I was in shock. I just started running toward the truck. Once there, I saw my grandmother, who is Delilah's mother, Mrs. Cesaria Alvarez, and she asked me, "Where's Delilah and Alexa . . . and your mom and dad?"

I told her that mom and dad . . . that they were dead . . .

My grandfather, Clemente Alvarez, came back from the ruins where my mom and dad were. He said simply, "Let's go . . ." because he wanted to take us to the doctor. Delilah had her ankle and foot all bruised up. I was bleeding where my wrist was cut, and I had a bunch of splinters in there.

At this point we went to Pecos . . . to stay at my aunt's house over there. Then we went on to the Pecos hospital the next day.

That night when we arrived at my aunt's house, I just lay down . . . to try to calm myself. I just lay down . . .

I marveled at the courage of this beautiful lad whom I had come to love and treat as a son. I was reminded of a quotation I cherished from Eric Fromm's excellent book *The Revolution of Hope:* "Man is strongest the more fully he is in touch with reality."

Brought near to the very portals of death, the heroic people of Saragosa, in facing the reality of that experience, seem to have grown stronger, indeed.

Seneca wrote, "Fire is the test of gold, adversity of strong men." The fires of adversity that swept the little town of Saragosa proved many strong men, women, boys, and girls, and to their everlasting honor, I applaud them.

* * *

Orlando Sanchez, a quiet-spoken resident of Balmorhea, owns and operates a modest garage, the principal auto repair shop in town. His youngest son, Matthew, was a member of that ill-fated Head Start class at Saragosa. Orlando, his attractive wife Becky, and other members of their families attended the graduation exercise.

Orlando related how microphone problems delayed the starting of the program, then how the program progressed. When Javier Lozano shouted his warning, Orlando dashed outside. His thoughts of leaving were drowned out by shouts of "Go inside! Get under the tables!" Scrambling back into the building with his family, he crawled under a table with them on one side by the wall. Others were busy doing the same, all of them soon waiting, frightened, wondering what was about to happen to them. The suspense was chilling as they waited for the horror to hit. Orlando Sanchez knew that horror.

Orlando Sanchez: The tornado came steadily on, and when it hit a few seconds later, it went "BOOM!" It was like some sort of unimaginable explosion. Glass from the windows flew through the air, slicing through it like shrapnel. Suddenly the walls were falling, and lumber and concrete came raining down! We — or I — watched a little and cringed a lot. But mostly I kept sharp eyes on my family, and somehow I knew that they were okay.

All of a sudden, it was all over, and after that thing passed, I went out of my hiding to see if I could help other people. It was then that my wife told me to go and open the car door. I couldn't find the car. It wasn't where I had parked it! Our car was gone . . . vanished!

Then Becky and the boys went out, walking across the highway to some buildings still standing over there, damaged, but they would provide some needed shelter from the wet and cold.

I stayed behind looking for my brother, Omero, and his wife Sylvestra. I found them, but they were both dead. They were under a wall which I tried to lift, but it was no use. That wall must have weighed a ton. Finally, jacks were brought and the fallen walls lifted, but it was too late for them and a lot of others down in there. In desperation I tried mouth-to-mouth efforts, but it was too late. Their little girl, Deborah, just five years old, was all right, thank the Lord. I have no idea how she managed to escape. Right after the passing of the storm, I made my way around the building and saw her standing up straight and all alone . . . in an open place . . . crying.

This puzzled me, and I think that when the wall fell on her parents, she was in a sort of sheltered, hollow space under there, and then she probably crawled out right away. Not knowing what to do, and in fear of doing anything, she probably just stood petrified with fear and released her emotions with tears.

I went to little Deborah and took her, intent upon leading her out and comforting her some. Suddenly, someone grabbed her from my hands and took her away. Knowing that she was being given care, I went then for my brother Omero and his wife. Both of them were dead. Their son Jacob was with me.

We stayed until about three or four in the morning . . . looking for people and trying to get others out. About two o'clock they started putting bodies into a school bus . . . seventeen or eighteen in one bus. I went into that bus to see if I could identify any of them, but it was useless. I couldn't figure any of them out. The problem was the mud . . . and blood. Their faces were mostly covered with mud — lots of it. Omero was the only person I knew for certain.

Jacob Sanchez, the son of Omero and Silvestra, was under the table with us, and his first concern was to find his parents. When he located them, Jacob shook them, crying, "Dad! Mom!" Then, being aware that it was too late for them (I suppose), he left, knowing they were gone forever . . .

My boys, Martin and Matthew, were both okay, but we took them to the hospital for a check-up later . . . Becky, my wife, was okay too.

After it was over that night, we felt really exhausted . . . physically and emotionally drained. The wind and the chill — we were all wet to the bone — everything took its toll. Home at last, we found that a warm shower and a comfortable bed never felt so good!

Becky Sanchez, a slightly built, attractive young mother, put in some afterthoughts for us.

Becky: When we were getting ready to leave for the program, I made the comment that I felt we shouldn't go. I'm not sure why I felt that way, but the weather was building up, and I had been at a bridal shower for Delia Matta there in that building last year when a storm blew up and hit the Center very hard. I guess I had this feeling that the old building somehow attracted storms! I remember how it rained and hailed and blew that day. I suppose I just had a lingering fear of it.

. . . Anyway, we went on over there . . . my mother and our boys . . . all of us together. Only our car was destroyed — completely demolished!

We were under a table, but when the wall started coming down, and the roof caved in, my mother was literally buried under all that debris. The tornado would actually pitch a car on top of the roof, and we could sense its added weight slamming around on that shaky pile of rocks and roofing and other stuff above us. It was truly a miracle that we were not completely crushed as so many others were.

There was a girl, Rachel Roman, who was sitting next to me at the meeting. This girl was trapped under there and partially suffocated for some time. One can't imagine the horror and helplessness of being trapped like that for a prolonged period of time . . .

* * *

One of the greatest joys of my teaching career has been my developing friendship with Delilah Alvarez. I taught her for six years — junior high and high school.

A great love of nature has long been one of the outstanding

characteristics of this ever-smiling, always-pleasant young lady. This was constantly reflected in her written compositions.

Once she wrote of her appreciation of Robert Frost's poetry because of its orientation to nature, a thing that was reinforced within herself when she read it. "He brings out his expressions and lets them take over your mind, so that you can have a piece of nature all the time," she wrote.

Paradoxically enough, that same nature that this attractive girl so dearly loves and enjoys also brought to her the greatest loss and pain she has ever experienced in this world.

But Delilah Alvarez today is reconciled to that paradox. "Nature has her moods like people have theirs. The most beautiful and gentle of us can fly into an angry rage at times," she reasoned.

When I heard that she had vowed not to attend her senior class graduation program, at which I had been requested by the class to speak, I understood. Her classmates did a beautiful and unselfish thing. They went as a group to visit her and prevail upon her to attend. She did.

Then Delilah declined to go along to Dallas with her classmates on the senior trip. I plead with her to go. "My dear little sister," I urged, "you *need* to get away from grief and sorrow and memories, and from Saragosa and Balmorhea for a few days." She nodded agreement and promised to go.

Delilah Alvarez kept that promise and gave herself permission to go on that senior trip and enjoy herself. I doubt not that this proved the "two roads that diverged in a wood," and Delilah Alvarez chose the one right for her at the time.

Today she is smiling that warm, embracing smile again as before. Not only did she write a journal entry for insertion here, but she also volunteered to type the final draft of my manuscript. In doing that unselfish labor of love for me, refusing all remuneration, she had to relive the horrors of May 22, along with that of other subsequent sad days and nights, all over again.

But this modest girl is mature and brave. She is as a kid sister to me, and that is how I regard her and love her.

Waiting At A Kitchen Window

Delilah Alvarez

This has been the worst experience of my life: I lost a beautiful sister and a wonderful brother-in-law. At other times when I had lost my grandmothers, the pain wasn't as great as the pain I feel now. To me, death to them was expected, because they were old and always in pain, but my sister and her husband were so very young . . . and so proud of their precious children.

They lived right beside us; so there wasn't a day that I didn't see her. If she wasn't here at my house, I was over at hers. We would always talk, especially about my problems, and she was always there to listen to me when I needed her.

I remember fighting with her once a long while ago, but I suppose that all sisters do that once in a while. On this one occasion we engaged in a fight over who had brought mud into her house, and we didn't talk to each other for about a week. My mother found out and tried to talk some sense into us. Mom said to me, "What if something bad happens to Sylvestra, and you never got to talk to her again? How would you feel? Could you live with yourself?"

That really had me thinking, and so I started talking to her again, forgiving my petty peeve against her. What my mother had posed as a possibility, I never thought would ever occur, that my sister that I loved so much might die.

I started getting ready after work to go to the Head Start program. Later I was to remember that Sylvestra had told me of an earlier tornado warning for Reeves County. She feared one thing in this world — bad weather!

All of us got ready except Omero, her husband. He would come over later on. Upon arriving at the hall, I noticed the rising wind, but thought little of it then. With Jacob, Alexa, and Deborah, my sister's children, I walked into the hall, and we seated ourselves comfortably, ready to enjoy the program.

The program did not begin for about an hour, and when it finally started, I noticed how very happy and proud of Deborah my sister seemed. Her smart little one was on stage and graduating. She learns fast, that little one, and I was proud of her, too. The program began, Omero arrived, and I glanced back, saw him, and whispered to Sylvestra that he had just walked in.

In short order we noticed rapid changes in the weather evidenced by brilliant flashes of lightning and very strong winds that were making their presence known through a broken window in the hall. Suddenly a man appeared as though blown in by the wind. He stopped and stood right by us and sighed in a noticeably worried manner. His wife darted down to the stage through the back. I thought they must be looking for a lost child. I was trying to dismiss their strange behavior from my mind, when suddenly everybody was on their feet, and my sister said, "Tornado!"

As she pronounced that terrifying word, she ran to the stage to grab Deborah. I leaped up and ran to the back of the stage in case the child panicked and fled. Corralling her, we then ran for the front door . . . in the midst of a scene of consternation where people were all pervaded with the same terrible sense of fright and confusion.

I gained the door and there before me was this great white funnel whirling right at us! We talked of going out, but my sister urged us to stay. She must have thought escape impossible, and so we all scrambled back into the hall and sat along the wall. The thought that I was about to die assailed my mind!

Frantically, I thought of the way we were seated: first, there was Omero, then my sister, then me, Alexa, and finally Deborah. Had Sylvestra kept little Deborah beside her, Deborah would probably have died along with her parents. It was as if she sensed that her youngest would be safe where she sat. I don't know, of course, but it seems so.

Just before the onslaught of the storm, my sister looked about for Jacob, and she told him something; I don't quite remember—if I ever knew—what it was. He was on the other side of the hall with Orlando Sanchez, Jacob's uncle, Omero's brother. Meantime, my sister kept yelling to Deborah to sit down and cover her head.

Suddenly, the lights blinked out, and windows started shattering! One could hear the voices of people mumbling prayers. Above the muffled prayers I heard the louder sounds of young children crying. Suddenly, without advance warning, there came a smashing of wind against the walls, and they caved in as if made of flimsy cardboard! I tensed all over with unimaginable fright, sure in my heart that this was the end. We were all doomed!

Almost instantly we were all buried under a mountain of rubble that had stood seconds before as massive sheltering walls. BURIED! We were trapped! The crumbled amorphous mass of masonry above me felt like a crushing mass of lead, and the air I struggled to breathe grew very thin and insufficient. My lungs were suffocating, but I was helpless, immobile, trapped. I simply sat there, ignorant of what to do to survive. Since I could do nothing else, I prayed quietly, confidently, that God would somehow get us out safely. I tried to scream, but no sound would come from my lungs. Perhaps I was too cramped, the air too thin, too impotent, too dead.

I yelled at Sylvestra, asking an irrational thing: "Get this wall off of us!" Her only response was that she couldn't do it. That was the last that I ever heard from her.

Omero seemed farther away than he actually was, but that

was because his voice was low . . . moaning . . . that's all I could hear of him. I knew he was in pain . . . actually, he was dying.

Suddenly, Deborah yelled, "Mom! Mom!" but my sister said nothing. That was when I knew something really was bad wrong. I felt her head, which was right beside my shoulder, and I called out to her, but still she wouldn't answer. I must have blanched as this chilling feeling came over me that she was dead!

Breathing grew difficult for me, and I pushed out Alexa's feet. They weighed across my legs. I pushed them aside so that fresh air could come in. Following that I had no choice but wait, and in time I felt the wall being lifted off us, and I was soon pulled out and placed where I was safe.

I felt no sensation at all in my leg . . . People had been piled on it, and I had this horrifying thought that I was paralyzed. It was soon dispelled, however, as the circulation returned once more.

I glanced about for Alexa and Deborah, but they had been found and were in safe hands. Jacob had dug himself out and was up and trying to help his parents, who were beyond human help. I was unsure of this and yelled for people to get my sister out. Omero was in my line of sight, being laid down. I knew what that meant.

I could not cry, although I tried. I could only yell. I was helpless and alone and hurting with grief and consternation. The moment was black and endless. Mr. Humphries came then and hugged me. I asked whether the tornado had hit Balmorhea, and was relieved — greatly relieved — when he told me "no."

After a while Joe Ortega came to me. He hugged me, too, a comforting thing, and gave me a blanket before leaving to help others elsewhere.

More moments crept by, and I looked up to discover my dad coming on the run. I told him all of us were okay except my sister and her husband Omero. Then they were pulling Sylvestra out. I didn't even recognize her! Poor thing . . . her face and neck were very blue! I could only recognize her by her shoes. Dad was telling me to take the girls to the truck. Alexa was hysterical. Deborah didn't even cry . . . she just whimpered softly, poor dazed little child that she was.

My tears still refused to flow, though I desperately wanted to let them all out. My emotions were sealed inside me, a pressure I must release somehow, but it only grew, a mass of misery within, kindling, building, from which there was no escape.

I found myself in Dad's pickup, not really knowing whether my sister and her husband were truly dead as had been reported, a reality I suppose I could not readily accept as fact. Mom was panicky and scared, but glad to see us . . . those who had survived . . .

Then Octavio Rodriguez, another student, appeared there, comforting me. I desperately needed to hold someone and to feel truly safe. Octavio provided that for me then.

Dad soon returned, ever so sadly shaking his head, a gesture and a moment that told me it was all over, that Sylvestra and Omero were gone . . . dead. My parents stood clinging to each other, weeping broken-heartedly, a grim reality crushing them, from which I must turn away. I desperately wanted this nightmare to end, to learn that my sister and Omero were alive after all . . . hurt, perhaps, but not dead.

Up to this very day, I still wake up wanting to hear her voice ringing out through the house. Sometimes, when I'm at the kitchen window, I wait momentarily to see if she is going to come out of her trailer carrying her usual load of wash to be laundered as she always did. The hope is futile as my fantisizing is unreal.

I know in my heart that someday I may be able to see my sister and her husband again — in the Resurrection to Life. Then we can live in true peace and happiness forever here on earth — where tornados appear no more, and the gentle side of nature at last prevails. This is my comfort based upon my Christian hope. Man's social system with its wicked elements will never give us true peace on earth. It is not to be until that "new system" comes from God. Only then can we live in Paradise here on earth. Until then, one can only carry the glory of that hope in his heart, "waiting for that blessed hope . . ."

September 19, 1987

* * *

Olga Mendosa, married to Joe Mendosa, is an attractive young mother and housewife. She was raised in Balmorhea, where she attended high school. Now she has a son, Joe Derrick, in school. Joe was in the Head Start school at Saragosa last year and was to have been graduated on May 22.

Mother and son arrived at the ceremony a little after seven, running a bit late, for Joe's graduation program was already under way. Then, with the singing and the ceremony finally over, the final portion was about to begin. Suddenly, one of Olga's friends, Javier Lozano, burst in and interrupted everything, his wife following but running down front. Olga thought a family fight was in progress, but her misconception was short-lived. Olga tells how Javier picked up his little boy, seemed a bit apologetic, and said, "Excuse me, but a tornado is coming," and left. The crowd and the graduation simply broke up at the word "tornado." Olga grabbed her boy and flew toward the door but could not get out and to her car. A confused crowd of milling people hemmed her in. She took her other son, one-year-old Robbie, and wedged under a table. Joe, her husband, was lifting windows, because "they say to open windows when a tornado is approaching," she told me, warming to her story . . .

Olga Mendosa: Suddenly, the walls began bursting, and Joe just took a big dive — he flew to the other side — and I was yelling for him. He shouted back, "I'm okay, I'm okay!"

We were near a wall in the center of the room. It just lifted up and toppled, crushing me! I felt myself being picked up and set down! When it all broke up and fell, I was finally deposited on the floor under it all. I felt myself in a sort of cavern where the wall section folded or fell onto something that partially supported it. I was not dead but thought I would die of suffocation. All that dust and closeness! I was on the edge of panic, couldn't breathe, but managed to push myself out a bit while overhead that horror was still hovering over us. The wind was sucking me up, and my baby with me. I pushed him further under the wall with my leg. It was a horrifying, desperate moment in which I sought to save him while just in front of me some people were crushed and killed! They were Jacob Sanchez's parents!

Mr. Sanchez — Omero — must have been alive for some time, because he grasped my leg and held on, apparently to keep me from being sucked out by the awful pull of that wind.

Jacob's mother, Sylvestra Sanchez, didn't die instantly, either. My brother, Randy Lopez, and my aunt, Livoria Lopez, both gave her mouth-to-mouth. She breathed a little bit, but not for long; that we know.

My husband, meanwhile, was trying desperately to reach us . . . from just a few yards away. He crawled as far as he could, then reached for us, stretching his arms to the limit, but couldn't make it. A wall lay between us! I could see his hand and recognized it by his white shirt.

I put my face all the way down during the blast. Many others did that too . . . and suffocated. I could scarcely breathe in there, and fortunately, I was not pinned down and helpless as were so many others there who were doomed. I was able to push myself out far enough that I could breathe.

Joe, my husband, escaped the worst with just several fractured ribs . . . but they still hurt him . . . I was banged up badly and was in a brace and a walker for a time.

It wasn't until about seven o'clock the following morning that they found the body of a little boy—Andres Morales. Both his parents, Anastacio and Corina Morales, died out there that night.

* * *

Javier Lozano was born in Pecos, attended Balmorhea High School, starred in football, excelled in track, and played basketball. He now plays pool and is good at it, or so he says. The thirty-year-old is also a General Motors mechanic employed in Pecos.

Linda Prieto (now Lozano) was born in Muleshoe, Texas, about twenty-one years ago. She relocated with her family to Saragosa and attended school in Pecos, but forsook academics for a handsome youth named Javier Lozano. Linda is now the pretty mother of a six-year-old boy named Billy.

As Javier reflected upon the afternoon of the tornado, he thought of something odd. Every Friday after work in Pecos he would customarily join buddies and play pool awhile before going home, but, on that Friday, he told them, "No, I'm gonna go home." He did not even stop and cash his check at the bank, but came on in "and there it was . . ." Dark cloud banks frowned threateningly to the northwest in the direction of Toya. Upon arriving home, Javier told Linda that "The weather doesn't look right out there." She was ready to take Billy Joe to his Head Start graduation. They left at about 6:30.

After a shower and a time of relaxation at home, Javier drove toward Saragosa, stopping in Brogado for a short visit with his mother. They stood outside talking, and that is when Javier noticed the bad-looking cloud rotating overhead. It was big, boiling, twisting, and swirling. His mother was urged to go inside, because, as Javier told her, "This is a tornado cloud. I'm going to Saragosa to bring my family home." His mother agreed that he should. Javier rushed off to Saragosa, and his story was soon upon the lips of many people, including his own.

Javier Lozano: When I arrived there, I was going in, but I kept staring at the clouds. I saw Rosendo out there, and I said to him, "They are bad-looking . . . they're tornado clouds!" Then I started in, but again stopped a minute and looked at the sky. I saw the funnel then . . . when I was outside the porch. I turned and walked over toward the highway to see better. Over near Hector Briceño's house I could see the funnel on the ground already . . . down toward Brogado . . . or the interstate.

I hurried inside, saw my wife by the door with some ladies,

and told her to go to the car. I went on in while Joey Hererra was giving his speech. I didn't know what to do, so I ran up onto the stage and grabbed up my boy. I just told them I was taking my family because a tornado had touched the ground. People were noisy, and some didn't hear. Others panicked. My voice was choking as I tried to warn them.

George Montes came rushing in and was dragging his mother out, and I had Billy, *but Linda was not there!* I kept yelling to her as I went out the door, and I waited for her outside, but she didn't come. I got into the car and kept honking my horn for her.

When she did not come after a bit, I looked back, and the tornado was coming closer, and by then I couldn't wait anymore. I had to take off, and I did! I drove north on Highway 17 as far as Curley's gin. It was hailing something awful, or I would have driven on to Pecos. Billy kept asking me, "What's wrong, Daddy?" and I told him a tornado was behind us.

About twenty people were already at Curley's — a bunch of them all around. When we began leaving after a while, I came back to Saragosa, where I noticed that Lucas Carrillo's mobile home was gone! Utility poles were down . . . wires too. Now I looked, and I couldn't see any Saragosa! I went forward, then backward, trying one way then the other, but I could not get into town. I worked my way around, detouring until I reached my father-in-law's house to the east of Saragosa. I picked up Eddie Mondragon's mom; she had a baby in her arms. It was Lucas's child. I later learned that the baby's father was dead.

Mrs. Mondragon told me that Linda was all right, but that a lot of people were hurt, maybe even dead. Leaving Billy Joe in her care, I went back to help if I could . . . That's when I saw you up there, Mr. Lane. I later found Linda, and she was okay, but when I looked at the rubble, I couldn't believe anybody could get out alive.

Linda Lozano spoke up then, telling us that, when the wall fell, it apparently broke the necks of a number of people.

Linda: Among them were my mother, Mrs. Matilde Prieto, and her dead friend, Mrs. Eva Meras, who was sitting in the meeting with her.

People out there in Saragosa had very little in their lives, and now they are left with even less.

* * *

A member of the Felipe Lopez family, Mary Jane Ontiveras is a sister to Thomas Lopez of Saragosa and Many Lopez of Balmorhea. Mary Jane grew up in Saragosa, attended school in Balmorhea until she married in 1981, and then moved to Andrews, Texas, to finish school there. She is married to Raul Ontiveras, Yvonne Machuca's brother (he is an Ontiveras by adoption, which explains the discrepancy in his name). Raul and Manuel Ontiveras, husband of Ninfa Ontiveras, were working in Van Horn, Texas, at the time of the Saragosa disaster.

Mary Jane had worked for the Head Start program as cook in the cafeteria since February before the storm. She now teaches there in the vacancy left by Lisa Carrillo, who was left tragically and permanently incapacitated by the storm.

She arrived at the Center around 6:30 that evening and helped Lisa Carrillo and Norma Rodriguez prepare the children for the program. The preliminaries were past and Joey Hererra was beginning his speech when the tornado warning was sounded by Javier Lozano.

Mary Jane was in the crowd that ran for the door, saw the funnel bearing down upon the building, and scrambled for cover under tables. She had just gotten under one when the windows began shattering and walls caved in on top of their tables. The legs of her table broke under its burden of heavy beams and chunks of cement banging down, trapping her and several others under tons of dead weight. A little girl, Alejandra Madrid, was there, as were Mary Lou Apodaca and her family.

Mary Jane held little Alejandra's hand. The child begged to be taken to look for her mother, Antonia Madrid. Mary Jane had seen Antonia just before the storm struck, rushing about searching for her son. Mary Jane elaborated on the grim consequences of that futile search.

> **Mary Jane Ontiveras:** Mrs. Madrid was killed, you know. I don't know how. Actually, she died later, after the collapsing building buried us all. I remember seeing her on the stretcher, and she was alive then. She really looked okay, but I think she died of internal injuries a little later on.
>
> . . . Mrs. Madrid was about fifty years old, one of the friendliest people you'd ever know — her husband too. Very nice people . . . from Mexico, you know. They lived in Presidio for a time, then moved here. But they spoke no English at all . . .
>
> Mr. Madrid worked on farms and ranches . . . I believe for Dale Toone, who lives just east of Saragosa.
>
> I actually do not know what happened to Antonia's husband — how he was killed. You see, as soon as the tornado had blown

past us, and we were able to get out, we went right away to our car. I did not see any of the injured then. It was raining, hailing, and *cold!* We went to our car seeking cover from the weather.

On my way to find our car, I looked around, and was I ever surprised. Things were gone! The town wasn't there anymore! I looked towards my mom's house across the highway. It was standing! I could see the roof, and I decided to walk over there since it was okay. Once over there, I put blankets around the girls — my niece Debbie, and Lucas Carrillo's daughter Lorinda. Debbie, who is only two and a half years old, would cry, and I kept trying to comfort her. Because she was confused about the tornado . . . and despair that had surrounded us, I used language she could understand, telling her it was a hard rain.

I stayed at Mother's place until my sister-in-law Maribel came. Lorinda was all right — no injuries — and I asked Maribel to stay with her while I went and searched for her mother. I wanted to be able to soothe the girl with the news that her mother was all right.

At the scene of destruction once again, I saw all those dead and injured people that had just been pulled from the ruins, and I turned away shocked and went on looking for Lorinda's mom, Rosie Carrillo. When I found her, she was with Lucas, her husband, who appeared okay to me, but was dead already! People think he suffocated under all the debris that covered him up.

Moving on, I heard someone pleading, "Give us a blanket over here!" It was for Amelia Carrillo, Corina Brijalba's mother. She was alive still, but died a bit later.

I couldn't stand any more. I just went! As I left I told Rosie that her baby was all right over at my mother's place. Poor woman . . . she was so crushed by her personal tragedy just then that I wonder whether what I said registered with her at all.

The Carrillos had another daughter — Christina, their younger girl — and she was missing. After some time little Christina was found by a neighbor in a house owned by Mrs. Aurora Briceño . . .

Mrs. Briceño had been injured while at the hall attending the graduation program. She was taken on to the hospital in Odessa that night.

As for her child, she was in that house alone, wrapped in a blanket. Nobody knows to this day how she got there, or for that matter, who found her, wrapped her in a blanket, and hurried on about his business of helping the needy. We arrived to find the paramedics already on the scene, checking her over just as we came in. Christina was okay, and we had them take her over to Mom's house to be kept with her sister there.

After the storm I couldn't sleep for some time. Memories of all those people — the screaming, the confusion, the praying, the dead and dying — it all kept controlling my mind, my thoughts, my emotions. I'd seen a little girl over there; she was all covered with blood from head to foot as if a bucket of red paint had been dashed all over her. Who could escape the horror of that in a million years? I remember, too, grabbing Lorinda from Mary Lou Apodaca, who had her hands full with her own two girls in an hour of total desperation. I kept reliving all of those frantic moments of horror until they gradually subsided . . . Life has become a winning existence for me and my husband once more.

The four smaller Madrid children now live with their half brother, Bernardo Guiterrez, in Pecos. I guess the family has pretty well settled down and readjusted to their losses by now. The deceased parents, Jose and Antonia Madrid, were taken home to Mexico and buried there.

* * *

Fernando Balderas is a tall, once-portly man, but who today seems to have lost considerable weight. He is a pleasant but reserved individual, soft-spoken and gentle.

Señor Balderas was born in Nieves, Zacatecas, Mexico, where he grew up and later married Maria del Socorro Avalas, also of Nieves. In 1980 the young couple moved to the Balmorhea area of West Texas. Fernando has since been employed as a farm and ranch worker for Larry Turnbough.

The Balderas couple have two little girls. Maria de la Luz Balderas was seven at the time of the tornado, and Ampara Balderas was five. She was in the Head Start program when the awesome tornado broke up the ceremony.

Fernando speaks only Spanish, and he related his story to Raquel, my wife, who interpreted his excellent Spanish for me.

He was preparing to irrigate on one of the Turnbough farms that afternoon, but at 6:00 P.M. stopped work and went home to take his family to the graduation program. He dropped his family off at 6:30 and promised to return for them immediately after Amparo's graduation, because they were having festivities at home instead of staying with the crowd.

Balderas returned to his irrigation pipes, set them to flowing, and about 7:00 drove back to the Community Center, arriving a bit early with a storm brewing overhead. Since he had on some "pretty muddy clothes" from his irrigation work, he did not go inside, and so waited in the pickup for the program to end.

Soon the wind blew furiously and rain and hail came down. Then the tornado struck with all its fury, blowing the windows out of his farm truck and moving it forward so forcibly he was helpless to stop it. He started the motor and shifted into reverse against the wind, but could not move it backwards, or even hold it at a standstill. The force of the wind kept pushing the pickup forward and sideways, and was about to suck him out, tugging on him with unrelenting force. Balderas dived and pulled the seat over himself as he grabbed the steering column near the floor and held on for dear life.

Suddenly the pickup was slammed into a big Oldsmobile. The pickup, wedged in against the Oldsmobile, held fast from being swept away. It tried and tried to leave the ground but was sufficiently stabilized where it lodged that it held fast, probably saving Fernando's life.

He lay huddled and frightened where he was until the fury of the storm subsided, then crawled from the truck with his eyes glued on the demolished building where his wife and children were buried. He was near despair as he visualized them possibly dead or badly injured. The world had come to an end for the distraught man.

He suddenly remembered that there was a high-lift jack in the pickup, for he always carried one. The truck was wrecked, but the jack was intact, and he feverishly removed it and tried to lift walls off the countless victims.

Apparently, Señor Balderas was the first rescue worker with a tool to plunge into the scene that evening. With the cries of the wounded and the dying ringing wildly in his ears, he worked like a man gone mad mounting an assault against a task too immense for one person. He stood facing what must have seemed like mountains of jagged, defiant rubble that he could never manipulate alone.

Fernando Balderas: Others soon began to join me, and we were not long in removing the first body. It was that of Nora Brijalba. In a little while we took two more bodies out . . . I don't even know who they were, if I ever did. I was so desperately grieved and trying to find and uncover my wife and my little girls that I hardly even saw those poor dead people.

Then I found her. She was crushed under the wall when it fell. Her head was down between her feet. [He assumed the same

> posture during the interview to illustrate.] That's how she was when we dug down to her and took her out . . . dead . . .
>
> I guess my eyes were wide-eyed with the terrible thought that my little girls had met death down there too. But at that awful moment, the darkest of my entire life, Elie Estrada, who had been sitting very near to my wife during the storm, called my name. She had crawled out a little earlier, along with my two little girls. She came to me and told me not to worry about them . . . she had gotten them out and had them safe in Floyd's police car outside.
>
> I continued to help a little longer, but police officers began arriving. Rescue crews came, too, and the officers sent me away out of the work area. Trained emergency crews were taking over now. I left and came to the home of Maria del Socorro's parents. They are Mr. and Mrs. Enrique Avalos. We were one grief-stricken, broken-hearted family that night.

I told Fernando of lying not far from his little girls that same night when we were bedded down at the school gymnasium. I only knew then that they had lost their mother, but their identities were unknown to me.

About this time, Mr. and Mrs. Avalos, with their children and the Balderas girls, came in. They had recently passed through another tragedy—fire. It struck their home situated about half a mile south of Saragosa. The devastating fire, started by a defective electrical switch, had deprived them of practically all their earthly possessions. As a consequence, the Avalos family had moved into the small cottage with their son-in-law, Señor Balderas. Their family included four children ranging from age fourteen down (Melchor, Marisa, Felipe, and Ricardo). Yet another son, Leonardo Enrique, who is married and lives in Saragosa, arrived only moments after his parents' arrival. He opened up and talked freely with us about the loss of his wife's parents, Jose and Antonia Madrid, and told us, "I wish you would go out to my place in Saragosa. I want you to hear my wife's story."

* * *

We found Lorena Avalos, wife of Leonardo Enrique, at home tending her three boys and visiting with her attractive sister Manuela. Lorena was herself a small, attractive young housewife. She was pleasant though obviously deeply pained, but once our dialogue about the loss of her loved ones was over, warm smiles wreathed her charming face as we said our goodbyes.

Lorena told us first of picking up her parents, Jose and Antonia Madrid, and taking them to the Center around 7:00 P.M. She spoke their hallowed names tenderly.

Lorena's older child, Richard, Jr., then five, was graduating from the Head Start program, and the grandparents were proud of him. Juan Ramon was only four and would follow his brother in Head Start the following year.

In addition, the Madrids had a young son, Lorena's baby brother, Omar Madrid, who was to graduate there too. The Madrids had another son, James, with them. He was one and a half years old.

They all sat together and later saw Javier Lozano run in for his boy, shout something, and leave, but they were uncomprehending — too much confusion already going on. The crowd was nervous and excited over the bad, brewing storm outside. Lorena thinks they sensed it, but did not know that a tornado was approaching at that very minute.

> **Lorena Avalos:** When I knew the tornado was about to hit, I took my baby and quickly rounded up the other two. I ran to the wall on the east side. My parents took their children, Irieneo, age fourteen, Josepha, twelve, Alexandra, seven, and Omero, four, and dashed to the west wall, where they sat with their backs to the wall.
>
> Lucas Carrillo was over there grabbing tables and shoving kids under them. That saved my little brothers' and sisters' lives! The funnel was close, ready to smash us, and everybody was braced, breathless, and praying. I hugged my three children to the wall, waiting . . . and suddenly it burst, caved in over us, but left us clear of heavy debris. The break in the wall was such that we could see outside . . . actually watch some of what was going by. Because of a pickup parked just outside the wall near us, I couldn't see very well. That was fortunate for us, however because that pickup saved us from the swirling storm of stuff that was smashing into it — things that otherwise would have bombarded us.
>
> I was beside Olga Mendosa and her children, and we all could breathe because of that breach in the wall. Others around us smothered and died during those terrible moments. As for my parents, the Madrids, the walls caved in on them, but they were deep down in the rubble, and their bodies were not really damaged sufficiently to have caused their deaths. We are convinced that they were asphyxiated down in there . . .

My little brothers and sisters, who were with my parents, were saved, as I said, by the alert efforts of that most unselfish man, Lucas Carrillo. He himself was killed. He had shoved them under the big table by the door where their lives were spared, but his body was crushed right there beside the place where they huddled helplessly but safe beneath the table. Not only did Mr. Carrillo help them, but he had already helped a number of other children find safety under tables. My brothers and sisters seem to have been the very last ones he saved, because of the position of his body beside them. Lucas Carrillo was a real hero that night, unselfishly sacrificing his own life for the lives of a good number of children. They are alive, but he is dead!

[My wife Raquel relates that many of her students gave Lucas Carrillo credit for saving their lives, crowding them beneath tables in those fast-receding moments just before time ran out for him. This brave man was described by witnesses as standing, straining, with another man, Anastacio Morales, to hold back a wall under the onslaught of the twister. But their human efforts were as frail as broomstraws restraining an onrushing locomotive.]

When he saw us crawling out through the gap in the wall, Floyd Estrada called to us. He told us to get over to his patrol car, out of the way and out of the weather. Our car was bashed in — totally destroyed!

I went to my car with my children anyway, because my oldest son, Richard, Jr., had a badly cut ear and was bleeding terribly. Once at my car, I left my children to wait for me there while I went to make a desperate search for Mom and Dad. Seeing that mountain of rubble heaped where they disappeared, I was forced to the conclusion that it was all in vain. They were entombed . . .

About that time all my little brothers and sisters came crawling out! I took them to my heart and then took them out of there.

I was intent upon taking those wonderful, alive kids to my wrecked car, where my own children waited alone and obediently for me. At that moment my inlaws, Mr. and Mrs. Enrique Avalos, drove up. I went with them then, taking all the children to their house which was located only about a half a mile down the highway south of Saragosa. Their home suffered some minor damage, mostly to the roof, because it was only on the edge of the path of the funnel. Only a few days ago, however, it was destroyed by fire, a second bad blow for them.

The only one of the children to suffer injury was Ricardo, Jr., who was taken by ambulance to Pecos County Memorial Hospital in Fort Stockton. He has recovered and is all right now. All of them suffered emotionally and psychologically, being extremely

> nervous at first. They reacted with violent fear to any bad weather, but are adjusting nicely now . . . except for the baby. The noise of a passing jet high above simply terrifies him, because he can't distinguish between that sound and the violent noise produced by the tornado.
>
> My dad was fifty-six, and my mom only forty-six. They were too young to go . . . and I'm still taking the death of my parents very hard. I am sad, and every night dream of tornados.
>
> [My parents' house] was wrecked, but it wasn't theirs. Tommy Martinez had loaned them a house to live in. My dad worked for Tommy, and as a friend, Tommy let him use the little house rent-free during their years of need before the storm.

Tommy Martinez — another generous, unselfish soul with a compassion for his fellow man. Like so many dear people around here . . .

[6]

Victims Who Fled

In 1942 a man, half French and half American Indian, left his home in Aguas Calientes, Mexico, and settled in Saragosa, Texas. He built a tiny grocery store which thrived there through the years. As those years came and went, he was able to send four of his five children to college. Two of them have master's degrees, and all enjoy success in the mainstream of American life today. Jose and Pas Candelas are rightfully proud of their children and their business success.

The success of the Candelas Grocery Store in Saragosa came to a pathetic end on the evening of May 22, 1987, leaving the distraught owners penniless. This handsome, aging couple, their brows creased with many cares these days, related the story of their personal tragedy, along with their grim determination to rise above adversity and make friends of prosperity once more.

Joe was inside his store that day, busily putting up grocery stock, and was ignorant of the gathering storm. For some strange reason he grew restless and went outside. There he discovered the expanding, restless clouds, and went inside and turned on the radio for news. Unsatisfied with the reports, he paced about with some agitation, checking the weather time and again. He checked for news on television and saw the tornado watch.

Joe went outside for another look, and there before his eyes, he saw two walls of clouds sweeping toward each other. They touched as if kissing one another, he said, and suddenly "just slammed into each other with a clash . . . and right before my eyes, a tornado!"

His nephew, Chonito Conception Lujan, was outside, about to leave for his home in Las Cruces, New Mexico. Suddenly, he saw the tornado, too, and "snatched all the kids into the pickup and took off." The kids were Eduardo, age seven, the son of Conception Lujan and his wife, Inez (Joe's sister); and Sergio, nine, and Yvonne, ten, both grandchildren of Joe and Pas.

Pas Candelas was very busy putting some winter quilts into plastic bags to store them free of dust. When she went outside for a moment, she too saw the two clouds described by Joe. It had suddenly gotten dark, so Pas lit a candle. That's when Joe burst in shouting, "Pas, a tornado!"

Pas Candelas: Joe came bursting in, yelling, "Pas, a tornado!" We lost a minute getting some blankets and clothes we might need. I grabbed my purse and ran outside, then I remembered that I had better put out the candle so there would be no fire from it. I returned and snuffed it out and ran again to the car.

Joe Candelas: In our big hurry to escape we forgot even to lock the store! Oh, well, what was the use? The place was a scrap pile when we came back later, and then during the night everything that was not blown away or destroyed, and that might have helped us get started again, was stolen! People carried off stacks of my stock pile of soft drinks and sixty-eight cases of beer! The furniture was gone through, drawers taken, *full of things,* right out of the dressers! They not only took our clothes but made our dressers worthless without drawers — useless, gone with personal effects as well! What kind of people make up our world?

Anyway, we just sped off up the highway, going north as fast as we could, heading for Curley's Gin, about five miles away. A glance back at the storm was all I needed to make me panic. The center of that giant cloud was black — very black — and with gray down under. It came down low — WHOOSH! I saw roofs in the air! . . . I glanced back over my shoulder just once as we raced toward the edge of town, and I saw the Morales's home rise as if on wings! Up into the air it floated, like a helicopter taking off straight up. Then, it banked over . . . over . . . over until it was upside down. Then, POOOF! It exploded! I learned later that the family had hidden in their car . . . eleven people escaped the storm, not by driving away, as we did, but by piling inside their car, and it almost went up too!

The funnel came on with a swirling storm of dust at its bottom;

> at its top were electric light poles swirling around like powered model airplanes, zooming and diving in all directions at once! I couldn't watch anymore . . . hail coming down, hitting hard, and me driving as fast as I could. The wind grabbed hold of us and kept pulling us back, whipping us about, slowing the car. Out there where the large fertilizer tanks stand, we were being blown off the road. I had to stop once just to regain control of the car. Further on, near the gin, there is a big pit beside the highway, and the wind whipped the car out of control there, and we almost went over! I somehow managed to maneuver it past the pit, only to have it lurch drunkenly across the highway in the opposite direction, striking the left shoulder before I could right it once more . . .
>
> A truck stood in front of us and a car behind when we finally pulled in at the gin. We were all pushing for a place under there with all that hail blasting down. With that huge truck in front of me blocking my path, I saw but one way through — I drove right in under it so that the car behind me could get in under the shed too.
>
> After the storm subsided, we attempted to return to Saragosa to look for our grandchildren and my nephew's family. We couldn't get through, and so took the long way around through the country roads. Trees were down on the roads out there, but with some effort and a lot of care, we picked our way around and back to town.
>
> My nephew had returned on Farm Road 1215 in his efforts to regain the town, and we came in the same way, looking frantically for them. That is when we saw Nita Brijalba's body beside her mobile home out there on the roadway . . . You just had to turn and look the other way.
>
> You asked me whether I plan to reopen my store. Oh, yes! I have cleaned up over there as best I could. I have no help, but I am going about it by myself, and I am molding cement blocks every day. I have a cinder block machine, and am making about forty blocks a day. I will get there eventually, for sure!

In the ensuing months a happy thing developed. Under the auspices of the Red Cross, a new cottage was built for Jose and Pas Candelas. The Catholic Charities have rebuilt his store building. Neither house nor store are anything near as spacious as were the old structures, but Mr. Candelas has plans to add to the residence.

As for the store, well, Joe shrugs, he has an empty store building without money for the stock to put inside. At present he sells a variety of drinks — sodas and beer — plus some candies out of his tiny living room at home next door. Joe Candelas hopes that a small business loan can be arranged so that he can open up for business once again.

* * *

Pete Vasquez has been a ranch foreman on the same ranch for twenty-five years. He and his wife Socorro are quiet, self-possessing, friendly people. For many years they lived in a ranch house owned by C. J. Kesey, Pete's boss and ranch owner. However, Pete recently began remodeling an old house he moved to Balmorhea from a site out in the country to the north of Saragosa. Pete smiles as he remembers his friends asking him, as he was moving the old house, whether he was taking it to the city dump! But the old house is now going through a complete transformation and looks beautiful inside, a tribute to this ranch foreman's imagination and ingenuity.

Pete shook his head in his quiet, somber manner as he remembered the horror of living through a "monster tornado," as he described it. He and his family had passed "about four long minutes," seemingly an eternity, inside a farm pickup nosed into a bar ditch. The pickup was totaled by the vicious assault of the storm when the funnel scored a direct hit upon them.

They had gone to the Head Start graduation of their five-year-old grandson, Liberty Ray Wofford, "Florinda's boy." The mother had taken Liberty earlier in her new Chevrolet Spectrum, and Socorro and Pete drove there a little later on.

Socorro Vasquez remembered how Javier Lozano shocked them with his tornado warning. Pete told of all the commotion of people running here and there, many outside and uncertain, while their grandson giggled as he misinterpreted all the excitement as the commencement of a big party. Pete grabbed the boy and hustled him and his mother and Socorro unceremoniously outside through the confused crowd.

Pete Vasquez: Once we were outside, we saw it . . . that monster . . . coming full blast straight at us! Florinda took a picture of it with her camera. Then we tried to get another, but the thing was too nearby then, and only the first picture came out very well . . .

Florinda rushed over to her new car and was about to get into it when I grabbed her and yelled, "Let's all go in mine; there's no time!"

We dashed over to my truck, and I was so nervous with fear

and excitement I couldn't find the right key to unlock the door. I fumbled as that monster came driving on, looming larger, roaring and bearing down upon us, just seconds away! People were screaming, some running for their cars, some just running. Why couldn't I get that darn key to fit? I fumbled our few life-saving seconds away almost as if with the very hands of death! Vital moments that seemed like eternities passed, and I finally fished out the right key from the bunch, and with a trembling hand, unlocked the stubborn door. We scrambled wildly into the pickup — all four of us — and we took off like mad! Florinda's brand new car was being demolished right behind us as we whipped out onto the highway, hell breaking loose all about us!

I hit that highway running . . . It didn't take me long to hit sixty miles an hour at the same time that electric high-line wires were swinging violently overhead and the utility poles were swaying drunkenly before us. Just then an electric pole snapped and crashed down right near us!

Socorro: Florinda screamed, "Oh, Mama, it's gonna hit us!"

Pete: We only drove about three blocks up Highway 17. The air was full of stuff . . . It all happened instantly as we pulled out into the highway, racing north in the blast . . . There was rain, hail, lumber, metal, glass . . . I don't know what all. And people! They were out in the highway running this way and that. I could barely see as it was, and at sixty quick miles per hour, or nearly that, dodging in and out to miss them . . . I was forced to hit my brakes a time or two and swerve around panicky people . . .

By the time I got to Gallegos's Bar, I was driving completely blind, couldn't see a thing. The air was alive with a solid sheet of mud. My windshield wipers couldn't move that stuff. You wouldn't believe it, but the mud was at least two inches thick on my windshield . . . and all over the pickup!

There was a pretty deep bar ditch on each side before you reach the creek bridge. I hit my brakes and cut to the right, nosing the pickup down into that right-hand ditch below the highway. We dived over and down that embankment head first! There we rode the monster out. It was blasting us full force, but from behind. The pickup danced up and down some, and we thought it was going to sail off into a pasture, but it didn't . . .

When we braked and headed down into the ditch, I reached behind our seat and whipped out a saddle blanket from back there. With that we covered ourselves, huddled head down there while the tornado did its worst above our heads outside.

The pickup was totaled out. The windshield went, then all the windows burst, the air full of glass missiles flying right there in the cab where we were. The heavy horse blanket was wonderful protection!

Our injuries were minor ones. Socorro got one arm outside the blanket while trying to hold it down as it flopped about, whipped by the wind. She had cuts and bruises all up and down her entire right arm. It had bits of glass, splinters of wood . . . gravel . . . all embedded. I had a small cut on my scalp and some little ones here and there on my hands . . .

You can't imagine what a mess our dress clothes were! All that mud came in at us after all the glass blew out of the pickup. It covered us, too, ruined our clothes! The stains won't come out no matter how many times Socorro has washed them . . .

The pickup was unrecognizable. With at least two inches of black mud plastered all over it, you couldn't find any of its blue paint. There were big dents and deep scratches everywhere. It was a total disaster . . . hubcaps gone . . . vanished! All the glass was out, broken and gone. Even the headlights and taillights were smashed. Rear window, gone, too . . .

And that horse blanket! I'll never use it again! . . . two inches of heavy black mud caked all over it . . . with gravel, slivers of glass, and splinters embedded in it . . . You could never put that blanket on a horse's back again . . . I'm just gonna keep that horse blanket like it is . . . as a souvenir . . .

[I asked Pete Vasquez whether he and his family owed their lives to the mud, since he had nosed his vehicle down below the highway embankment due to the mud blinding his vision.]

No doubt about it. That pancake of mud on the windshield forced us to stop, to turn aside. The mud had put us into a frenzy of desperation at that moment, but, there is no doubt about it, that same mud plaster saved our lives. It forced me to wheel off the highway and park when and where I did—just in the nick of time . . .

* * *

Delia Rodriguez graduated from Balmorhea High School in May 1986. I taught her English and speech. We were friends, and she was a pleasant young lady to have around. She attended Texas State Technical Institute during the past year, and had just recently returned home to Saragosa when the tornado struck on May 22.

One day Delia came into the Salvation Army storage facility for food and clothing for her family. I was doing volunteer work there, and during our visit she told me her story, the horror of its painful memories obviously crossing her vision.

Delia Rodriguez: I was at home . . . with my parents. We were watching the cloud, and we saw it touch down once, then again. The second time it just kept on coming toward town . . . and us!

That was when we jumped into our car. Kiki [Ramon Meneses] was at our house with us, and his car was the first to take off. We stopped at the place where the kids' graduation was in progress. The funnel was zig-zagging, but was moving on the ground toward the Community Center.

George Montes told some people inside about the storm coming. He ran in to get his mother out about the time we stopped outside. The crowd panicked but stayed, seeming to think it was safer in there.

We took off toward the gin up highway 17 toward Pecos. We stopped and went into the gin, and pretty soon we could hear the windows cracking and breaking up. The funnel itself did not come that far north, and after waiting a little while we went back to Saragosa.

By this time it had gone and torn the town to bits. We couldn't go into town by the highway, and so we drove through some back roads . . . Coming in from the west and south on the farm-to-market road, we came to a wrecked mobile home lying across the road. We were forced to park on the right shoulder, and that was when we saw the body of this lady beside the mobile home . . . Anita Brijalba.

After that I saw wrecked cars, pieces of cement, wires thrown around everywhere. A bus was parked near the Community Center with seventeen bodies inside. I was asked to identify the people who were dead, but I couldn't! My mind was confused . . . I soon left and went to the Pecos hospital with friends . . . to find my parents.

We found them around two in the morning — okay, but worried about me. They thought I had gone to that graduation program with my two aunts, Irma Garza and Olivia Contreras. Both of them had died there . . . And Tia Irma's baby boy, Lionel, Jr. — he was killed there. The two little girls, Joanna and Abigail, were safe.

* * *

Dora Vasquez, the beautiful daughter of Onesimo and Virginia Vasquez, grew up on a farm north of Balmorhea some twenty miles or so from town. Her father farmed out there in a neighborhood named Alamo. Dora rode the Alamo Bus to Balmorhea Public Schools until her family eventually moved into town when Dora was in the sixth grade. She continued attending school in Balmorhea until her graduation from high school in 1982.

Dora is now employed at two places in town, working as secretary to the justice of the peace, and employed part-time at the Balmorhea Post Office as an assistant to Postmistress Marilyn Moore.

Still single, this ambitious young woman is saving what money she can from her employment to apply toward nursing school. She aspires to become a nurse so that she may serve beyond the boundaries of her community, and thus "see something of the outside world."

I asked her to tell me what happened with her on May 22. In the mellowest of tones she told how on that Friday she had to work at the post office the entire day — a kind of dreary day for her — gloomy somehow. Dora cannot account for unusual low spirits that day. She merely worked, and that was all.

Her little nephew, Jose Mendosa, four years old, was to graduate at the Head Start program at Saragosa, and he had reminded her all week how much he wanted her to attend.

Dora left at 7:00 "to go hear him sing." She noticed the threatening weather on her way over and thought it looked "weird . . . kinda like . . . maybe a tornado!" But like many others, she shrugged the dark thought aside, thinking that "tornados never strike around here — they're always in the news and far away."

Once in the hall, Dora found a place and sat down to wait. She enjoyed the ceremony, but the wind came up and she had trouble hearing the children singing. The place became uncomfortable — chilled. She grew cold. Suddenly, there was complete calm and the singing became bell-clear, audible now. The three-year-olds were singing to the four-year-olds "a very touching little song, and waving goodbye as they sang." For Dora it was dramatic, "so touching it wrung tears from my sentimental eyes." Even now, Dora choked up on the memory. She continued with an apology.

> **Dora Vasquez:** Excuse me . . .
>
> My very best friend was sitting right next to me . . . Corina Morales . . . She was seven months pregnant. I remember her . . . just smiling and smiling . . . just very happy those last closing moments of her life.
>
> Nobody was expecting anything — any tragedy, you know . . . My sister thought it was weird that the wind was blowing in so powerfully, then just stopped. It was suddenly so perfectly calm, and she feared that something was wrong . . . She seemed apprehensive; I guess she knew in her heart that something was wrong . . . something brewing . . . something dangerous. We were

sitting there listening to the little kids sing during those moments of Elida's and my apprehension, and that's when Mr. Lozano ran in, warned us, and left with his son.

We ran out the front door ahead of the stampeding, screaming crowd, and there before us was this great towering . . . like a big dark-like cloud . . . a tornado of tremendous size on the ground and not very far away! . . .

People were disagreeing, some saying to stay in the place, others starting to go. My little sister, Elida Mendosa, and her daughter Lisa, along with my nephew who was supposed to graduate, we all wanted to leave, but people held my brother-in-law and my nephew back, not wanting them to go. We were already out the door, ready to get in the car and take off, but we had to go back and drag them out of there against the restraints of people shouting, "Don't leave, don't leave!"

We were screaming, "Let's go! Let's go to Joe Gallegos's house." For some unknown reason we thought of going there for refuge from the storm that was about to crash down upon us. We finally scrambled somehow into the car and raced away. Other people were driving out of there, too . . . There was an awful lot of confusion in that desperate swirl of traffic, but we somehow escaped and soon found our way to Gallegos's Bar . . .

Into the bar we ran and glimpsed there an old man, standing over by the wall alone. I told him, "Sir, please hide, because there's a tornado coming!" [Raquel knew this man to be Ned Briceño. The Woods family had not yet arrived.]

I looked desperately for a door. I saw one leading into the Gallegos's house, and we dashed into their home, looking desperately again, now for a place to hide. There was nobody in the place as we took it over. They had already gone . . . to the Toya Creek bridge, as we later learned. Then we found a bedroom closet, and we all crowded into it — a sort of walk-in closet without a door.

My sister, my niece, and my nephew dived in first, and there was just sufficient room for them. I sat by the opening of that closet — like them, with my knees up. My brother-in-law was hiding with his face to me.

When I first came in, I saw a suitcase there, and I emptied it in a hurry and put that suitcase over my head . . . Then we felt IT — the tornado — coming! We felt . . . rumbling.

The roof just ripped away then. We felt the thing pushing the walls . . . where we sat on the floor. The wall behind us was suspicious, might go any second! I kept bracing it, holding back with my feet. I felt it push and push, and I thought for sure it was gonna take me with it any second.

One of my shoes left me, but I stayed, sure all the time I was gonna go. Stuff was falling everywhere, and there was all this deafening noise. That house was being ripped to shreds — everything just being torn apart! You could hear the windows break . . . I couldn't breathe . . . In that awful low pressure, I felt as if I was about to suffocate.

But I could scream. We did, too, feeling terribly, utterly helpless! It was just God who helped us there. We prayed and prayed . . . it seemed like forever by the time it left us . . . like forever we were in there at its mercy.

Then it was gone, and we were too paralyzed with fear to move. I think we feared it might return in those awful moments of breathless suspense. Then the rain came down, and hail with it. My brother-in-law looked for something to use to cover our heads, because the roof had gone, and hail was falling very hard. He found a mattress under a whole bunch of boards, and pulled it over on top of our heads.

I still had the open suitcase over my head, and Guadalupe took it from me so that I could get under the mattress with the others. When he took the suitcase, he discovered a big blade of glass, like a large knife, or a sword, that had stabbed through that suitcase, just missing me! That long shaft of glass, probably split from a window pane, had been hurled with great force by the wind and stabbed all the way through the suitcase. Fortunately, I was holding the suitcase up high, and the glass did not pierce my skull as it could have otherwise . . . had I not been under that suitcase, that long blade of glass might have gone through my head!

We were there until the rain stopped. It had gotten cold again. Some jackets in our closet had fallen all over during the storm, and now we put them on and started trying to pick our way out. It wasn't easy, for we had to crawl under a tangled pile of boards and other stuff.

Once out of the house, we could see nothing in any direction except piles and piles of boards and other rubble . . . no town! It was unimaginable . . . terrible! Then we discovered that we were all muddy . . . It had plastered us while we hid in the closet . . . My skirt was full of mud, and I have not been able to remove all the stains from it to this day. My hair had rocks lodged in the piles of mud that plastered it over . . .

My concerns were a few miles away, bothered about Balmorhea. Had the tornado smashed it too? I must get home and see whether my parents were alive! Saragosa was a mess . . . If Saragosa looked so devastated . . . what about . . .? I ran all the way from Joe Gallegos's place to the wrecked Community Center. In spite of all the electric wires down along that road with other debris, we made it safely somehow . . .

There at the Center I could see nothing else but wreckage . . . nothing but rubble. The bodies had not been brought out yet, and I saw none of them.

Then I saw a friend of mine — Nancy Prieto, or Nancy Matta since her marriage. She had just crawled out and kept crying, "My mom's in there; get her out! Help me get her out!" It was as if she was calling to nobody at all, but pleading for help when there was none to be had.

Some friends of mine drove up from Balmorhea then — Norma Barragon and Dora Valerio. They offered to take us home as they were taking out people who were stranded. We came on home with them.

I wasn't hurt or anything, but when I came home, I discovered that my leg was bleeding . . . there are still little scars there . . . something blown, glass fragments, perhaps.

It was incredible how quickly people arrived at the site of the Community Center. We were there very early after the storm passed on. I saw Nancy about five minutes after we arrived there. Then Norma and Dora came within ten minutes. Floyd was there too . . . and Mr. Rhyne . . . and the highway patrolman, Mr. Bourland. They came so soon because of their radio communications, and they summoned others from afar who also came in an unbelievably short time.

Speaking of communications, my sister Sylvia from Pecos has a scanner, and my brother-in-law takes pictures for the newspaper. He and she both work for the *Pecos Enterprise.* She heard on the scanner that there was a tornado, and she called my mom. Sylvia did not know that we were at Saragosa. While she was talking on the phone, the line went dead . . . That's when the tornado hit out there . . .

Later, my sister went to a friend's home, and this friend asked her if she knew about the tornado that had hit the Head Start graduation. Since my little nephew was to have been in that program, Sylvia knew that my other sister was going there, but she didn't know that I was to be there as well . . .

Sylvia drove to the hospital in Pecos and waited there . . . Finally, someone came in, and when Sylvia asked about the family, those people told her that they had seen my sister Elida, that she was all right, but that they couldn't find me, and they thought I was dead . . . She spent some time then looking for me — running around all over the hospital in needless concern. When she could learn nothing of me, Sylvia called my brother in Odessa, because she could not call Balmorhea.

My brother searched at the hospital in Odessa for me. It was a mess! He could find me nowhere, and there was no way for either of them to call and learn anything about me. So, they went through hours of anxiety. My oldest brother, Tino, in Odessa, finally called another brother, Feliciano, in Fredericksburg and informed him that I was missing.

I have *six* brothers. Arnulfo works for WTU and was on his way to help rescue people in Saragosa. Knowing we were there . . . he was greatly concerned and kept yelling my name and my sister's name while they were digging out and searching for bodies out there. He saw our car, wrecked out there, and was filled with fear for us . . .

None of them could contact us until the next day. Imagine their concerns! And I couldn't sleep the whole night . . . About five o'clock that next morning Tino arrived from Odessa, and my daddy told him that I was all right and still asleep. He was too overjoyed and relieved to believe that I really was all right.

Once the phone system was back in service, Feliciano finally was able to contact us from Fredericksburg. He couldn't believe the good news that I was all right, either, and he kept calling back every ten or fifteen minutes to talk with me again and again — to make sure that I had survived, that it was I, almost as if I had been raised from the dead.

Sylvia came down from Pecos; others came too. Everybody gathered around me, rejoicing.

[Upon Raquel's asking who they had lost, she named them.]

Amelia Carrillo, Nora Brijalba, Lucas Carrillo, Olivia Contreras, Irma Garza, and Sylvestra Sanchez — mostly all on my dad's side of the family. And besides family members, there was my best friend, Corina Morales, and her husband Anastacio. She was seven months pregnant, and was to have her baby in July. Of their two little boys, one died — Andrew, their baby boy. The other boy, Armando, who was to graduate, survived and now lives with his grandparents, Mr. and Mrs. Armando Morales in Saragosa.

. . . For a while after the tornado, I was very nervous. I couldn't handle it. When I'd hear tornado warnings on TV, I'd fall apart. Before the storm they never used to bother me, but now I still have nightmares about the tornado. Each time I see news or read about a tornado somewhere else, I have bad nightmares. Really, I have them most all the time! I suppose that when you have been that close — right in the teeth of a horror such as a tor-

> nado — your subconscious preserves a vivid impression that surfaces time and again and is easily triggered . . .
>
> Sometimes when it is windy, I'll have to call my mom from work to have her look at the news and see if there is anything on TV about the weather . . . She tells me not to be nervous over such things. But, at night, too, if there is a thunderstorm, I never can sleep, and am the first one up, anxious about the weather. Florinda Wofford, Pete Vasquez's daughter, called and asked me the other day whether I ever have nightmares about the tornado. When I assured her that I do, all the time, she was surprised. She told me she thought she was the only one who still has them.

* * *

Miriam Mondragon lay in a bedroom inside a mobile home in Balmorhea. Her Saragosa home had been destroyed, and this was her place of temporary residence in the home of a cousin, Nancy Prieto Matta, and Nancy's husband David. The storm had been gone almost a month now, and she had recovered sufficiently from her injuries to be released from the Odessa Medical Center.

I was ushered to Miriam's bedroom, and as I entered, a broad, happy smile spread across her lovely face. She rose upon an elbow and reached for me. I was almost afraid to hug her for fear I might hurt her. God knows, she had been hurt enough in those past weeks during and after the storm.

Miriam, an eleventh-grade student, is a quiet, beautiful, sensitive, and sensible young woman. In time she told of being in her front yard, of noticing the neighbors, the Tomas Lopez family, in their yard nearby pointing toward the sky — only there was no sky . . . just clouds, dark, turbulent, and threatening. Then came the shock of seeing the tornado descending out of that broiling cloud mass above. She called to her unbelieving parents, but their family car was gone, her younger brothers, Manuel and Michael, having earlier taken it away.

Miriam dated Octavio Muñiz, who was there visiting and they all scrambled into his pickup and dashed over to her grandmother's place. Her parents stayed there while she and Octavio dashed off to search for her kid brothers. The search was short and fruitless, with the funnel closing fast. They fled north on Highway 17 when the truck gave out, its gears locked as the terrible pressure of the storm slowed and stalled it out. There they sat in the path of that onrushing funnel, stalled in the middle of the highway.

A mobile home stood just east of the highway, and the youths ran for it, bursting inside just as the twister struck it and rolled it over. The ceiling rushed up from below, and Miriam took a smashing blow to her right shoulder just as everything went black. She lay with a broken clavicle, a fractured vertebra in her lower back, and less serious cuts and bruises. Octavio had a badly lacerated scalp and ear. The owners of the mobile home, Herbert and Dorothy Berdan, an older couple, were dead. Their son Myles had two broken wrists.

In the desperation of the moment, Octavio snatched Miriam into his arms and carried her back down to the highway. At that timely moment Yvonne Machuca and Norma Carrasco drove by on their way from Pecos, picked them up, and carried them back to the heap of rubble that had been the Candelas grocery store. No ambulances were on the scene yet, but a small white car was, and some unknown driver took the couple to the hospital in Pecos. Octavio remained there, but Miriam, in far more serious condition, was transferred to Odessa Medical Center.

She smiled as she talked, her tender and lovely eyes holding my own. I had taught her something of the enduring significance of loving, caring, sharing.

"Others were far worse off than I," she said, "but thank you, Mr. Lane, for your beautiful love and concern. It shows in your eyes. People have been wonderful. I am happy, too, and thankful for so much."

She was enrolled that fall in my English IV class, the "same ole Miriam," quiet, smiling, perhaps a bit more knowingly. She will graduate with scars upon both her body and soul. But much healing has taken place. I find great joy and comfort in this for her.

[7]

Victims at Home

He was twenty-three when a call was made to his home in Sequim, Washington. It came from a casual acquaintance, Bill Wendt, of Saragosa, Texas. Mr. Wendt, engaged in farming and supervising the Saragosa Mission of the Seventh Day Adventist religion at the northern edge of Saragosa, urgently needed help for their farming operation. That was in 1981, and young Myles Berdan left his government job with the YACC, a young adult corps program for youth, and answered the call for help. He is an L.P.N. (Licensed Public Nurse).

In March of 1987, his father, Herbert Berdan, retired and moved with his mother, Dorothy, to the Adventist community. They resided with Myles in a mobile home.

The Berdan family had never met Miriam Mondragon and Octavio Muñiz until this young couple suddenly banged on their door and burst inside in a desperate race from death as the killer tornado pursued them. There was no time for introductions.

Myles let them in and they all took cover without ceremony just moments before the killer struck, rolling the mobile home over, turning an exploding world upside down for them all.

Youthful Myles was knocked unconscious momentarily, but soon was on his feet, his mind foggy and confused. His eyesight wasn't right, his vision coming and going. He seemed to remember a strange girl lying next to him, and "maybe there was a guy." He was not sure if they were hurt. While he concerned himself with his parents, the young couple vanished. His parents lay side-by-side near a window.

> **Myles Berdan:** My dad lay there with his jugular vein cut. I pinched it off to stop him from bleeding to death, but it was too late. Nothing flowed through that collapsed vein. He was dead.
>
> Mother was in a lot of pain, her legs immobile. She was soon en route to Odessa Medical Center in an ambulance. I never knew the extent of her injuries when I visited her there during the following days. She was in intensive care, then was soon released to stay with Sue Moore, a friend who lives in Odessa. This enabled mother to be near the hospital for checkups and further medical attention.
>
> Then, on Sunday evening, around seven or eight o'clock, my mother collapsed and was rushed back to the hospital, but it was too late. A blood clot lodged in her chest, and her heart stopped. She became death victim number thirty of the tornado.
>
> I came here and worked as a service, trying to help out with the mission, working practically without pay for these six years. I have no money saved, but have been given a mobile home. I'm proud of that. But I have no trade, and I can't lift things . . . you see, I have two broken wrists! My right wrist suffered multiple fractures, while the left one received a clean break. I'm just not sure what the future holds.

Our hearts went out to this clean-cut youth who evidently has lived a life of caring for others and selflessness for himself. Others told me that Myles, under the impression that Floyd Estrada lived out there somewhere, was concerned for his welfare. He searched the blacked-out desolation for his esteemed friend that night, carrying about two broken and unattended wrists to which he seemed to give little or no thought at the time. Call that what you will, but I view it as the genuine love in true heroism.

* * *

Esther Lansberry, eighty-seven-year-old president of the Saragosa Mission, Inc., lived alone in her comfortable and attractive home just northeast of Saragosa across Toya Creek. Her house was situated beside the Berdan family's mobile home in the small Seventh Day Adventist missionary colony situated about a hundred yards east of Highway 17.

Mrs. Lansberry, a widow, had taught school in Oregon for forty-two years before retiring and later relocating to the Saragosa area in 1972. An artist, she formerly taught art and loves to paint in oils. Proceeds from the sale of some of her paintings paid for the construction of the mission school which the tornado destroyed.

When the tornado came, Esther had no warning except "a sudden deafening roar like that of a freight train running wild and racing down a grade." She was alone in her house studying her Bible. Hearing the unearthly rumbling, she arose and peered out her large picture window and was shocked at the size of the huge hail balls pounding the earth. Suddenly, a murky shadow appeared beyond the glass, and she strained her eyes attempting to make out its identity. Her split-second curiosity was satisfied when a gigantic hail ball smacked into the window within fifteen inches of her face. "It was a wicked-looking thing with sharp, jagged edges . . . simply terrifying!" she told me, making a wry face.

She felt that her house was going to be wrecked when she beheld the gigantic funnel half a mile away, ripping at the vitals of Saragosa. She watched a roof rise, shift a few yards to the right, and then slump back again just before it disintegrated before her astonished eyes.

Then came the overpowering urge to abandon her house as she cast about for a place to hide, but she felt she dared not go outside. Now the roof of her porch was already down by her door. She had once made a leaded glass panel and had it installed in an opening beside her entry door. Suddenly, it was blown out and away. Impulsively, she squeezed through that opening, fell to her knees, and crawled, keeping as close as possible to her house . . .

Esther Lansberry: I came to a stop about twenty feet from my door and sat there in the drenching rain. I then asked the Lord to take over: "Lord, I have no way to turn," I prayed. There, in the wild, raging storm where death and destruction raged about me, I felt a sudden, settled calm assurance of His love, and I knew that He would never leave nor forsake me.

My home was utterly demolished, and I sat right there, miraculously safe except for some relatively minor injuries—a head wound and an injured cheekbone. At the hospital they put six stitches into my head . . . My left arm suffered temporary injury, but is all right now.

I was among the first to go to the hospital in an ambulance. I was treated at Pecos, then was taken in and cared for by friends, the Cauls family there . . . until I could return to Saragosa. But while I was in the hospital that night, poor Bill Wendt and his family searched for me most of that night, not knowing where I was, or whether I was dead or alive. For them, I was missing three whole hours! I also learned later that Myles [Berdan] spent a lot of time hunting for me and calling my name in the night, beside himself with concern for my whereabouts, health, and welfare.

* * *

Victor Mondragon is a tall, athletic youth and a varsity football star who speaks with a slow West Texas drawl. He was a member of the junior class, of which I was sponsor at Balmorhea High School. He lived with his parents, brothers, and grandmother in a house adjacent to the Candelas store in Saragosa.

Victor had gone jogging on the afternoon of the storm, and upon returning home took a nap for about half an hour until his grandmother awakened him, excitedly explaining that a terrible tornado was coming. He was skeptical until the house began to be bombarded by flying debris only seconds later. His family bolted to the kitchen and took shelter under tables. The frenzied wind made off with part of the roof, but the house suffered only minor damage.

He ventured outside, where an unearthly calm surrounded him. Suddenly, he heard a lot of voices — screams. They came from the wreckage of the Community Center two blocks away. He was drawn to that bedlam on the run until another scream, lone and compelling, drew him aside to investigate. Trying to run, Victor kept stumbling all over himself, because the debris out there was almost impassable. He pursued the voice a hundred yards or so until he faced the ruined site of the Tomas Lopez residence. Just beyond it he saw Raul, the son, the source of the calls, lying under their truck, seriously wounded and yelling.

The youth was bloody all over — muddy too. Victor could not see the deep cuts under his shirt, but could see that Raul's right arm seemed "cut to the bone."

Victor Mondragon: I bent down and held him close in my arms for a moment; then I eased him down again and told him to lie still while I went for help. "Please don't leave me!" Raul pleaded, but I told him it was best that I go get help and get him to an ambulance. He saw the sense of that, and I took off running. By the time help came, his father and uncle had taken him to the hospital in one of their cars.

I hurried on to the Community Center wreckage, where I had started initially, and I arrived there about the same time Floyd and

Glenn did. I jumped in and worked furiously, all of my emotions shut down, leaving me without feelings or senses. I worked like a machine, a maniac, moving rocks, helping to uncover bodies . . . until I felt two people clawing at my back and shouting for me to slow down. I was deaf to them, driven by desperation to work, claw, move stones, reach for bodies, dead or alive . . .

Sometime later I found myself on the outside of that wrecked building, helping to move bodies and injured people to waiting cars and ambulances. When we caught up, I went walking out in the dark, sort of scouting for people down out there. That's when I came up on your group, Mr. Lane, you and Floyd and others, and I worked with you all the way down to the Ramirez house on the west side.

[I told him that was about the time we came upon the body of Kathy Escovedo.]

Yes, I was there, and Floyd thought she was Erica, his niece. I didn't say anything, but I knew it was Kathy . . . I had seen her before, when it was daylight, right after I left Raul to go for help. I knew it was her . . . her long black hair and all . . .

[I asked him how she was lying, on her back or on her face, earlier, and how she was dressed initially. I asked this, because it had been reported that her clothes had been blown off, that she was nude, or nearly so.]

She was lying face down with the ground all around her clean — swept very clean. She and Raul were about twenty yards in front of and to the left of the car. She was lying about fifteen feet to the east of his position under the truck. She showed signs of life then, seemed to breathe. I was afraid to move her and hurried away to get help.

As to her clothing, she was partly unclothed. She still wore her shorts, but she was bare from her waist up, except for her bra . . .

I wondered then how it came about that Kathy was fully clothed when our group found her. I had observed that she wore not shorts and a blouse but a very pretty little dress — dainty and almost formal. It was beautiful, trimmed in white lace, clean and wholly unruffled. No mud, no blood, no tears. I told him that someone had clothed her and laid her to rest face up. I wondered. Raul's father and brother had been there and taken the youth away; had they, or Mrs. Lopez, cleaned Kathy's face and dressed her? I had to know and would inquire.

I pointed out to Victor that somebody had made her presentable, and he agreed. She was dressed differently than when he first found her, was turned over, face up, and she had been covered with a clean-appearing spread.

I learned later that Tomas Lopez had thoughtfully and respectfully covered this lovely girl. Urgent as was his trip to the hospital with his son who might be dying, he and his wife had consumed extra moments for that act of respect. Those dear people might have been poor and desperate, but they were the salt of the earth, rich in Christian graces and sensitive to the concerns of a fellow human being. As to who had dressed Kathy, since the Lopez family seemed to know nothing of it, I was never able to learn. The mystery remains.

* * *

Kathy Escovedo was taken home by Sammy Carrasco after driver's education class on Friday, May 22, 1987. Sammy had dated Kathy for a long time, and it was not unusual for him to drive her out to Toyavale, four miles west of Balmorhea. There at Toyavale, the Escovedo home was located across Highways 17 and 290 from the Balmorhea State Park and swimming pool.

Brenda Lopez of Saragosa had visited with Kathy before she left for home that day, and they discussed the possibility of Kathy visiting Brenda at her home that evening. Brenda's brother Raul was home from Texas State Technical Institute in Sweetwater, where he was a student. Since he and Kathy were friends, Brenda wanted Kathy to come over and visit with them.

After arriving at home, Kathy and her father drove into Balmorhea on an errand. Meeting Brenda and her sister Elizabeth on the road, Kathy waved and motioned to them to come to her house and pick her up. When Kathy arrived at the home of the Lopez girls, Raul suggested that they go "cruising." Kathy was glad to be with Raul, it was reported. Her long-standing relationship with her boyfriend was going sour, and since she planned to break with him, she felt free to be with someone else. Brenda declined, saying that she had a lot of studying to do in preparation for the following week's final exams. That decision probably saved her life.

Raul and Kathy drove toward Balmorhea to the southwest, then circled back to Saragosa, stopping at the baseball park to the east edge of town. They were watching the weather, which appeared threatening, and then rain commenced coming down and with it heavy hail. Concerned for the paint on his red Camaro, Raul thought at once of the sheltering carport at his father's home in town. In his frantic drive to outdistance the hail, Raul never noticed the tornado that was closing the distance from the south and to his left. He and Kathy slid into the driveway just as the tornado pounced upon them there.

The louver assemblage over the rear window of the Camaro was ripped away as he braked to a stop. Almost instantly, the sun window in the roof above their heads was yanked out, up and away. Out went the window on the driver's side, and as suddenly, a large wide board slammed against that opening and stuck fast there, affording some protection from the barrage of debris slamming into the car.

The Camaro was rocking about, almost leaving the ground, and in moments, flipped over, smashing its roof flat down onto the tops of the seats. But first, a second piece of heavy lumber came out of nowhere and smashed through the opening left by the now-vanished sun window above. It slammed into the passenger's front seat, separating Kathy from Raul. He had just screamed to her to duck down below the seat. Now she suddenly reached across to him, pleading, "Hold onto me!" Raul grabbed her hand a split second before the board came down between them.

As the incredible story tumbled from Raul's lips, other members of his family assisted in piecing the tale of disaster together.

Raul Lopez: The car began bouncing up and down and was just beginning to roll over when I lost consciousness. I don't know what happened; everything just went blank for me. I must have come to myself short moments later, and I was flat on the ground some distance from the car. I was covered with mud . . . and, I learned later, blood. I felt no pain, didn't even know I was hurt, and rose unsteadily to my feet . . . a big mistake! That gale of wild, howling wind and stuff driven by it slammed into me like machine gun fire. I tried to run, but things and the wind kept knocking me down headlong. I kept trying but could not stay on my feet. Then I was knocked out cold.

When I regained consciousness, I felt something plastered on my face and over my eyes. I made another serious mistake then by reaching up and rubbing at my eyes. That totally blinded me, but I kept moving . . . I knew not where . . . through that howling gale. Each time I reached my feet, I would be hurled headlong, again and again, on my feet but a step or two. Blind and staggering, I slammed into our truck and somehow crawled under it, trying to escape that horrible storm. The howling wind and the sound of things slamming into other things was positively deafening. I lay through all of that, just stunned out of my senses, and scared out of my wits, blind with all that mud smeared into my eyes.

Suddenly it was over . . . quiet from the storm, the roaring of the wind and the slamming of things together. An unreal nightmare was over — except I suddenly heard a clamor of voices — people trapped in the rubble of the Community Center ruins. At that time I had no idea who they were or why they were screaming, but suddenly, I began screaming, too — ten times, I suppose, as loud as I could . . .

Someone came to me then — Victor Mondragon — running to investigate their screaming . . . and mine . . . then he ran for help, and I did not see him anymore.

[Raul did not mention Kathy Escovedo, a subject possibly too painful for him. I allowed the conversation with Raul to shift from myself to Raquel. As it did so, I turned to Brenda Lopez on my left and opposite from Raul. We are very close friends, and Brenda felt comfortable with me as we talked with lowered voices.

She related to me what her brother had told the family. Kathy evidently had been swept out of one window of the Camaro when Raul was swept out the other, a blast as violent as it was unimaginable. Brenda told how her father, Tomas Lopez, had found both Raul and Kathy just moments after the storm passed on. He found a sheet and covered her, then found a curtain and used it as a stretcher for the removal of his son.]

Brenda Lopez: Raul was seriously injured with a clean gash across his left rib cage and stomach. There was a bad cut across his back with wood splinters associated with it. His left arm was cut to the bone . . . wounds his doctor could not figure out.

Mr. Lopez: We were all at home except Raul, and I kept watching the storm until I saw a great funnel drop out of the cloud. I shouted to the family and they joined me in the yard where I pointed to the funnel and told them, "Let's go!" We took off, my wife and our girls. [His daughters are Elizabeth, seventeen, Brenda, sixteen, Erica, thirteen, and Edna, eleven.] We drove toward Balmorhea along the farm-to-market road, almost right into the teeth of the tornado.

Raul and his friend Kathy had gone to Balmorhea, and we went that way to find them. On the way out, we saw the tornado on our left very near and sort of in front of us. Things were in the air, swirling, turning, moving at great speed. We saw a huge steel basket off the top of a cotton picker just sailing through the air like an airplane out of control and blown by high winds. It was gyrating slowly as it flew . . . a fearsome sight, and with it the sky was peppered with stuff like lumber, pieces of sheet metal, and all kinds of other things. We almost joined those flying objects when our car was jerked about and slowed to a crawl by the wind. I geared down until I was in low gear and barely moving until we made it around the curve near Turnbough's barn and finally escaped from the force of that awful thing.

At the Fina station near the interstate toward Balmorhea, we met my brother Felipe and inquired about Raul and Kathy. He informed us that they had returned to Saragosa only a short time earlier.

We followed Felipe back to Saragosa the way we had come and drove as far as we could. The tornado had done its awful work, and we went on foot to the place where our house had stood. There was Raul, down and bleeding pretty badly. My brother was ahead of me a bit and was yelling to me to hurry when we arrived.

Brenda: My dad ran up to where my uncle was, and that's when he saw Kathy's body. He found a piece of cloth and covered her up, because she was dead. He found some more cloth, a piece of drapery material, I think, and made a sort of make-shift stretcher, for carrying my brother down to the highway. There was no ambulance available then, and my mother drove the car around there to them. They put Raul into the car and rushed him to the hospital.

Raul Lopez recovered after a lengthy convalescence and several early false reports that he had died. Months later, Tomas Lopez told me that Kathy Escovedo's body was lying right beside a tree whose trunk was about six inches in diameter. He is convinced that she was blown into that tree trunk and slumped there beside it, either dead or dying from the impact to her face, where her injuries were most evident to me.

* * *

Ernesto Bordayo, about thirty, is a handsome Mexican-American of medium build, with quick, warm, friendly eyes. His wife, Isela, is pleasant in conversation, to all appearances, warmhearted. Both of them give every evidence of being serious, responsible parents. My wife taught their Jason, the older son, and describes him as "a very good boy."

Ernesto and his family were returning from Isela's father's home the night of the tornado. When the cloud was spotted, they raced to their mobile home to escape the hail. The electricity snapped off, and Ernesto ran out to his pickup to catch any news reports on the radio. A tornado was reported four miles northeast of Balmorhea — near Saragosa. At that, Ernesto and his wife took off.

They met Ruben Carrasco down the road and stopped to chat. Ruben advised them to take the farm road in the back way rather than the blocked-off highway as one goes into Saragosa. Filled with growing anxiety, they raced toward tragedy past Larry Turnbough's heavily damaged barn, aware then that the tornado moved in a line directly toward Saragosa. Isela was crying now, concern for her mother, Mrs. Roman Muñiz, gripping her. In moments they arrived at the Muñiz home near the western outskirts of town and were immensely relieved to find the house intact.

Lisa Lopez, Isela's niece, was there and informed the Bordayos that Lisa's mother and father were out looking for their son Raul. Brenda Lopez, Lisa's sister, and Roman Muñiz (III) were out somewhere searching for Brenda's horse that had broken out of the corral during the storm. Ernesto walked down the road to assist Brenda and Roman with the horse. She had a rope in her hand and a look of defeat on her face, and she told him they had given up on finding the horse in the growing darkness. Ernesto took the rope, sent Brenda home, and went on to join Roman in rounding up the horse.

> **Ernesto Bordayo:** I went to the pasture and tried looking for the horse. This was at the same time that people were being rescued and removed from the collapsed Community Center only a few hundred yards away. I kept calling to Roman until he finally answered, "Over here!" We found the mare but were unable to catch her. The storm had spooked her, and that mare wouldn't permit me anywhere near . . .
>
> I was in the mood to give up and send Roman home when suddenly the whole world around me flashed in a blinding, thunderous white explosion! The next thing I knew I was coming to on the ground. I couldn't get up. I don't know how long I had been knocked out, nor how long I lay in the mud and blackness of the night, helpless, unable to get to my feet. *Lightning had struck!* I don't know how long it was before I heard a voice calling, "Ernest, where are you?" I yelled weakly, "Here . . . over here!"
>
> Lisa and Roman came then. They turned me over, and Lisa stayed with me while Roman ran for help. I was paralyzed, totally helpless. In time Roman returned with help, and I was brought to an ambulance down the road and taken to Pecos.
>
> I kept choking and feeling the need to spit, but nothing would come. After several feeble tries, I did spit . . . blood! That

meant internal bleeding and worried me. What had that bolt of lightning done to me? I was scared! But by the time we reached the hospital, the use of my fingers and toes was returning. My limbs felt like your leg when you pinch a nerve and it goes to sleep; but the feeling gradually returned during the two hours I was with nurses in the emergency room at the hospital. They put me into a hospital room for another two hours, made X-rays, and found me to be okay and released me. I was sore for days!

The hospital was filling up fast with the injured coming in from Saragosa, and they released me at three in the morning . . .

Reuben Chavez's wife's grandmother was there for a cut on her hand. She had been in the storm, and was let out about that time, and those people gave me and Isela a ride back to Saragosa.

The lightning scored a direct hit on Brenda's horse . . . I was about twenty feet from her when it came down. Several times I had been only three or four feet from that mare . . . you know, almost able to reach out and bridle her, but, thank God, she was not that close when the lightning struck! I'd be a dead one now, just like her!

Isela Bordayo: I thought he was dead. An incorrect report was brought to me at my mother's house. It reported him killed by lightning! As if the horror of the tornado was not enough, now this personal catastrophe! It was a shock upon shock for us.

At the hospital my first and terrible concern was soon relieved, and I was overjoyed when I learned at last that he would recover. With that news the problem of being so far from home and afoot at 3:00 A.M. did not hit me at first. Then I had two things to be thankful for at last: my husband was going to survive, and we had a ride home!

* * *

Mrs. Gertrude Cruz is a diminutive, graying grandmother who manifests a delicate femininity like that of her lovely granddaughters. She sits now among her grandchildren, composed, serene, and brave, her careworn face an index to a heart of smoldering grief. Sorrow does prove, however, the fact of living, and in sorrow life goes on for her. This courageous little grandmother, with a new and youthful family (the Casias family) to assist in rearing, is obviously making the most of life as it comes.

On the afternoon of May 22, Señora Cruz, along with Juanita Bejaran, a friend, and Mrs. Juanita Casias, the daughter-in-law of Señora Cruz, arrived home from a grocery-buying trip to Pecos, thirty miles away. Elsa Casias, the two-year-old daughter of Juanita, was with the three. At 3:00 P.M. Juanita dropped Mrs. Bejaran off at her home, then went on to the bus stop about halfway to Balmorhea to pick up her children. After picking up her children, Juanita dropped Mrs. Cruz at her home next door, then parked at her own. They did not see each other at all for the rest of the afternoon — nor, for that matter, ever again.

Mrs. Cruz scrambled into the bathroom just before the tornado struck. The bathroom soon collapsed. Her husband was separated from her in the wreckage, but each could hear the other calling. In some mysterious manner they managed to join each other under a table that toppled, leaving them exposed, huddled, terrified, and holding hands.

Suddenly it was over, and Mr. and Mrs. Cruz found themselves in an unbelievable desert wasteland of smashed homes and automobiles. Their daughter-in-law's home, the Casias place next door, was laid waste, wholly demolished. They picked their way through the uninhabited ruins strewn about them, and then found Juanita Casias, thirty-four, Elvira, her eldest daughter, aged sixteen, and little two-year-old Elsa — all of them dead. Nearby lay Mrs. Bejaran, seriously injured. She had come over to visit and wait out the storm.

It was too horrible to believe. However, the story told by Adrian Casias, a third-grader, his eyes bright with excitement, made believers of us all. His story was expanded with comments from his siblings, Manuela (eleven) and Albino (fourteen).

> **Adrian Casias:** We had all been in the same bedroom, but when the wind hit, we ran to a space where another room had been. Then the window blew off, and the walls went, and the roof came crashing down on us. I was standing by the window when the wall . . . blew away. I got a bad wound on my head and a hole in my left leg, plus a broken leg. There were nails, splinters, and glass and rocks all in my leg.
>
> **Manuela:** I was in there with them, and I had some cuts in my forehead and in my back, and in the calf of my right leg. I just thought it was going to rain . . . *no mas* [no more]. I was hugging my mom when the wind knocked me down and rolled me over and over on the floor. I was grabbing for her, but I couldn't find her. Later, when the wind stopped, my sister Angelica told me to move Elvira, but my dad came then and took me to the car. I was cold then, and my grandpa gave me a blanket to warm me.
>
> **Adrian:** Angelica ran to our room right after the tornado hit. The wind had knocked her down and then rolled her up in

the rug, tight, like a cigarette. Pieces of things were falling on her, but the rug which was wrapped around her saved her life. When it was over, she couldn't get out for a while! When she finally wiggled her way out, she came to us . . .

Grandmother Cruz: She was frantic. She then ran out into the street, screaming, without her shoes on . . .

Manuela: Her godfather, Rogelio Miranda, picked her up and took her to his house at Balmorhea. My dad was in Balmorhea also. He was fixing his car, and he missed the storm. He must have been driving in the edge of it on his way home, because his car was moving off the road, and he went back to Balmorhea.

Albino: I went to Balmorhea with Manuel and Michael Mondragon, Miriam's brothers. Eddie Lopes was with us too. We saw the clouds—just dark and scary and just rain at first. We had to drive very slow as we were coming back through Brogado because we couldn't see through the rain. On a curve the wind caught the car and swayed it. That's when we turned around and went back to Mr. Billy Lozano's Exxon. After a little bit, we left and went and parked under the overpass. When everything had happened, we went on over toward Saragosa and saw all the posts down and cars turning back. We couldn't make it, and so we turned into a back road and drove another way into town. We had to drive under hanging lines . . . and over some.

When we came to a mobile home across the road, we went off and passed among some trees, trying to see where our houses were. But they were gone! We couldn't find any of them!

When we saw Manuel's father, who had a bad cut on his head, that's when Mickie started crying, and we all got scared then.

A car was coming out as we went on, and the people at the graduation place were holding hands up — everybody screaming for help. We went on by, looking for our folks.

Soon we had stopped, and I was running when Angelica called to me. I saw Dad's car then. I ran and was almost there when I saw Kiki . . . just lying there, face down and moaning. He was pretty banged up — all bloody and still.

I went where our house was and asked Angelica who those people were . . . all of them just lying there — dead. She told me then that they were Mom, Elvira, and Elsa! I started crying, and Dad tried to get me to stop and go find an ambulance. Israel Mondragon came to us then, and he went along with me to the road for an ambulance, but we couldn't get one. They were all on the highway afraid to come on in, afraid the lines were hot there, down on the streets. Then a policeman stopped by and told one of them that some people needed it badly, and the ambulance went for my folks.

Lydia Meneses came running then, screaming, asking for Kiki. I told her where he was, and she told someone there to go pick him up. I went then with Ernie Ramirez, my friend, to a policeman's Blazer and asked if we could get in: we were cold. He sent his wife with us to Pecos — to the school which was open for people to rest and sleep and get out of the cold.

I wasn't hurt myself, and later they called one of my cousins for me, and she came. Later, my grandma and Angelica came too.

He stopped then, brave little guy, and looked about. That must have been the biggest speech he had ever given, and about the weightiest topic ever for a little boy who usually says very little. But he had lost his mother and two sisters, his home and way of life, and all the meager possessions his family owned in this world. He couldn't keep quiet about his colossal tragedy, and no doubt his reliving and talking about it was the therapy he needed most.

His oldest sister, Elvira, was gone — a very beautiful and gentle student who reminded me of a lovely flower lifted to the beauty she saw in the world about her.

* * *

Lolo Escovedo is my friend. Since Kathy Escovedo's tragic death we have developed a relationship close to brotherhood. My wife, Raquel, and I visit the Escovedo family on a fairly regular basis as time allows.

Lolo has worked at the Balmorhea State Park for quite a few years and is highly respected by everyone who knows him. He exhibits a keen intellect and a warm, caring heart.

Lolo seems to have adjusted to the loss of his lovely daughter well enough despite his understandable inner pain.

Señora Escovedo is small and strikingly quiet. She is sweet, attractive, but not overly outgoing. Still in the twilight of trauma, she lives under the oppression of pain resulting from her unimaginable loss. She does not comprehend English, and my Spanish is limited, a situation that causes us to turn to her husband and my wife for translations.

These people were stranded at home on the evening of May 22. They did not have a car there, because Shorty, their son, had taken it a little while after arriving from school. "Shorty" is Arturo, their only son, a senior in high school.

Daughter Kathy came home after her driver's education class. Her boyfriend, Sammy Carrasco, had driven her to Toyavale, where the Escovedos live. When Sammy left, Lolo mentioned supper and Kathy said she did not wish to eat at home. She suggested they go into town and get something different.

Kathy accompanied her father to Balmorhea, where "things for making sandwiches" were purchased. On the way to town the two of them kept watching a "bad-looking cloud" to the east beyond Balmorhea toward Saragosa. Once they imagined they spotted a funnel cloud but could not be certain, and then they laughed about their "tornado." Although the cloud appeared dark and dangerous to Lolo Escovedo, he did not really take it seriously. With food in hand, he and Kathy hurried home.

En route Lolo noticed the Lopez girls in their car, "waving to Kathy as if making signals to each other." The girls followed him and his daughter home.

Kathy had no interest in sandwiches anymore and walked out with her friends. Lolo remembers that they called back saying they were going to the swimming pool (across the highway in the Balmorhea State Park). He cried bitterly at this point, saying, "But they lied to me! They went to Saragosa instead!" The deeply buried hurt in his heart showed up in his eyes.

I suggested that perhaps they did intend to go to the pool, then for some reason decided to drive over to Saragosa. Lolo was silent, mentally nibbling on this thought, then said that the pool would have closed in five minutes. Perhaps the girls had not thought about that at the time, I said, and when they realized how late in the afternoon it was they decided to go driving. I parleyed tactfully, knowing full well that I might not be on the right track at all, but I wished, above all else, that he be open to options rather than place blame and remain bitter.

The girls had not been gone very long when Arturo Escovedo (Shorty) left in the family car. He was shortly followed by Floyd Estrada and Glenn Humphries in the deputy sheriff's car, racing east, lights going, siren wailing. Lolo thought for sure that Shorty was being chased for speeding. "But, no, Shorty wasn't being chased," he said, because when Shorty returned home around 10:00 he called his father outside and slowly broke to him the news of the tornado and of Kathy's death.

I then filled in details for him that I felt would interest him — of how a shockwave spread through that whole crowd of students, and we all wept together, when we learned Kathy had died. Something in every one of us died out there in that blackness, silhouetted under the hard glare of emergency lights. During those awful moments we briefly forgot that other victims were being exhumed from their burial places in the ruins before us. We were only aware of a monstrous personal loss that had wholly occupied our minds and souls.

Lolo Escovedo reflected upon that indelible moment I had witnessed in his stead. Vicariously, I was his eyes, his ears, his memory, as I recounted an event of supreme consequence to him.

I told Lolo that Kathy wrote often of her love for her parents in her journal. Kathy learned the beauty, the necessity of human love and of the love of God in our hearts. She was always so beautiful, like a little kid sister of mine.

"I'm missing her, too, sir," I told him, "hurting just the way you are, deep down inside. We both loved her, and right now, and for all time, the thing Kathy would want most of you and me is that we love each other and be as true brothers forever. That is how it must always be between us."

He voiced his warm agreement with tear-moistened eyes and a quiet, solemn voice.

"This is what all the world so desperately needs, Mr. Escovedo — love. Kathy always did her part down here to make it so. She went about spreading sunshine." My voice grew husky, and I could say no more.

Lolo Escovedo voiced concern for his wife, Gloria: "She is having a hard time." I reminded him that time heals broken hearts, although they are left deeply scarred. I was delighted that Señora Andrea Ortega, Gloria's mother, had been able to come up from her village of LaJunta in Mexico and spend some time with her distraught daughter. We all need mothers and grandmothers like Andrea Ortega, with her deep, abiding Christian faith, her strong, loving shoulders on which her family can cry. Señora Ortega had only a temporary permit and it was necessary for her to return to Mexico.

I have heard it said that "Joy is not the absence of suffering; it is the presence of God." When people like Andrea Ortega reach out and touch other people, they are the representatives of God on earth — the presence of the God of all love. Kathy Escovedo believed that. Her beautiful grandmother most assuredly does.

During one of our many intimate visits together, Lolo revealed that he thought Kathy knew she was going to die. "I feel this very deeply because of several indications she gave," he said. As I sat looking intently into Lolo's eyes, I was wondering with him what really went on in Kathy's mind that night. I asked him to tell me what he meant.

> **Lolo Escovedo:** One week before Kathy died she was talking with me about death. She sat with those tender brown eyes focused upon her grandfather's picture . . . She sat right there on the floor, and it seemed that she was totally absorbed in that picture. As she looked searchingly into her grandfather's eyes, Kathy told me, "I wonder how it is up in heaven where my grandfather is. What will it be like to be with him up there in heaven?" she asked me.
>
> I told Kathy that we don't know, but that we will find out when we die. I went on to say, as I recall it, "I imagine that he is doing pretty well up there where he is." She looked up at me and said, just matter-of-fact like, "Well, Daddy, I am going to die . . . I'm going to see my grandfather and be with him, and when I die, I want you to bury me right next to my grandfather. Will you promise to do that for me, Daddy?" We did; we granted her that request. She is buried right next to my dad in the cemetery at Fort Davis.
>
> On the following Friday she was strangely anxious to be off in the evening, to be gone somewhere. She was curiously anxious, restless, agitated at home, as if she was on fire to be somewhere else. It was as if some unknown summons or force was drawing her, compelling her to be gone — that there was an appointment with destiny to be kept! . . . After we drove all the way into town and back for the things she said she wanted for supper, she wouldn't eat . . . just walked out and ignored the food! She left as if she had to go and must not be delayed . . . and I guess she just barely made it over there in time.

Yes, Kathy Escovedo, one of the dearest friends I have ever had, rushed off from her father and mother, from the safety of her home — and her appointment was kept.

I was inspired to write a poem as a tribute to Kathy Escovedo and Elvira Casias, a verse of which reads:

In retrospect I cry and contemplate
How sudden stormy winds can seal one's fate
And hurl sweet life into a headlong flight,
Paled out and gone . . . blended with hues of night.
Their tender touch lent charm to each caress,
Enduring time in memory now to bless;
Like lovely lilies, given once to me,
That time would wither, fade, and free
Of further pleasant charm to human touch
I never can again reject as such!

Let pleasant memory live, though they be gone . . .
The sweet and silent spell live on and on!

* * *

Israel Mondragon, another of my former students, is a heavily built young man, outgoing, and always identifying in his own heart with those who suffer. He had a brief, modest story to relate after the passing of the storm.

He was at his home when it occurred, then rushed out afterward to lend a hand. But his adventure took a turn that moved his responsibility from the mangled and beaten town to a hospital bedside in Odessa.

Israel Mondragon: The tornado didn't last long, and after it passed, we crawled out and looked around. We saw that everybody in our family was okay, and then we ran to the church where the graduation was taking place.

Pretty soon they sent me with two babies to Pecos in a police car. Those babies were Lionel Garza, Jr., and I believe the other was Mr. Joey Hererra's baby.

Those babies did not seem to be very seriously injured at the time; they were alive then, but thirty minutes later, they both passed away at the hospital.

Then the ambulance came in with Miriam Mondragon and Octavio Muñiz, who was with her during the storm. Both were seriously injured, but Miriam was hurt really badly. After she was installed in a room in the Pecos hospital, they soon removed her to the Odessa Medical Center. I was right there and was asked to go on to Odessa with Miriam in the ambulance, because she requested that I go along. She's my cousin, you know . . .

I went with her, and I stayed there two days and two nights. Because of this I missed all the subsequent action that took place in Saragosa.

Octavio remained in the Pecos hospital since his injuries were less serious than hers. She had sustained a broken clavicle and some damaged vertebrae. Later, I asked Octavio how he and his car had fared, and he informed me that he had thirteen stitches across his left scalp, and beyond that, had been almost scared to death. His red pickup was totaled out. The wind had picked it up from the highway after he and Miriam abandoned it, and had thrown it to one side of a field off the road. I guess it was wise of them to have abandoned it. That act saved their lives! Thank God for that!

* * *

Bob Walker, a horse rancher, has lived at Saragosa for many years. In 1944 he built a large and sturdy rock home across the highway off the southernmost edge of town. On the grounds just west of the Walker home stood the first building ever constructed in the town. It was built 105 years ago as a tiny mission. This historic landmark was so structurally impaired by the force of the tornado that it was judged unsafe and torn down.

Bob Walker arrived home from the Gallegos Bar only moments after 8:00 on the evening of the tornado. He had been visiting with his longstanding friend, Joe Gallegos. Entering his home, Mr. Walker found his wife Peggy busy at the sewing machine. He had noticed her car parked near the archway in front, and since the weather was unsettled, he thought he should move the car in case there was hail with the rain that was already coming down. Not wishing to disturb Peggy's sewing, he went out and parked her car in the garage, then parked his pickup in the barn nearby.

By that time the rain was cascading down in torrents, and hail with it, creating a clatter on the barn roof that was almost deafening. Mr. Walker decided to wait out the rain and hail, and since the pickup afforded the best place for him to sit in the barn, he stayed in it throughout the storm.

He had not noticed the approaching tornado, probably hidden from view by the rain as he drove into the barn. Once inside, his view of the clouds was blocked. There was no point in his going to the house in drenching rain, so there he sat.

Bob Walker: Suddenly, something happened that startled the wits out of me . . . BAM! The barn blew away right over my head! The pickup was undamaged, and I was unhurt. After the siege of the storm had passed and things quieted down, I went to the house . . . or, what had been a house. I heard screams! It was my wife screaming in the subsiding wind.

Peggy had continued her sewing until the big wind struck with sudden, shocking violence. A large picture window in the front room was suddenly sucked out with a horrifying force and a big clatter. Startled, she ran to the bedroom closet and pulled shut the door behind her.

[H. C. Krietz, a friend of the Walkers who had come up from Yorktown, Texas, to assist as a volunteer carpenter, was standing nearby, listening to Bob Walker's story. He led us to the spot where Peggy Walker had hidden. Wall partition patterns were plain on the now-clean concrete floor. Speaking in the absence of Mrs. Walker, Mr. Krietz repeated details of her near-fatal misadventure.]

H. C. Krietz: While the tornado was wrecking the house, Peggy was in here struggling to hold the closet door closed against force that yanked it open again and again. Each time she would pull it back, using all her strength to slam it shut. As the tug of war went on, one of the Walkers' black cats dived into the closet during one of those moments when the door was partially open. The next second the roof went from the house, and the wind lifted that cat above Peggy's head! Chilled with fear, yet charmed in disbelief as the cat floated birdlike above her, she watched it float, out of control, around and around above her head like a cowboy spinning his lariat. Then the cat vanished with the roof and the rest of the house, and has never been seen or heard of again!

[He then led us into the yard area, promising to show us some striking evidence of weird things that tornadic winds can do.]

Look at this piece of wood about the size and shape of a wooden paint stirrer that comes with buckets of paint. This piece, as you can see, is driven straight and rigidly into the huge body of this tree with no apparent damage to either. You can't pull it out!

[He also showed us slivers of metal, no larger than 3x5 cards, protruding from various trunks and limbs. He told us that it was impossible to pull any of them out. I visualized the debris-laden wind blasting to its death and destruction every living thing within its grasp, and I thought of what such things did to some of the unfortunate neighbors and other creatures caught out in the open. Back inside the framework going up where the old Walker house had stood, Bob Walker continued his gripping story.]

Walker: We had a thousand-gallon propane tank out here west of the house. My wife went out to find me when the storm had gone. Upon reaching that rocky archway out front, she found her passage blocked by that big propane tank right in the archway . . . spewing propane gas! Moving her car from that spot wasn't a bad idea!

Well, she just turned around and wandered about, circling the house, crying, upset . . . in some sort of a daze . . . I don't know. But a big tree had been uprooted just off the west side of the house . . . Krietz here showed you the pit . . . well, my wife tumbled right off into that hole!

Out in the road near the west edge of my land, a mobile home, or what was left of it, had been blown across the road and left there, making passage of traffic impossible. I walked out there nosing around and found the body of its owner, the elderly Mrs. Anita Brijalba. There she lay beside the remains of her trailer . . . dead . . . and not a very pretty sight. I came to the house — the wreckage of mine — and found something to wrap up her body in, and then I left her where she was. I could do no more. Others would have to remove her when they could.

He paused for the better part of a painful minute while all our minds reeled under the impact of his narration. I remembered something I had once read from Christopher Fry, "In tragedy every moment is eternity," and so it seemed to us then — as now.

* * *

Mrs. Lydia Meneses, outgoing and vibrant, was picked up at the Odessa-Midland airport by two neighbor friends, Lydia and Ramona Machuca. Mrs. Meneses had left her van with them so that they could pick her up at the airport when she returned from visiting her daughter in Houston. They drove directly to Lydia Machuca's home in Saragosa, where the unsettled weather went unnoticed until the wind later blew open the van door just as Mrs. Meneses was about to leave for her home. Her friend prevailed upon her to stay longer until the weather calmed down.

Then Kiki Meneses, her son, came by and borrowed $25. He was going to Balmorhea and needed the money. His mother gave it to him, asking whether he had unplugged the TV set in their mobile home. Lydia Meneses lived with Ramon, Sr., her husband, and Ramon, Jr. (Kiki), in the mobile home beside one occupied by Manuel and Ninfa Ontiveras.

Her son had not unplugged the TV, so she told him to be sure and do so because of the threatening weather. Since he insisted that he had to hurry off to Balmorhea, she dismissed the matter from her mind and doubted that he went to unplug the set. She would never know.

Mrs. Meneses was later told that her son drove down the streets of Saragosa yelling warnings to everybody he saw: "Tornado is coming! Tornado is coming! Run for safety!" He drove on to his home, and nobody knows what happened after that.

Relatives surmised that Kiki tried to save his "aunt," Ninfa Ontiveras, and that the tornado caught both of them at that moment, taking her life and critically wounding him. His car stood in the driveway, relatively untouched except for mud and a few minor damages. Automobiles all around were smashed to shambles, overturned, and tossed about like rag dolls. Kiki, badly injured, was found some distance from his car and some distance from the spot where their mobile home had stood. Mrs. Ontiveros's badly battered and lacerated body was too disfigured to describe. She was killed instantly.

Ramon Meneses, the son, was first placed in the Odessa Medical Center, then at the Institute of Rehabilitation and Research in Houston. He has since been receiving physical therapy at Pebble Creek Nursing Center in El Paso. His prolonged therapy has resulted in disappointing results to effect his recovery from a comatose state following massive injuries in the Saragosa tornado.

I taught Kiki Meneses in my English classes in the Balmorhea Public Schools, from which he graduated in May of 1984. He had been an all-around athlete, popular, and generally "a lovable guy." Un-numbered friends and relatives are hurting with him and his mother, who found him badly hurt following the storm . . .

> **Lydia Meneses:** Mr. Isidro Casias was there near his own wrecked house when I arrived and asked him to help me pick up Kiki. The man looked frightful . . . terribly distressed . . . and he told me . . . us . . . that he had been picking up all his dead and injured, a terrible ordeal for that poor man . . . and that he didn't have the strength to do any more. He had lost Juanita, his wife, and his two daughters, Elsa and Elvira. His little boy Adrian, and Manuela, his little daughter, also — that is, they were injured and went to the hospital. I understood his plight, his utter extremity.
>
> They finally got Kiki into an ambulance and took him away . . . I didn't know where. The next day we began our search — Van Horn, Pecos, Fort Stockton. Finally, we found him near noon on Saturday in Odessa at the Medical Center, where I have been ever since.

I had heard that Kiki was picked up right after the storm by his former coach, Michael Barrandy, who had gone out there following the tornado to engage in rescue operations. Weeks after the storm had gone, I made inquiries of Michael, who was my next-door neighbor. He was still pretty shook up and told me that he preferred not to talk about what had happened on that frightful night. He did confirm the report, stating that he and Ted Woodruff, his assistant coach, had picked up Kiki and gotten him to an ambulance. "He was a fun-loving, crazy kid who loved football and fast cars," Michael told me rather grimly. "He also loved people and tried to be a friend to everybody."

Thinking of this tribute, I remembered a verse:

> Although the world is full of suffering,
> it is full also of the overcoming of it.
> —Helen Keller, *Optimism* (1903), 1

* * *

Joe Gallegos is a six-footer, sixty-three years young with the demeanor and bearing of a seasoned West Texas rancher, sure of himself and friendly. Mr. Gallegos has owned a ranch near town and the Gallegos Bar in Saragosa, as well, for many years.

Amparo Molinar was born in Terlingua, Texas, near the Big Bend National Park. At age sixteen, the beautiful Amparo was employed at the Kandy Kitchen, a snack bar and jewelry establishment in Alpine. During another period the graceful young *señorita* worked for the J.C. Penney store in Alpine. In 1945, as World War II was winding down, Amparo married Joe Gallegos, and nine years later the young couple moved to Saragosa and settled down to industry, investment, and hard work. The Gallegos Bar, ranch, and the Chevron station and restaurant at the busy intersection of IH 10 and Highway 17 resulted.

Out of the family growth sprang nine children and their separate families. The Gallegos clan has been successful, indeed, in and about this land of cotton, cattle, and cantaloupe, where mountains eternally hover about in a distant opaline silhouette.

Joe Gallegos and a friend, Ned Briceño, who worked for him, had gone to the cow pasture at around 4:00 that afternoon on some errand having to do with the Gallegos cattle. Both in their going out and their coming back, the men were struck by the remarkable build-up of clouds over the basin. "We kept our eyes on those dark clouds, because they spelled very disturbed weather . . . boiling like water . . . very disturbed."

He continued watching those clouds, which were later "really boiling back toward the Davis Mountains." Joe's mind was so distracted by the threatening weather that he paid scant attention to his customers as afternoon gave way to evening and his wife drove in. He told them it looked like a tornado might develop. They bought some six-packs and took off for Pecos. Bob Walker came by, and they commented to each other about the "huge cloud extending to the east of us," and then Bob left for home to watch boxing on TV.

It was around 8:00 when Mrs. Gallegos arrived from Fort Stockton and parked under a large tree. He had her move her car so the storm would not blow the tree onto it. Their daughter-in-law, Regina Gallegos, Jimmy's wife, and Linda Briceño had come in with Amparo from Fort Stockton, dropping Linda off at her home just down the street near the Community Center. She noticed Rosendo Carrasco taking pictures outside, but she did not see the tornado. It was behind her. The weather then looked so dangerous that she told Joe he had better go for Linda.

He had his eyes on the cloud, too, and suddenly saw four small funnels, one after the other, come and go, come and go. The big funnel was now in sight, and Joe Gallegos went for Linda and returned, taking flight behind his family who had dashed on foot up the highway to the Toya Creek bridge. The troop consisted of Billy Gallegos, his mother-in-law Dorotea Hidalgo, his wife Anita, and their boys, Ringo and Billy Joe. Regina was with her husband Jimmy Gallegos and their baby girl.

The family scrambled down into the creek, then clambered up the concrete incline to the wedge-shaped point where it joins the overhead structure bearing the roadway. There they huddled and hoped and waited through eternal seconds before the twister struck.

Joe and Linda were right behind the others, racing madly toward the bridge in his pickup. Rapid-fire events followed, told now in Joe and Amparo Gallegos's own words.

> **Joe Gallegos:** I arrived right behind the family, but those seconds were almost fatal . . . It was so noisy I couldn't describe that deafening sound! I just leaped out of my pickup as it leaped too! It stopped a hundred and fifty feet from the bridge, as I learned sometime later. I wasn't measuring distance then — except in leaps toward the creek and the bridge. As I tore down into the creek, time had run out. I couldn't reach the family; the storm was upon me! So I locked my arms around a bridge piling and

held on while the wind whipped and beat me around pretty badly. Debris was everywhere. There was no safe place at all, even under the bridge.

Amparo Gallegos: The air was filled with sheets of tin, tumbling automobiles, large rocks and gravel — all smashing into everything in sight. Even the big bridge above us shuddered and moved a little, ready to go — and with us beneath it! It was worse than a battlefield!

Now the angry wind was sucking us — all of us, eight people — out, whirling us through space. I lost my senses as we dropped in a heap of human bodies together in the creek below! I came down head-first, and stayed like that, head down. That's when I lost my pair of new glasses I had just picked up in Fort Stockton that day — never found them! Joe lost his too; Ringo too. Regina's legs and arms looked bad — skin gone, blood thickened with sand . . .

Joe: I saw my family dumped in that tangled mass with limbs protruding in assorted directions, right next to a willow tree in the bottom of the creek. I was fighting savagely to hold onto the cement column right nearby.

Amparo: It whipped him around and around that post. Later, we went and looked at it, and where he hugged it, there is a lighter band all the way around the pillar — polished, I guess by his arms. The rest of it is much darker and chipped and pitted from the gravel bombardment it withstood.

Joe: When the family was sucked out from under the bridge and thrown in a pile down in the creek below, the boys were both swept from under there too . . . and vanished! When the storm subsided, we limped and crawled up to the roadway above, and there they were — Ringo and Billy Joe — where they had been blown and deposited up on top of the bridge. They were both on their feet, but not in very good shape!

Amparo: The boys had blood running down all over them. They were a shocking sight with some very deep wounds. Ringo had cuts on his face . . . on his cheek, and Billy Joe had some deep cuts too. Sand, rocks, and no telling what all had blasted them, matting with blood and wounds alike. Both boys had a deep cut across the middle of their bodies, alike and in the same place — strange!

Joe: . . . like a piece of sheet metal sliced by, not making a direct hit, like a soldier swinging a sabre . . .

You know, when we all made our dash for the bridge, Nate Briceño, who had gone with me to look after the cows, stayed behind in the bar. He had just stood calmly by one wall the whole time that the place was bursting apart and falling in on him. When we came back from the bridge, there was not just one but eight or ten people in the bar, all looking pretty dazed — the Woods family, Nate, and several others . . . Dora Vasquez and her folks . . .

"Nate, are you all right?" I asked him, and he said, "Yeah. About a minute after you left, the roof went. Sounded like a bomb hit . . . The walls gave way and burst into the room. I just grabbed me a Pearl and washed my mouth!"

Amparo: When I came out of the creek, I couldn't see a thing, but I remember babies crying. My mind went blank at some point. I never even noticed that our home was gone!

There we stood, many of us injured and needing to go to a hospital. The boys had those cuts, and Dorothy had a badly damaged right arm. Amber, Linda's baby, required surgery.

[Linda Briceño, the Gallegos's daughter, tall, attractive, pleasant, and prone to be quiet and attentive while others of us rambled on with our talking, now spoke up.]

Linda: I was struck a blow on the head during the storm. I passed out and let go of Amber. I guess she fell — I don't know — but she had a fractured skull.

Amparo: I had bumps all over my head too; needless to say, I couldn't sleep that night!

Joe: Anita, Billy's wife, was bloody all over . . . as were the boys . . . blood running everywhere!

Amparo: After we looked things over a bit, we caught a ride with some people who came along on their way to Mexico. We rode the three miles south to our service station, then Tony, our son, took us on to the hospital in Alpine, where we all checked into the hospital together.

Linda: For a long time none of us could sleep. We all hurt too much . . .

When I could, I went to Odessa, where I spent some time with Amber. They had to do surgery on her fractured skull . . . My mother-in-law here, Mrs. Aurora Briceño, was at the Head Start graduation. When my dad dashed down there in his pickup for me, it was maybe two or three minutes before the tornado struck there . . . I looked across toward the Community Center, and I saw a bunch of people boiling out of that building. A man was making motions with both hands as if to calm the crowd.

I could see the giant funnel then — just behind Bob Walker's house. A hard driving rain was coming down, and the atmosphere had turned murky and dark. The tornado was just about to hit there when we took off for shelter under the bridge. As you know, the rest of our family was already there ahead of us, and Dad and I almost didn't make it!

You asked about my daughter Marlene, who once was in your English class. She was visiting in California, but rushed home the next day. I'm glad she wasn't here.

* * *

I taught her when she was Regina Ramirez, first in junior high, and finally in high school. She always wrote fascinating compositions and daily journal entries about nature, and about God, and about the need for improved interpersonal relationships. Regina married Jimmy Gallegos in the summer of 1986, and the two of them now have a daughter named Jo Gina Lee Gallegos.

When termagant nature unleashed her rampaging tornado on the evening of May 22, Jimmy and Regina, with their child, joined Jimmy's family in their hundred-yard dash to the Toya Creek bridge. From that harrowing experience none of the Gallegos family will likely ever be quite the same again. Here is Regina's story:

Regina Gallegos: Gosh! We couldn't believe it — a tornado was actually coming! When we saw it, the funnel had already touched the ground just on the other side of town.

Moments later, the wind was roaring around us, and the sky was sooty black. We all took headlong flight to the Toya Creek bridge, located about a hundred yards north from our house. My husband, with our baby, and my inlaws ran breathlessly, as fast as we could while the monster tornado gained on us, gathering speed right on our heels as we charged down the embankment into the creek . . . We scrambled up again, now toward the supporting beams high above our heads. Once we were wedged up under there, we all huddled and squatted down, hushed and still, fear clutching at our throats. Our hearts were pounding violently from our exertions and from stark terror as the shrill wind shrieked about us. This could well be the end for us all!

The sand began mercilessly whipping at our feet, paining and torturing them until we lost all sense of feeling of the pain. Stronger and louder grew the raging wind, a deafening and constant shriek and roar. I held my baby tighter and tighter while praying for mercy. In seconds that wild, senseless wind stripped her from my arms and seemed to place her into Jimmy's arms. She landed there unhurt as if God Himself had placed her in stronger hands.

As she was sucked away, the wind tugged me from under the beams of the bridge. Jimmy, seeing me about to go, grabbed my hand and tried to rescue me, but it was useless. The wind prevailed, dragging Jimmy along with me! Then everyone was grabbing someone else, hanging on, forming a human chain, a frantic lump of hopeless human beings being dislodged from their place of concealment and hurtled ruthlessly down, down, down toward the creek bed below! Almost instantly there was a tangled heap of human bodies at the bottom of Toya Creek.

I glanced up and saw that horrible black funnel plowing its way into the creek only a few yards away, and hurtling menacingly down upon us. In that mad moment of time I thought, "Oh, God, this must really be the end!" Helpless in my own frailty, I was praying, yelling against the shock of that tempest, "Oh, Lord Jesus! *Help* us!"

The others joined in, and before the funnel, looming ominously before us, could bear down and strike its fatal blow, it just seemed to melt before our very eyes. I don't know what happened, and I can't explain it, but we were spared. I now know, as I had never realized before, that the Lord does step into our lives in our extremities to help us. In some mysterious way He is able to come to our rescue when we are utterly helpless and call upon Him. He is truly "a very present help in time of trouble."

After the storm moved on I began to look at the destruction left in its wake. I thought that everyone was injured, myself included. My legs were numb but so pained I could not stand after I struggled to my feet. Somehow I dragged myself up the slope and out of the creek, reaching the top, only to be further devastated with shock as my unbelieving eyes swept over a scene of houses ripped asunder, where debris, driven like an artillery barrage, had leveled the landscape that had been my home and my neighborhood. My town was gone, utterly wiped out! Were we the only ones left upon this ghastly scene? That thought tore through my mind for a long minute, a mind torn into as many pieces at that moment as my little town. I thought, "Oh, no! Can it be we are the only ones left alive?" Not a soul stirred. What other conclusion could one have just then?

Another part of my shredded brain seemed to engulf my consciousness: "I've never had a death in my immediate family, but today I've lost them all in just a matter of moments!" I was assuming my family all perished when I did not know, and I realized that I was doubting that the One who had saved us could have saved my family as well.

I desperately wanted to run through that wasteland of torn and shredded human habitations to my parents' home, to my grandparents' place, but I was barely dragging my own body . . . Both my hands were bleeding profusely, and all sorts of pains wrapped my body in flames. I wanted to cry, but no tears would flow, I couldn't even talk, couldn't yell, much as I felt the urge to do so. My state of shock immobilized me, and I could do nothing, my plight a helpless one. A prayer for the Lord's help for us all crossed my mind, and then a passing truck driver, seeing my destitute family and me huddled by the highway at the edge of devastation and death, stopped and gave us a lift to the Chevron station down by the interstate. My brother-in-law, in charge there, urged us to take his car and be off to the hospital in Alpine.

En route to the hospital I had thoughts only for my family, and particularly for my grandmother, two years then in a wheelchair. Would I ever see her sweet face again? How could she, helpless to run, have survived? . . .

At 9:00 P.M. they wheeled me into the hospital in Alpine where emergency personnel attended my wounds, X-rayed me, and sewed me up where I had raw and torn edges. It was 3:00 A.M. when they finished overhauling me, and I was soon peacefully asleep in a quiet room.

I awakened the next afternoon to face visiting relatives, whom I quizzed about my family. Their uncertainty was overwhelming! Nobody knew anything, and something inside me tried to convince me that they were all dead and nobody wanted to expose me to the awful truth. Then, the following day, Nora, my sister-in-law, came from Pecos and promptly informed me that she had seen my folks, and that they were all okay! Yes, my grandparents were fine too! Oh, thank God for them all!

With that relief came such happiness in my soul that I had the sensation of swimming in a great sea of serenity . . .

After my discharge on the 25th of May and my subsequent sessions of physical therapy were over, I could only sit and face one reality of this life: that the most tragic things can really happen to me after all . . . The secret of victory in one's own soul is that he be at peace with God and have the settled peace of God within. Then, when he looks forward, hoping for the best, knowing the worst can come, it is not a hollow, empty hope nor a groundless faith, for "The Lord knows how to deliver the Godly out of tribulation."

* * *

Raquel and I have long cherished the Ramirez family as friends. I have taught Alex, long since graduated, Regina, now married, and Rene, still in high school. My wife taught Ramiro in first grade and then again last year in the fifth.

Frank Ramirez, the father, is an automobile mechanic employed at the time of the disaster in Verhalen, north of Saragosa. Natividad, better know as "Nati" to her friends and co-workers, works for the Balmorhea Elementary School as an aide in the special education section. She is an attractive middle-aged lady with a warm personality, a dedicated aide who shows genuine caring for the children with whom she works day by day.

Although their residence was almost totally demolished by the tornado, the Ramirezes were fortunate to have escaped with their lives. With the exceptions of Alex and Regina, the family was in their house when the tornado struck. Happily, they all survived, due in part to the location of the home on the far west end of town, where damage was less severe.

Nati told how the heavy clouds mounted up that afternoon, growing darker as the wind grew intermittently gusty and still. Lightning crashed and thunder rumbled, growing louder and more frequent. Frank grew worried and young Ramiro sensed that "something funny was going on." Nati peered out again and again, and finally went outside where a startling sound as of a roaring jet plane crashed upon her ears. The clouds to the east were clashing, boiling wildly. The family went inside after that and had barely reached the middle of the room when it struck. With the sudden shock of the blow, they dashed into the bathroom located in the back part of the house.

Off came the roof, literally exploding in the thundering wind. The earth was shaking something akin to an earthquake. The walls trembled back and forth, and for a minute Nati thought the end had come for them all. Suddenly, the bathroom wall to their left came down upon them. Nati's aunt, seventy-nine-year-old Mrs. Doribia Bustamantes, was there, and Nati was desperately trying to shield her from flying debris. Nati had just huddled down over her aunt when the wall came down, but the older lady was saved.

Nati did not fare so well, because the wall fell on her back. She was left with numerous bad bruises but no broken bones. She tells how she glanced up into the open sky where the roof had gone, and suddenly a board smashed in and down, striking her on the head. It scared her more than it injured her, incredibly doing only minor damage.

Rene and Rose Ann dived under the bed just before the walls came down. They suffered no harm beyond a bad scare, and both remained surprisingly calm and quiet. Rose Ann did later complain of soreness resulting from the weight of the fallen wall, which caused the bed above her to give way and place some pressure on her arm.

I told her how I had been involved in a house-to-house search after the storm that night, and that we had probed about in their wrecked house. "Your home was a real victim of violence, but I was relieved that we found nobody at home! Naturally, I wondered where you folks were," I said.

Nati Ramirez: The storm seemed to go on forever while we were in there waiting it out. I thought it never was going to stop banging the house about. When it did pass, Frank and I had to jump over downed walls and climb over smashed furniture. Once we had gotten outside, everything was deathly quiet and still for some minutes. We then thought that everybody in the whole community had been killed . . . everybody but us! What a strange sensation!

Then I heard a blast of voices. "Get us out of here!" It was sudden and electrifying, this big, big bedlam of hollering, yelling, and crying. The clamor came from the Center, but we had more immediate concerns now. Frank went back inside our heap of ruins to help the children out as well as my mother and father. Everybody was still in there, and we didn't know what we would find. Everyone was safe, and we all went across the street to see about my sister, Monse Guevara, and her husband Rodolfo. Both of them were okay, but their house was badly damaged . . .

We had no home then, and went to Barstow, just east of Pecos, and lived for a time with Juan Ramirez, Frank's brother. Later, we rented a place in Pecos where we will live until our new house is eventually built in Saragosa. I may not be at all comfortable out there, however, because I'm terrified of clouds. I do hope that all our fear and dread will in time wear away, but I still wonder . . .

PART III
The Caregivers

Caregivers

'Tis said that "into every life
A little rain must fall" . . .
'Tis true, but now and then some soul
Is near drowned in a squall.

Good fortune for myself is just,
But has no sound defense
If, when misfortune others strikes,
I show indifference.

I'll only pass this way but once,
And while here on the road,
Let me some Good Samaritan be,
And lighten someone's load . . .

Someone who's down, a fellow man
Who needs care I can give . . .
When I'm identified with him,
I'll the more fully live.

— Derwood Lane

[8]

The Givers and Takers

The monstrous killer tornado left, in a manner of speaking, many dangling human feet at Saragosa. And many ladders of human assistance were needed for the rescue and support of those dangling feet. Many such ladders showed up in a surprising complexity of forms and in expressions of generosity worthy of great people. Our nation and the rest of the world were moved to extend helping hands — ladders of support for those helplessly dangling feet.

Bill Collier, staff writer for the Austin *American-Statesman,* described how Austin donations "were among tons of clothing, furniture, food, and other aid that swamped Saragosa and Reeves County." (January 18, 1988) Collier wrote, in the same story, "Donations flowed in — some cash, but mostly clothes, furniture, appliances and toys." In a story the day before, he wrote, "But rural Reeves County . . . was not prepared to handle the tide of donations that rolled in for Saragosa." In his January 18 account, he correctly observed that "county officials and volunteer disaster workers say they were unable to keep track of all the donations, and many were stolen." Thus a door was left open to the unscrupulous.

I was on the scene myself and continuously distressed that there was inadequate organization for responsible handling of the influx of gifts. Records should have been kept, but in the bedlam and confusion there was only partial and inadequate recording of donations.

It is beyond the realm of possibility to pay deserved tribute to all the donors of foodstuffs, clothing, money, and medical supplies, along with countless other means of human support. The disaster struck with such swiftness and force, the need was so dramatic and urgent, and the response so generous and widespread that accurate and thorough record-keeping was virtually impossible. Tons of clothing, food, furniture, and other kinds of gifts came in from countless numbers of unnamed people. While this was taking place, almost every responsible able-bodied adult among us galvanized into emergency rescue action at once. Everyone kept busy beyond imagination. Clothes had to be received in haste and thrown into assorted piles that grew into mountains — who gave what nobody knew or even gave a second thought. Disaster relief agencies were caught up in much the same current and never sent the promised summary reports; thus, acknowledgments will have to be given general treatment.

While isolated larger donations and gifts of money through checks should have been recorded, in many instances they simply were not. Some assessment of guilt and fraud may, in time, prove to be in order, but accusations are not a part of this story.

Since an exhaustive chronicle of the caregivers is impossible due to lack of records, I can but record my personal gratitude to the multiplied thousands who responded to our horrendous emergency. They came with open hearts and open pocketbooks, and sent every conceivable kind of material necessity to soften the blows of the victims. The spiritual support, conceivably far more important at times than the material, came in all shapes and sizes as people prayed, offered counsel, and gave encouragement. " 'Tis not enough to help the feeble up, but to support him after," wrote Shakespeare, and I watched the practical aspects of that in the families victimized at Saragosa. On their behalf, I express my thanks and appreciation to all the caregivers everywhere, even in the act of writing this story.

In a few cases I can be specific, and it is incumbent upon me to be so as limited space and information allows. Unnumbered people came from far and near to give their time and skills in the rebuilding of the town.

The Meadows Foundation has built and donated a $250,000

multipurpose center at Saragosa. George C. Harrison of the Baptist General Convention of Texas superintended construction. His charming wife Juanita was there doing her part in the field office. Their time and labor, along with that of numerous others, was as remarkable as it was unselfish.

Prominent among those who furnished invaluable labor and skills toward the rebuilding of the homes was the Texas Baptist Men's Retirees and the men of the Mennonites. We applaud all of these unselfish friends of humanity for the practical caring they have shown.

The Catholic Charities rebuilt the uninsured grocery store that Jose and Pas Candelas lost in the storm. The Diocese of El Paso is constructing a new Catholic church at Saragosa.

The senior class of Richland Hills High School in Fort Worth, Texas, sent a cash gift of over $1,100 to the senior class of Balmorhea to help with their senior trip. Balmorhea seniors were from both Balmorhea and Saragosa, and the gift was a godsend for them. All of us were grateful to the Fort Worth students and their families.

The Salvation Army gave an original gift in excess of $2,000 between May 22 and June 4, according to Major Neil Sanders. The agency remained in Saragosa almost four months. We regret having no complete summary report of all their commendable help following Major Sanders, Ernest Branscom and his wife Star, and others early on the scene, until the last volunteer had gone.

Besides countless lesser gifts, there were others of significant magnitude to warrant notice here. Ruth Weidman of Bernice, Louisiana, donated a modern air-conditioned mobile home to Saragosa. It was delivered by Mr. and Mrs. Don Keelins of Monroe, Louisiana, at their own expense and the donation of their time.

Ed James, a resident of Fort Worth, donated a $27,500 catering trailer, described as a "restaurant on wheels." From it untold numbers of Saragosans and volunteer workers were fed on the site of the disaster for many weeks that summer.

Members of the Texas Used Cars Association donated sixty used automobiles as gifts to the dispossessed people of Saragosa.

Furniture, food, housewares, air conditioners, televisions, building materials, and beverages inundated us and filled all the available warehouse and storage spaces in the area. A large eighteen-wheeler loaded full of paper goods came in as a remarkable donation from the Kimberly-Clark Company of Paris, Texas.

Involved were civic groups, religious organizations, radio and television stations, businesses, individuals, and governments. Appreciation also extends to all the taxpayers across the country, for the federal government made grants of $5,000 through the Federal Emergency Management Agency (FEMA) to qualifying families.

The Red Cross made a nationwide plea for donations and reported contributions in the amount of $985,245. Many of the checks made out to the Red Cross were sent to the Reeves County sheriff's office in Pecos, and I personally examined photocopies of those being kept in the office of District Clerk Juana Jaquez in Pecos. Most of them were from concerned people in Florida, but a scattering of other states were represented: Illinois, Georgia, Indiana, Arkansas, Louisiana, Missouri, Colorado, New Hampshire, Montana, Pennsylvania, Texas, and New Jersey. These must have represented only an extremely small percentage of those who gave through the Red Cross in these states. Of course, most of the states were not represented in this partial listing, but we are aware that they gave unselfishly.

There were records showing that the C. C. Hutton Saragosa Celebrity Golf Classic/Mission Dorado Celebrity Golf Classic, held at the country club in Odessa, netted a $12,190 donation.

Songwriter-singer Tony Joe White responded to news of the Saragosa tragedy by enlisting the aid of his friend, country singer Waylon Jennings. The plan to conduct a small benefit concert in Austin included these two and Johnny Cash, Jessi Colter, Johnny Rodriguez, Neil Young, John Anderson, Rex Allen, Jr., and Steve Earle. Tyson Foods, Inc., of Springdale, Arkansas, joined in a corporate sponsorship of the show. While the Austin concert fell short of expectations, it did net $5,000 for Saragosa.

The Hidalgo (Texas) Saragosa Relief Fund made donations of $4,505.38, $462.88, and $3,000. Through their Interfaith Community Services, Newberry, South Carolina, made donations of $7,435.25 and $2,097.16. Among the other distant contributions was one from the Hispanic Cultural Association of Hawaii, Ewa Beach, Hawaii — a donation of $654.

A check for $23,000, representing the donations pooled by the lobbyists, legislators, and state employees of Austin, was presented by State Representative Larry Don Shaw to Reeves County Judge Bill Pigman on August 18, 1987.

Myra Michaelis, Bobby Bell, and Robin Maples, employees of

the Security State Bank of Pecos, opened letters that came in with contributions to the Saragosa Relief Fund. They reported receipts in excess of $12,000 from people around the country. A large proportion of these gifts came in from residents of Wichita Falls and Sweetwater, where tornados have been a part of their recent experience.

A temporary mobile home park was set up on land donated by the Seventh Day Adventist Mission at Saragosa. Forty pads were designated for mobile homes. FEMA gave monetary contributions to some victims for rent of apartments.

Probationers from Midland County were allowed to work in Saragosa sorting out salvable items from the rubble piles, reported Tyson Eisholtz, a Probation Center official.

Twenty-five volunteers from Sandia View Academy of Corrales, New Mexico, came by bus to assist in salvage and clean-up operations. "This place is worse than I ever expected," commented Brian Oster, a student member of the group.

Sid Stevens of Montreal, Canada, called Reeves County officials and offered clothing and toys from its clothing bank there. He further offered to receive sixty youngsters from Saragosa at a summer camp in Montreal.

On May 26 Governor Bill Clements traveled to Saragosa to announce that President Ronald Reagan had declared Saragosa a major disaster area, eligible for federal assistance. "I have to say it's the worst I've ever seen!" the governor remarked. Some twenty state and federal agencies, including FEMA, set up field offices at the Balmorhea schools to assist and aid families victimized by the tornado.

Early on the scene after the tornado struck were Red Cross units from Midland and San Angelo. Volunteer Cindy Reed was among the earliest to arrive at the temporary quarters set up by lantern light in the Balmorhea High School. Ann Chapman, executive director of the Concho Valley Chapter, arrived early Saturday morning. Soon the high school cafeteria, with its regular manager Gloria Garcia in charge for the Red Cross, became the base of food operations. School offices were used by the Red Cross as staff offices for the ensuing summer months. Food was catered and carried by mobile canteens running between the school cafeteria, where meals were also served, and field operations in Saragosa.

The San Angelo Police Department collected several hundred dollars and a ton or more of household items, clothing, furniture, and food. Their radio appeal resulted in streams of cars and trucks loaded with donations for Saragosa, according to Master Patrolman Armando Vasquez, who stated, "The people really opened up their hearts."

Similar hearts were opened in many widely separated places — Del Rio, Fort Davis, Odessa, Austin. In Odessa the American Legionnaires auctioned off a gold-plated eagle and raised $3,000 for the tornado victims. Jim Leonard of Valley Motors in Pecos furnished automobiles for emergency use at Saragosa. Henry Galvan of Carlsbad, New Mexico, arrived in his own truck at Balmorhea with a load of gifts and money. Additionally, the concerned people of Carlsbad sent three semi-truck loads of donations. Marion Jenkins of Radio Station KCCC was a key figure in helping to accomplish this herculean feat of human response by airing requests and needs of Saragosa on his radio programs.

The list is more endless than we know, because our records are not all-inclusive. Although all the facts are not in and details are missing, all the caring from all over was deeply appreciated. It would be indeed wonderful to be able to develop a glossary of all the names right down to the last individual who contributed in any way, shape, or form. Donors are reminded, therefore, that in the end God is the rewarder of all who sacrificed to aid their fellow men in hours of dire distress.

In the inevitable circumstances of chaos and confusion, where so many goods and so much money was involved, selfishness and greed were sure to raise their ugly heads. While it is beyond the purpose of this narration to explore some deplorable incidents of mishandling the donated gifts and funds, we must take note of this flawed facet of our story.

In the following pages are recorded the individual stories of a *mere fraction* of those who rushed in to answer the call of the crying needs of their fellow men, women, boys, and girls. I doubt not that each of these caregivers did far more than he could remember or cared to relate. Others in droves came and worked as diligently, felt as deeply, and gave of themselves as unselfishly, but due to human limitations, not all of their stories could be gathered. It is impossible to imagine what might have happened had none of these people chosen to appear in Saragosa after the tornado struck on that ill-fated night.

[9]

The Rescuers

When you meet Floyd Estrada, you meet a short, stocky man who appears about to break out into a smile at any moment. Perhaps it is his eyes that suggest a reserve of humor that betokens tolerance and friendliness. As the arm of the law in this part of Reeves County, Deputy Sheriff Estrada embodies a just cause that needs no interpreting. His spirit of respect and enforcement of the law holds the confidence and respect of the people around here who know him.

Born and raised in Presidio, Texas, he served in the Armed Forces of the United States until 1972, and upon returning home from the service became a deputy sheriff in Fort Davis, then in Alpine, and finally in Pecos and Reeves County. He has served there since 1976. Floyd and Elie Lopez of Saragosa were married in January 1985, and seemingly have "lived happily ever after."

Returning to Balmorhea from a special detail in Pecos, Deputy Estrada noticed people in front of Gallegos Bar in Saragosa watching the threatening clouds. He was watching them, as well, as he drove through town very slowly. There stood a lot full of cars at the Community Center, and he remembered that he was supposed to have gone with Elie, his wife, to the Head Start graduation.

On the western outskirts of Balmorhea, Floyd found Glenn and Larry Humphries watching the weather. After a short visit with them, he invited Glenn to get in and ride with him since Larry was leaving. The men drove west to the county line in the foothills of the mountains for a better view of the turbulent weather. Out there, Glenn called Midland Weather Service to inform them of weather conditions. A tornado watch was put out after his report. On his radio Floyd alerted special officer Darrel Rhyne and highway patrolman Rob Bourland to stand by.

Bourland called from mile marker 222 on IH 10, east of Balmorhea. He was working traffic and would begin moving westward toward Floyd. It was almost 8:00 when Charles Towry called Glenn and reported watching a wall cloud and a rotating cloud formation nearby. He was out at the lake. Moments later, Bourland called to report a tornado in sight at the 210 mile marker by the old experimental farm east of Balmorhea.

Floyd Estrada: We came off the hill then, taking off for Saragosa. A twister out where Bourland reported one would give it a possible bearing on Saragosa! I hit my lights and sped through Balmorhea. A tree was down at the experiment station, and a sign was on the ground nearby, but we found no tornado. We raced on to Saragosa, noting a number of cars and trucks under the overpass as we passed under Interstate 10. Moments later, just before the gin, we saw telephone lines down, posts strewn about . . . electrical power lines down too. We had to drive over one high-tension line on the roadway, hoping it wasn't hot. We saw Dale Toone's house with stuff coming off the roof in the wind. His barn was gone. Our car was becoming light, tending to float, or drift, tending to go out of control . . . as if we were overtaking the twister . . . and we could scarcely see.

Dust, rain, hail . . . thick enough to blind you in spots, then we would pass through that swirling mess, and it would seem as if the lights came on. Suddenly, there was pitch blackness again, and we were plowing through a dense wall!

Suddenly, there was the Saragosa crossroads, and I saw that the hall wasn't there anymore! I couldn't see the Apodaca house across the highway. I found myself calling Pecos, "I've got a hell of a thing on my hands . . . the community house is down, people trapped! Send all the help you can!"

All was quiet except for the frogs in the night — thousands of them it seemed, hopping all over the place like a plague . . .

Darrel dashed in right behind me, and soon after the sounds of moans and voices pleading for help began to reach our ears. I spotted a body and rushed to check it out. I found Lisa Carrillo, but there wasn't much I could do for her. She was in bad shape. I saw a stick through her arm, and part of a two-by-four was through her leg. We covered her up — all we could do for her just then.

People started arriving — fire department, farmers, lots of people, all wanting to know what they could do. I shouted, "Get high-lift jacks, rescue people!" Bourland arrived, and asked me what to do. I said, "Direct traffic!"

I really didn't do much myself. Somebody had to direct people, and I did that . . . just directed people. I hollered at the sheriff's office in Pecos to call the Balmorhea school for buses. Two came, one driven by Charles Towry and one by Bob Clanton. I believe one was used as an ambulance . . . Once the big effort got under way, things sort of fell into place. The sheriff arrived, and we organized house-to-house searches while most of the volunteers plowed through the ruins at the hall. I remember you being there in our search party, Mr. Lane.

People came all night . . . from all over an area of about 150 miles radius — from Alpine, Marfa, Fort Davis, Midland, Odessa, Fort Stockton, Carlsbad, and Artesia, New Mexico. They sent rescue squads and ambulances, as well as law enforcement officers.

One man and his family were just passing through in a camper. They stopped and set up a stand, served coffee, sandwiches, and offered clothes for people who were chilled. I wish I knew their names . . . unknown heroes — and unsung.

From Pecos — from Safeway, from Furr's, the donut shops, and, I guess, from all the merchants — food and other necessities came in for our emergency use. We needed only ask, and they all pitched in and responded wonderfully.

The telephone company set up emergency telephone lines at Saragosa for our use . . . that night, I think it was.

Jim Wafer Oil Company brought in a tanker truck of gasoline and gave fuel to every emergency unit vehicle as it was needed. James Garlick brought in the tanker and did a great job.

Later that night some of us heard a suspicious noise out in the blacked-out town. We investigated and caught three people inside one wrecked house. We arrested them for stealing rifles. They were from out of town. The house was Elie's father's home. Because of this and other looting, we sealed off the town.

Things quieted down for a few weeks, with people busy taking care of their injured, attending funerals, picking up pieces, trying somehow to get their lives back to normal once more.

. . . But the thing that impressed me was the way the disaster brought us all together. There were lots and lots of people out there that night with just the right tool or idea. Charlie Oats showed up with a cutting torch. He cut the rebar that held large chunks of concrete masonry together so that they could be managed and removed. Once we smelled natural gas — leaking from somewhere. We needed flashlights in a hurry. Norma Barragon dashed out to Balmorhea Lake and picked up all the flashlights in the store out there.

Not only did local people flock in; they came from everywhere . . . Bill Calloway, director of the Calloway Funeral Home in Pecos, was a big contributor. The Red Cross bore the expense of the funerals from their donated money, but Mr. Calloway went a long way toward bearing much of the expense himself. People were wonderful with their offerings of emergency vehicles and equipment. Weldon Brookshire of B & B Wrecking in Pecos sent down refrigerator vans for the frozen goods that started pouring in. Foster Frozen Foods and Dick Morrow of Coors Distributors also sent refrigerated vans for free use there. B&B Wrecking also sent air bags, a wrecker, and an electrical generator that night — all of them manned by owner Weldon Brookshire's own crews.

The air bags were for lifting the heavy cement walls. Those things are normally used to raise overturned tractor and trailer rigs wrecked on highways. If you looped a cable or a chain around one of those huge trailers, it would cut it in half, or rip it apart. With the huge air bags, those big rigs can be set upright without damage to them at all . . . one of [the air bags] was ruined lifting those sharp-edged cement walls that night, and they cost about $4,000 each!

Of the many others who came in to help or sent equipment was Billy Riley of Monahans. His ambulance crew came the next morning and did a house-to-house search for injured people who had not reported in for emergency treatment. Some were given patch-up jobs right there, then sent in private cars to hospitals in the region.

Mr. Art Getty, of Blair, Texas, built the new building where the Head Start is now located — a very generous gift of kindness that we all appreciate very much.

One could go on and on. People were simply wonderful to us . . . I was impressed by the way this terrible disaster brought us all together. Of all the people who came and worked, I never saw anybody trying to play the hero. It didn't matter whether people were young or old, rich or poor, men or women, Catholic or Baptist . . . there were no self-styled heroes . . .

It's a miracle that there were no accidents out on the highway that night. People in droves were returning from Pecos to Balmorhea and Saragosa. There were lines and poles down and strewn over the highway, people were milling around — confused, excited, some pretty much in shock. But there wasn't a single mishap on that dark, dangerous highway — none at all!

Joey Herrera, the Head Start speaker, was fortunate in many ways. A wall was on top of him. He's built like me — stout — and he was suffocating. "I can't breathe! I can't breathe!" he was yelling down in there. I helped get the wall off him and take him out. Joey was one of the first people trapped in the wreckage to start hollering. He even called me by my name!

He was okay but pretty shook up — and scared. In trying to release him, I put the base of the big jack down in there, and it was beside a woman. Joey was down in there too. He said, "That's my wife." We got him out alive and pretty much okay, but his wife and little boy were dead. Joey could walk, and after quite some time, he came back . . . looking for me, I was told. He didn't find me to help him. He was looking for his wife Elsa and his baby. Both she and little Jonathan, eleven months old, were dead, Jonathan in the Pecos Funeral Home, and Elsa in Fort Stockton. The poor man was beside himself. It is a wonder he didn't get himself killed that night racing around from town to town trying to locate his lost loved ones the way he did.

* * *

Floyd Estrada's wife Elie is a charming lady. She is petite among women as the hummingbird is among birds. Elie loves people and demonstrates such in the caregiving for which she is known. Elie and Floyd are loved and respected far and wide and enjoy numberless friends all over the area. Elie knew most of the mothers and their children involved in the Head Start graduation program. Not to have attended herself would have been unthinkable.

Now, looking back upon that singular disaster, she shudders at the horror of her experience. On the other hand, she is glad that she could have been there to offer her ready hands when they were so desperately needed. Like so many of the survivors of that spring storm, Elie appears as one whose present happiness is but a tender shadow of the sorrow she has seen.

She regrets that the program was so late in starting; but for that, it "might have finished ahead of the storm."

Elie Estrada: The meeting was about over but for the awards, and as they were about to begin, Javier Lozano ran in sounding his tornado warning. That was the only warning that I know of. People panicked, some left, some came back. I just assumed it was a strong wind, but suddenly realized that it was a tornado for sure, and right there! Windows began shattering above us, and the screams really started then!

The wall beside me broke off just as I flung myself and two little girls to the base of it and onto the floor. That wall broke in the middle and tilted in and downward at such an angle that it left an opening below. The three of us were lying flat, closed in by that triangle formed by the tilted wall. There was the terrifying sound of heavy thudding masonry and the slash of falling timbers. Through a hole I could see all sorts of debris racing by. After about thirty seconds there came the crackling of hail all around and above our heads; it was followed by rain which flowed in and reached us down below. I could see a hole beyond my feet, large enough a hole for me to wiggle through with some difficulty. I did so, and the girls crawled out with me.

Once free of my trap, I saw a pickup parked adjacent to the wall just outside. I moved the children to it and put them under it for protection from the rain. The little girls were Maria de la Luz and Ampara Balderas — sisters. Their mother had been killed. Mr. Balderas was reportedly waiting in the pickup on the parking lot where he sat out the entire storm, unharmed!

Just at the moment I was about to crawl under the pickup, a car from the sheriff's fleet burst into the edge of the yard. It was Floyd, my husband! He came running toward me and the wrecked building . . . where many people were trapped inside. I had just seen them, some dead with walls on them. One girl was dead, countless others injured. That was the most horrible moment of my life . . . and it could have been worse. My injuries were mere scratches and bruises . . . no injuries worth mentioning. Worst of all, I guess, I was all shook up . . . but there were people about needing assistance. I turned to their needs.

* * *

Darrel Rhyne has the build and bearing of an All-American quarterback, but his profession is that of park superintendent and peace officer under the Texas Parks and Wildlife Department. He is presently assigned to the Balmorhea State Recreation Area. Both he and his tall, trim wife Nita were among the earlier persons on the scene at Saragosa on the evening of May 22, 1987.

At the park, Darrel Rhyne and Mike Henderson, a park ranger, kept monitoring the cloud. Rhyne kept an ear to his radio scanner, listening for law-enforcement calls. A radio call from Austin alerted him to a local tornado warning. Then he heard Rob

Bourland of the highway patrol report a tornado at mile 210. Suddenly, Floyd called Rhyne to "stand by."

While Mike Henderson was taking video pictures outside, Floyd whizzed by, lights flashing. Darrel and Mike jumped into the truck and followed Floyd to Saragosa. Mike continued his picture-taking all the way over there.

Upon arrival at the scene of the disaster, Darrel was asked by Floyd to take over communications. He did, then was interrupted to drive a county employee, Armando Mondragon, over to the baseball field for a front-end loader to help dig people out of the wreckage.

A large group of people was gathering by the time they returned. Rescue operations began with all available car jacks, attempting to lift the sides of the demolished building.

In short order a Balmorhea ambulance arrived, manned by Ike Ward and Rita Lozano, and Lisa Carrillo was placed into it for an emergency run to Pecos. She was "in a very bad way when we found her," Rhyne said. Lisa's husband Larry had been employed by Rhyne, who knew Lisa very well. Although she was scarcely recognizable, Rhyne knew her at once when he saw her down and helpless, and in great pain.

> **Darrel Rhyne:** It made me sick with pain myself to see her. She had a stick about two and a half to three feet long stuck about four to six inches into her leg. It *had* to come out, and it seemed to have fallen my lot to do it. She was in such bad shape it didn't seem to matter. It had to come out! So, I yanked it free . . .
>
> Floyd had gathered a bunch of kids into his car, and I some in my Blazer. Rachel Carrillo, Lisa's little girl, was in Floyd's car. She saw me and shouted my name. I took her out, and since her mother was on board and about to leave in Rita's ambulance, I halted it and took little Rachel over there. She, too, was seriously injured with a chunk of flesh gone from one arm . . .
>
> Later that night, we stacked bodies — a lot of them — in a row on the side of the highway. It was a grim and growing assemblage that blocked both Floyd's and my car from being able to move. Later this bunch of bodies was loaded into the Adventist bus and taken by Bill Wendt to Pecos.
>
> Paul Deishler, a police officer from Pecos, brought a K-9 car and loaded all the children from our vehicles into it. The bodies and breaths of those children gave off a lot of warmth and humidity, and our car windows were fogging up constantly. The kids kept wiping the windows clear so that they could see out, and

they were gazing upon a gory pile of horror just outside the car windows. We were pressed to remove the children from their morbid spectacle out there, and so we removed the kids. Even so, we had to carry them over the bodies of all those dead in order to transfer them to the K-9 car, which removed them to the Balmorhea school gym shelter, I believe.

I came on home around 2:30 that morning. After viewing all that death and pain, I needed to see my own kids. Maybe that's odd, but I needed that! Nita, my wife, was out there working too. Other than being bone-tired like me, she was okay, as were my girls, and that was a comfort, believe me.

I returned to Saragosa the next day and for many days after that. We used a bunch of dogs and made a house-to-house search the next day, but found no more injured or dead people in the town. The police dogs were a real help. They had come in from Midland, Odessa, DPS [Department of Public Safety], and from places all around. No more bodies were found, but there were lots of poor injured animals out there.

Our catastrophe changed a lot of people — brought us all closer together . . . I've been around death on numerous occasions before — you know, auto mishaps, drownings, and the like — but nothing like this. So much devastation, so many injured — almost like the aftermath of war . . . a battlefield.

Nita Rhyne, Darrel's wife, is the former Nita Cushenbery, born in Garden City, Kansas, and reared in Houston, Texas. There she attended public schools, and later, San Jacinto College. Nita met Darrel in La Porte, Texas, and soon became Mrs. Nita Rhyne. In time he settled into his chosen career with the Texas Parks and Wildlife Service and eventually was assigned to the Balmorhea State Park.

As of May 22, 1987, Nita was employed at the Western Cafe in Balmorhea. Business was quiet; the main activity in town was all the cars speeding through, heading east. Curious, Nita called Kate Crenshaw, her husband's secretary at the state park, and inquired of Kate what was going on. That is how Mrs. Rhyne learned that Saragosa had just been destroyed.

Nita promptly closed the cafe and took Enadena Morales, a co-worker, with her to Saragosa. Mrs. Morales had a number of relatives attending the Head Start program: her son Anastacio Morales and his wife Corina, their baby son Andrew, and Armando, who was in the Head Start graduation class.

Nita Rhyne: We raced over to Saragosa, arriving right after

Darrel pulled in, arriving so soon after the storm that we could drive right to the scene of destruction. In a little while the bodies of Enadena's family members were taken out . . . all of them died except little Armando, the Head Start student. Interestingly enough, not a single member of the Head Start children was lost! However, they did not find little Andrew, the baby, for some time. He was dead when they found him later — he and both his parents.

I busied myself covering up the bodies of the dead until Kelly Davis came to me and handed me a baby, asking me to go with Donna Davis, his wife, to Pecos to carry a load of four adults and the one baby to the hospital.

En route we encountered a world of debris on the highway. Besides that clutter, we ran into heavy hail and rain, plus traffic rushing both directions. Many people would not yield the right-of-way, consuming precious time against which we raced trying to reach the hospital with possibly a dying cargo of human lives. As it turned out, two of those people we were carrying were dead when we left, and two more died en route. I don't even know who they were. At the hospital, several nurses flocked out, one taking the baby, the others unloading the bodies. We then drove on to the LEC [Law Enforcement Center] and gathered a load of blankets needed at Saragosa.

Upon arriving back at the scene of the disaster, we found that most of the people, both dead and injured, were already taken out of the ruins of the main building, the Center. I then went out by myself, wandering around through the darkened and devastated town, hunting bodies. I had no flashlight, and so confined my efforts to the area that was made visible by the cluster of emergency floodlights blazing at the Community Center operations.

At first, bodies had been everywhere in that vicinity. You stepped gingerly over and around them, but as I moved further out from the clearly lighted area, my view was obscured somewhat. Out there in the semi-darkness all alone, I encountered many uncertain, lumpy shadows on the ground, and many of them made me cringe as I hunted for bodies I hoped I wouldn't find!

After all the bodies were found, we turned our attention to other matters and saw two injured horses. One had a badly mangled leg; the other, a deep gash in its stomach. The officers wanted to put them out of their misery, but there was such a big crowd of onlookers milling around, they decided against that.

Someone found two halters. We brought Floyd over with someone else; a vet, Mr. Ron Box from Pecos, had been called. A horse trailer was sent for and brought in. The poor animals were in shock because of serious unattended injuries and pain. Suddenly, a reporter turned a spotlight on those suffering creatures, filming their wounds. It was ghastly! The poor horses, spooked by the glaring lights, went crazy again, and I said a few unprintable things!

Around 2:30 A.M., everybody having been accounted for, I left there, soaking wet and cold. It had been a long night. I drove home to obtain changes of clothes for Darrel and myself and to check on my kids. En route, I stopped at the Balmorhea school, because I had heard a shelter had been set up there. A Red Cross woman had several boxes of food that had come in. She was sorting through them, and I helped her finish that before I left.

After going home and changing into dry clothes, I came back by the gym once again. In that short time, it was running over with food and clothing that had been sent in already.

I returned with the dawn to Saragosa, and with the coming of color in the eastern sky, the devastation was gradually revealed to me in all its enormous totality. What I saw was unimaginable! In last night's darkness, I had been only able to see the place piecemeal — bits and pieces here and there, disconnected, and presenting no comprehensive view. Now, with the dawning of the day, all of it was visible at once. What a nightmare of unreality under the harsh light of day . . .

I picked my way through the wasteland to the western edge of the town, where a narrow fringe of houses still stood as if sentinels guarding the remains of their fellows struck down before their time. People were arriving now — those dispossessed home owners, almost as zombies in a nightmare, picking their uncertain way through what remained of their demolished possessions.

But a couple I took to be strangers were poking around. Family pictures were scattered about along with such documents as marriage licenses and birth certificates. I was gathering them in a basket, which I left right in front of the house plot where a home had stood. A little boy with the strangers nearby was preoccupied with a toy truck. I asked him whether he lived there, and he said, "No." I then told him to put the toy back where he had found it, because that little truck might be the only thing that some little child had left in the whole world. He put the toy down and left.

When I returned the next day, the basket of items I had collected remained there, untouched. I took them to the justice of the peace, who eventually returned them to their owners, the Madrid family.

One of the hardest things I did was seeing that town leveled, knowing as I did that it was full of people when it all came down . . . so many families smashed, so many hopes destroyed . . .

I later took the Escovedos to Marfa to make arrangements for Kathy's funeral. She was in the preparation room in the back, and Lolo, her father, was unsure of procedures. I stayed with the grieving Gloria up front while he went in there to spend some time with his daughter. Gloria was in no emotional state to be seeing Kathy yet. After the arrangements were completed, I drove them on to Fort Davis to eat, taking our time to allow the funeral director plenty of time to finish with Kathy and then transport her to the church in Fort Davis. We already had gone to the cemetery site in Fort Davis to select a burial spot beside her grandfather . . .

We went to the church where Kathy had been taken by that time, and Gloria, her mother, was alternately hysterical and mute. She had not yet seen her daughter since she died in the storm . . . All the bottled-up emotional stress now broke loose. She needed that, needed to confront the reality of her terrible loss.

Sunday, I went to the funeral home in Pecos, where there were a lot of bodies still in the refrigerated truck. Enadena had to climb up into the truck and identify Anastacio Morales, Corina, and Andrew — her family. There were her son, her pregnant daughter-in-law, and two-year-old grandson.

Joann Williams and I went together to the funeral services in Wink. The Morales family members were to be buried in Kermit, but they, along with Jorge and Roxanne Martinez and Socorro Rodriguez, of Wink, were all brought to the Civic Center in Wink, where they were arranged in a great horseshoe-shape . . . six coffins. Later, some of the bodies were removed to different religious services, then regathered in Kermit for burial there.

After the funerals were all over, we went in many directions and occupied ourselves with different efforts to help out wherever we felt needed — the Red Cross, the Salvation Army, and other efforts, both in Saragosa and in Balmorhea.

* * *

James Garlick is not physically the typically tall, rangy West Texas cowboy. Rather, he is of short to medium height, range-toughened, blue-jeaned and booted, with a bearing of positive assurance, giving one the impression of strong manliness and strength of character without the facade of machoism so common these days.

Recounting his experiences incident to the tragedy left in the wake of Saragosa's tornado, Garlick's deep human warmth and tenderness surfaced repeatedly. Months now after the tragedy, the persistent spectre of horror and heartbreak still bridged the passage of time, and empathy appeared as poignant now as then.

James and his little nephew were at the Gallegos's I-10 truck-stop unloading a truckload of fuel when his attention was drawn to "this unusual flat cloud that had quickly formed overhead and slightly to the west." He called a cowboy friend, Jim Moore, to come outside and "have a look at this strange cloud." A small funnel appeared, and Garlick called the whole crowd inside the cafe to come and see the tornado. It moved closer, the "stinger coming out of the cloud and going back." He called his wife to come for the boy, but she informed him that it was hailing too hard for her to come just then.

During this conversation, James kept glancing out the window near his telephone and suddenly yelled into the phone, "Oh, hell, honey, it has hit the ground, and it — it's kinda like an atomic blast!" He saw the dirt mushroom up and out as the mammoth tornado dropped out of the cloud about half a mile to the northeast, "out toward the Cuban's house where Jack Gray, a retired school superintendent had lived." Garlick broke and ran to his truck, tucked in his hoses, and dashed off to Balmorhea, where he was a member of the volunteer fire department. On his way he watched the thing grow into a half-mile-wide monster and slam head-on into Saragosa. It was not like the little "dangling rope twisters with the 'J' in their tails" such as James had seen so often in Oklahoma . . . this one was a vast wall, "wide like a curtain, like a drape."

Garlick ran into Craig Huelster at home. Craig's wife Dwana and their little girl Michelle were in their pickup with its windshield knocked out and the pickup a general mess. They had been in the edge of the tornado but miraculously escaped death. Craig, another fireman, and James took off for Saragosa, where the front-end loader was just arriving at the Head Start building wreckage. The first body they saw was Omero Sanchez, Garlick's friend who worked for Balmorhea Feeders — "just lying there . . . dead. The place looked like a combat zone!"

He plunged in, scooting crossties under the rubble lifted by the loader, then crawling under the mass, into the cavern thus created. At once he saw the legs of three people. He touched the legs of a woman; they were cold, clammy, and he knew she was dead. A man moved, but when he pulled, cried, "Oh, don't, *don't!* My arms hurt!" His arm was pinned under a wall. Now James saw it . . . and the blood

. . . and a little baby. He grabbed it by the feet, and they felt like the little feet of a plastic doll. It was Joey Herrera's baby — dead.

Garlick said something, and a babble of children's voices responded from down below — schoolchildren he had taught, and they recognized his voice. "Mr. Garlick, help us! Please!"

"Well, what was I going to do? Here was this eight- to twelve-inch-thick concrete wall . . ." He was helpless.

Hacksaws and flashlights were sorely needed, and Garlick dashed back to the plant to fill this request by Pat Brijalba, Jr. It was then he realized how wet and cold he was, "about to freeze to death!" After returning with the tools, Garlick found himself involved in the rescue of Corina and Pat Brijalba, as well as Tommy Martinez, his wife, his daughter, and granddaughter. Other details were lost in the confusion of pulling bodies out and piling them on the roadside or into the bus, or putting the injured on stretchers.

The hour grew late, and Garlick joined a search party made up of a group of Fort Davis cowboys. We choked up when he remembered their coming across the body of Kathy Escovedo out there in the heartbreaking horror of that night. He and Kathy had been close friends when he taught school at Balmorhea.

> **James Garlick:** The next morning a couple of boys helped me, and we rounded up all of Joe Gallegos's show calves . . . and some hogs . . . and took them over to my place for a week or so. There was a gruff-looking cowboy who came over from Fort Davis with Larry Baldwin and Bob Diller, and he said, "I've been through a lot o' things. I spent nearly three years in Viet Nam, but I never seen anything like this!"
>
> We had a bunch of people at my house that night, and we were without electricity. Christy Dillard, who writes and photographs for the paper, was there, as were Kim Perrin, Greg Perrin's wife, and my sister-in-law . . . anyway, we were all so shocked and afraid, and had only a candle for light. We had plenty of bedrooms, but we all huddled together on the bed and on pallets on the floor, all of us in one room. We all felt the need to be close together.

* * *

Leroy and Eva Miller moved their family to Balmorhea from Midland, Texas, in 1979. Miller had retired from the U.S. Air Force and wanted to bring up his boys, Paul and Frank, in a small town. Paul was then in the sixth grade and Frank was in the fourth. Paul had graduated from the Balmorhea High School in 1986 and was back home for the summer from Texas Tech University in Lubbock. The tornado had happened weeks before when Paul visited in my home. I asked him about the tornado.

Looking smart and every inch a marine, Paul Miller told me in a quiet, solemn voice about his night of volunteer work after the passing of the storm. He was doing summer work as a lifeguard at the Balmorhea State Park swimming pool. A strong wind had blown all day, and at 8:00 P.M. they had closed the pool. He came in for dinner at 8:15 and had begun to eat when the lights went out. In about ten minutes a call came in from Cenesa Chance, saying that her stepfather, Jack Ivey, had just left for Saragosa and wanted to let Leroy Miller know that a terrible tornado had just hit Saragosa and that help was needed there at once. Mr. Miller and his two sons left immediately, taking a flashlight and a blanket.

The place was alive with people, and the Millers had to park half a mile away. They dashed to the downed Center on foot and plunged into the frenzied rescue activity.

A front-end loader using heavy cables was attempting to pick up wall sections. People were under there, some in crouched positions, others just lying. Paul Miller and other helpers crawled beneath the hiked-up wall sections and picked up bodies and handed them to waiting hands above. Then the operator would drop the wall section back into place once more. Paul recognized quite a few people as they were being removed and piled with the other dead bodies.

Finally, a bus came, a bus without seats, and he helped put bodies on stretchers and remove them to the bus. Judge Carrasco, the local justice of the peace, was there, and Miller assisted with the identification and tagging of the bodies. Once he picked up a little girl, already dead, her neck apparently broken. "It just clunked over onto my shoulder — limp. Her little body was as cold as ice, no blood circulating. She was unbelievably cold . . . like an ice pack . . . Some of the adults we could not identify, because their faces were all bloody . . . Noses were broken, one man's ear falling off, hanging by a shred of skin. Nobody could identify him.

"Judge Carrasco's secretary, Delilah's sister, was another person I picked up and put on the bus. We identified her and put a wrist band on to identify the body. The judge pronounced her dead. I never saw him cry until that moment, but then the tears came down. I had talked to her just a few days before . . ."

Paul Miller worked on through the night and for days afterward. He sorted incoming clothes and food, helped out at both Balmorhea and Saragosa, and when he worked there he would "just fill up with emotion and cry," because he was hurting with them, feeling their hurt. "I just wanted to be there, to help helpless people, and to see how they were doing." He saw his friend Kiki Meneses's automobile "with a big light pole that had been driven right through it." Later, he served as a pallbearer at Kathy Escovedo's funeral. His services were endless. When the navy later learned of Miller's work following the tornado, they gave him a merit award, for which he is justifiably proud.

His former football coach, Michael Barrandy, described Paul Miller to me as "tough." Michael said, "Both in high school and on the football team, he was a very tough kid, not just physically, as in football, but in his thinking. He had a resilient mind and rose to any challenge physically or intellectually. And, as you know, he shows, as well, a deep tenderness, real feeling. He is sensitive, and that's important."

Miller told me that his heart was filled with cruel anguish, but that he wouldn't for anything have missed being there to lend a helping hand, to be with his friends in their hour of personal tragedy. I remember him saying, "Their loved ones were torn from their families and maimed as was Kiki, or killed as were Sylvestre, Omero, Elvira, and Kathy, along with so many others out there that terrible night. It was the highest privilege I could have ever had to have been identified with them as I was . . . and still am!"

* * *

Jack Hoffman is the high school principal at Balmorhea. A West Texas rancher and farmer, he stands tall in his western boots as well as in the hearts of those who know him well. He is a man always ready to pitch in where there is any human need, a man who could be expected to be found at the Saragosa tragedy.

Jack had been watching with George Rodriguez, the vocational agriculture teacher, as the ominous cloud developed. George left, and then the phone rang. Sue Toone, a Balmorhea teacher, informed Hoffman that the power lines near Saragosa were down, that a tornado had just hit over there, and an ambulance was needed. Jack's efforts to call Ike Ward, an ambulance driver friend, were unsuccessful. Moments later he heard the ambulance speeding down the highway and supposed it was him.

Jack and his son Bill, a seventh-grader, took off for Saragosa.

"I thought something was definitely wrong over there, but I never dreamed it was that bad," Jack said.

On their way over they met Pete Vasquez, his wife Socorro, and their daughter Florinda. Jack, watching his driving, failed to see what Bill observed, that "things were wrong with their pickup; you know, all muddy, banged-up, windows and windshield out." The Hoffmans arrived amongst screaming and yelling, total destruction, and general confusion.

"The place looked like an atom bomb had hit there! Right away I saw Orlando Sanchez, the mechanic, standing there before his brother, Omero, Jacob's daddy . . . and another man I couldn't recognize. Both were dead."

Jack Hoffman worked in the Community Center wreckage all evening, never leaving it. James Garlick and others began coming in with hi-lift jacks which were used in attempts to raise wall sections. The efforts failed until a front-end loader operated by Armando Mondragon, Sr., was brought in.

> **Jack Hoffman:** We found Mr. Herrera down in there, pinned down by the wall . . . on his left arm. We tried for at least an hour to release him, but it was no use. The front-end loader was worked into position and hooked under the wall, and that raised it enough to free Mr. Herrera.
>
> I could hear one little baby or child who was really screaming loudly near the center of the building . . . under the rubble. Suddenly, it gave it up, got quiet. I guess it died then.
>
> After droves of people pitched in to help, I felt I could do more good arranging for transportation, and so I climbed out, found my wife Krish, and we put an injured lady into her Suburban and Krish took her to Alpine. Later on I was needed at school, and I came on over here in the middle of the night to help open a school shelter. Then for two or three days and nights Krish and I worked here, helping out wherever we could.
>
> One thing that really impressed me was the way people really pitched in and helped . . . you know, our students. Some of them really worked — Armando Baeza, Junior Iniguez, Rosa Sotelo, Paul Matta, Cynthia Dutchover. I can't begin to remember them all.
>
> I was also impressed by a man from Dell City, Jack Wendt, a Chevron dealer, I think, who brought in a large forty-three-kilowatt generator to restore our power here at school for our use and for the Red Cross and Salvation Army. Then another, somewhat smaller, power generator was brought in by Mr. Lee Davis from here in Balmorhea. Those two generator units really saved

the day for us here, and that truly impressed me. Another generator— a really big one—was brought in by an oil-drilling outfit in Fort Stockton to restore power for the entire town, but the electric service company had our power back on before that one was pressed into service. I believe it was Diesel Energy Systems who sent in that rig for us. In any case, the efforts of those people really impressed me.

* * *

Lanky, six-foot Larry Humphries lounged easily in the sheriff's temporary field quarters situated in the blight that had been Saragosa. He presented a casual but imposing figure in his officer's uniform as we passed a few words, warming to a full-blown conversation that ended in general merriment.

After Glenn and Larry parted on the afternoon of the storm, Janie, Glenn's wife, contacted Larry, asking him to find Glenn's car, locked with the keys inside; she would bring her set of keys and take out some spare radio batteries Glenn needed. Larry was to take them to Gallegos's station and leave them there for him to pick up. Larry figured there had been an auto accident somewhere, and on his way to Gallegos, he kept wondering about the accident he had invented in his mind.

On the way out, Larry spotted Ted Woodruff and Eddie Rivera, a former girls' basketball coach, picking up hailstones. Larry smiled, musing to himself, "What a world of tastes and interests we live in!" About that time the Balmorhea firetruck whizzed past him, and Larry thought, "This accident must have resulted in a blaze. I'll just follow that firetruck and see." He raced after them, saw a man with a very bloody leg at the Gallegos station. The blood appeared to be flowing from a smashed-up knee. In efforts to walk, the injured man was hobbling clumsily about behind a little girl. Larry wrote that off to his "auto accident" somewhere ahead and raced on behind the firetruck.

A large assortment of cars and trucks parked under the interstate evoked a chuckle from Larry, who thought, "This is really going to be something! It must have been a real smash-up!" Suddenly, up ahead he saw the winking of several red lights. "It is at Saragosa," he mused to himself. "That really must be a bad accident," he thought, holding to his theory of an auto accident. On he rolled, bearing down rapidly upon a scene that was to surprise him into stupefaction.

The first downed buildings evoked the thought of high winds — "the winds must have blown things that distracted some driver, causing the accident." Suddenly, there it all was, the tell-tale evidences of the killer tornado — a real monster! Larry was dumbfounded, appalled. He mechanically stepped from his car in a numbed state of shock. He couldn't believe it — "a town shaved right off the face of the earth!"

Larry Humphries joined the few others already there, and they plunged into a night of hard work. He joined in the feverish removal of rubble from the wrecked Center. He helped take out a lot of bodies — some dead, some badly injured. More people poured in until the volunteers were almost walking on each other in there. About 2:30 in the morning, Larry went home.

He and Glenn went out fairly early the next morning and began a search for Billy Gallegos, who was reported missing. They reasoned that he might have been blown completely out of town, and as a consequence, they searched open pasturelands downwind where the storm had gone. Their search turned into a five-mile hike out into the wilds, but they found no bodies. Personal belongings were widely scattered — pictures, bits of furniture, household utensils, clothing, tin, trash. Larry shrugged knowingly. "I shot a hog out there. It was badly injured, with a very deep slash across its back, severing its spine . . . it couldn't have lived."

Later, the word made its rounds, and Larry was confronted with requests to take care of other hurt hogs since he was the expert at killing wounded ones. "They wanted me to put a bunch of them out of their misery, and I could have done it, but then, so could they!" Larry chuckled, then laughed outright as he remembered the incident. "I just took off and left them with their hogs and their problem, and I never came back!"

* * *

As was his habit, Bill Wendt drove over to the cluster of Adventist dwellings situated across Toya Creek, just northeast of Saragosa, to check on the Berdans and Esther Lansberry. The time was around 6:30 P.M., May 22, 1987. Bill visited with Herb Berdan for a time, and he detected a certain melancholy that clouded Mr. Berdan's usually jovial spirits. Herb spoke of discouragement, a sense of futility about his work. He told of recently going around to everyone he knew and "making things right," asking forgiveness for any wrongs he might have done them. "He told me he was ready to go . . . that he would see me *much later*," Bill remembered. "I told him, 'tonight at evening worship,' and he corrected me, saying 'no . . . *much later.*' He must have meant in another life. He seemed to have death on his mind, a sort of premonition that he was at the end of a long hard fight, and I was later to realize that his death by the tornado that very evening came as an answer to a prayer!"

After family evening worship with his wife Hazel and their children, Bill Wendt noticed the wind growing violent, blowing over a small barn on his premises. When the radio reported a tornado at Saragosa, about five miles away, Bill and Hazel Wendt dashed over to the mission "to assess the damage done there."

As the missionary couple passed the Community Center in Saragosa, they noticed people extracting themselves from a great rubble heap, "some screaming, running about holding injured heads, and blood gushing." They hurried anxiously on to the Berdan place.

A wheelchair normally used by Esther Lansberry's sister stood in the yard, Esther sitting in it, more or less okay. Her house was gone. Myles Berdan sat in the family van, hands in his lap, both wrists mangled, broken. Lying in the rubble strewn about the yard was the body of Herbert Berdan. He was dead. His injured wife Dorothy sat beside him.

A mobile home parked in front of the one owned by the Berdans had blown headlong into theirs, sending it and Myles's station wagon flying. The first mobile home came to rest across the road and about three hundred yards toward the highway.

Bill Wendt and his family pitched in and helped in all-out search and rescue work there immediately, and at Saragosa later. Scott Wendt and his wife Kay joined in the desperation efforts.

At Saragosa, Bill soon realized the need for a large vehicle for the disposition of the growing pile of bodies. He asked Floyd Estrada whether they needed their church bus, and the deputy's quick affirmative sent Bill and Scott scurrying for it. They cleaned out the bus, loaded seventeen bodies, and drove them to Pecos. Scott became so ill and upset during this operation that his whole system seems to have "frozen," and he was forced to retreat. He took his family to Montana.

In days that followed, the Saragosa Mission's Pathfinder youth group, made up of local young people, pitched in and folded the incoming donated clothing and bedding and made deliveries to people in Saragosa. Tons of clothes and other gifts arrived in three semi-truck loads coming in every week for several weeks, and those kids distributed the mountain of donations.

The Saragosa Mission suffered the loss of five homes, their school building, the bakery, a community service room, clinic, and storage building. In addition, the lives of Herbert and Dorothy Berdan were tragically taken, leaving large, empty places in the hearts of all who knew and loved them.

* * *

Alvaro Machuca was thrown from a pickup a few years ago, leaving him virtually invalided, and leaving to his wife Ramona the responsibilities of caring for the needs of the family which includes Yvonne, their daughter who was a junior in high school, and Roy, an eighth-grade student at Balmorhea Junior High.

Mother and daughter served as volunteer workers under Richard Friday, a member of the Salvation Army team with whom I also worked at the time. During some slack moments I learned their story.

They had watched the approaching tornado blow Bob Walker's house apart, scaring them into their closet where the mother, father, and son safely rode out the blast. Yvonne and Norma Carrasco, a cousin, arrived from Pecos to tell Yvonne's parents that "there are no houses left in town!"

Ramona Machuca hurried off to the blasted Center and helped out with rescue operations until past midnight, leaving then for Pecos to look for Kiki Meneses. They drove from there to Monahans, Kermit, and Odessa, looking for her sister-in-law, Ninfa Ontiveras, her brother Manuel's wife. He joined them in the search for family members, during which they encountered high water at Penwell, and again at Odessa.

In Odessa their pickup flooded out for a time, then ran long enough to get them to a motel, where calls were made to the hospital. "My sister-in-law Ninfa was there," Ramona said. "She was dead, they told us. Kiki was there too . . . in critical condition."

They could not negotiate the high water; besides, the street was barricaded. Dry pavement was two blocks away, and a man's truck was there. The man, Santana Porros, had to wade with Manuel through hip-deep water from the motel to his truck. Mr. Porros drove Manuel to the hospital, then returned, waded in, and led Ramona through the water to his truck. He drove her to the Odessa

Medical Center, where Kiki lay in a coma. Ninfa Ontiveras had been removed to Wilson Funeral Home.

Yvonne Machuca and Norma Carrasco, returning from Pecos, had arrived in Saragosa "about two minutes after it all happened." Just north of town the girls picked up Miriam Mondragon and Octavio Muñiz, who had just been injured in the Berdan mobile home and had hobbled to the highway. As they began seeing the wreckage of their hometown, Norma started crying for her child, and Ramona started crying for her mom. Minds distracted, they let their injured friends out near an ambulance and hurried home, there to find the Machuca family all right.

Norma Carrasco told of their going in search of Kiki — she and his mother. "Isidro Casias told his mother and me that Kiki was alive . . . but badly injured. We found my little son okay there at Yvonne's home, but we learned that my aunt, Ninfa Ontiveras, the one who died, had been found two lots away from her house, all her clothes gone except a string from her nightgown . . . and her underwear — that's all!"

She told of Kiki's injuries — blood clots in his brain, cuts all over, a coma-like condition, a big cut across the base of his skull. With her words and the sweeping gestures of her arms, Norma had worked us into a tangled snarl of concern, of empathy, and of memories of a better day.

I asked her if she were related to Kiki and was told that she was by marriage. His sister Rita was married to Norma's uncle. When they divorced, she and Rita remained close friends.

I asked if she lived in Saragosa. "Yes, my house was destroyed in the storm . . . swept away. I never knew where the furniture went. Even the tile cemented to the concrete slab where my house had stood was swept away!"

* * *

One of the most significant caregivers in terms of manpower, time, equipment, and outright personal expense was Weldon Brookshire, a mild-mannered and modest man of Pecos, Texas. With Jeanne, his attractive, youthful middle-aged wife, Weldon owns and operates the B&B Wrecker Service. He commands a "SWAT" team, his Special Wrecker Assistance Team, which takes to the highways to set upright such heavy vehicles as overturned buses and eighteen-wheelers.

"I think the first thing Floyd Estrada did was to make a call for our assistance, and he had the foresight to request that we bring along our air bags. That was real foresight," Brookshire mused. "He called the dispatcher and asked him to call us for the SWAT team and heavy equipment. We were there in thirty minutes after receiving the call from the sheriff's dispatcher."

Brookshire mobilized his crew of eleven people and eighty pieces of mostly heavy equipment for the emergency. They fought heavy hail, rain, and heavy traffic as they dodged debris on their rush to Saragosa. "There was so much hail on the highway those last two or three miles that it looked like a snowstorm had gone through leaving three or four inches of snowfall. One could scarcely see where the roadway was, and a lot of people out on that road refused to yield the right-of-way to our convoy of racing emergency vehicles!"

The equipment consisted of an air bag van, a large and a small wrecker, flatbed trucks, two refrigerated trucks, floodlights, and gas torches. The rescue truck is a refrigeration unit comprising a lot of compartments, and is built somewhat like a motor home. It stands ready to go at all times, full of fuel, maintained and loaded with all the essential emergency equipment. The air bag van hauled the air bags Floyd requested. They only require seven pounds of air pressure, but their volume is so great that they do a remarkable job of righting overturned buses and trucks, something a big winch truck with a steel cable cannot do because the cable would slice apart the overturned vehicle. At Saragosa the bags raised cement slab walls enough to allow rescue workers to remove bodies of the dead and injured trapped and buried below.

The bags were unloaded from the van, and driver Debbie Bertelson, Brookshire's oldest daughter, turned the van around and parked it heading north in the southbound traffic lane, now blocked off. They used it through the night as the primary emergency command station and light plant for emergency lighting.

Members of the eleven-man crew were Jack Brookshire (Weldon's son), his daughter Debbie and her husband Keith Bertelson; Eddie Jo Hardwick, another daughter; Rufus Spivey and his two sons, Robert and Allen; Fred Brookshire (Weldon's brother) and his son Steven; Terry Metcalf; and Weldon Brookshire.

Jeanne Brookshire had gone directly to the hospital as a volunteer to help organize and prepare for the anticipated injured soon to be coming in. She worked endless hours that night and during coming days handling blood-soaked, cut, injured, and dying people who flooded in.

There were not enough coffins in town to handle all of the dead, so Mr. Brookshire sent in a refrigerated trailer with a truck for transfers to the funeral home.

Weldon Brookshire explained his continued involvement: "We were all down there the first thirty hours without once coming home. Then, at least one or more of us was there every day for all the balance of last summer, moving water tanks, trailers, and a lot of cars. We furnished three trailers for three months for use as temporary warehouses for donated food, clothing, and furniture." Those trailer-warehouses, as well as two furnished by Roadway Express and Central Freight lines, saved the day at both Balmorhea and Saragosa. Brookshire helped further in the matter of storing donations by making fifteen or twenty trips hauling commodities into Pecos and storing them in the city's old aircraft hangars.

One of the Brookshire daughters, Eddie Jo Hardwick, had earlier told me a bit of good news which her father now confirmed. An air bag costing nearly $4,000, which had been ruined in the rescue operations, was later replaced by fellow members of the International Wreckers, Inc. "The manufacturer was good enough to supply it at, or near, factory cost," Brookshire told me.

In all the chaos of the rescue operation, the SWAT team saved eight or nine lives and was instrumental in releasing fifteen or more bodies from the ruins. They gave no thought to possible rupturing of a bag under the sharp, rough-edged walls. This was the first time air bags had ever been used in this sort of service.

The Texas Towing and Storage Association presented Weldon Brookshire with a special award plaque at their 1987 annual banquet, a beautiful gesture to a most deserving man and his associates. The modest man shrugged praise aside and himself praised others. He spoke of the forty men of the Pecos Fire Department, of which he is chief, who served. He told of Johnny Barbee, of Barbee Wrecker Service in Fort Stockton, who came in with his huge, portable floodlights. He spoke of the scores of law enforcement groups from towns all over, and of how Texas highway patrol sergeant Milton Rasberry, of Reeves Precinct 4, came onto the scene and assumed command, bringing order out of the virtual chaos and turning it into one giant, efficient team. He had praise for the heavy equipment operators who were so very careful in pushing walls aside. "You push a wall out of the way, but, in doing so, you can easily pull off someone's head under there," he remarked. Brookshire exuded praise of Ismael Dutchover, who was "everywhere that night, hauling out bodies, and never once let up during that entire horrible night." I could not agree more, remembering how Dutchover and his wife Anita drove 250 miles to Sweetwater one night to bring me and a load of antiques home to Balmorhea after I was involved in an automobile accident.

Caught up in commendations, Jeanne Brookshire voiced her admiration of a Dr. Zeke from Odessa. He had come to Pecos to assist at the hospital. "His manner was positive, tender, and reassuring as he went about doing a most wonderful job of comforting people waiting at the hospital . . . Other wonderful doctors came, too, each doing his great, unselfish service for his suffering fellow man, and I regret that I do not know their names," Jeanne concluded.

"Heaven knows them," I told her. The Man of Galilee, almost 2000 years ago, expressed it classically, "Greater love has no man than this, that a man lay down his life for his friends."

* * *

She is a remarkable lady, a mother, and both a tornado victim and a volunteer. Mary Lou Apodaca is short of stature, attractive, bouncing with energy, concerned and caring — an involved woman. Even though her home was lost in the Saragosa tornado, this lady volunteered immediately afterward for full-time work with Project CARE in their offices set up in a Balmorhea school building.

Her smiling eyes twinkling, she told about her little Erica being in the Head Start graduation program, of the singing of the children that drowned out the sounds of the approaching storm, of the warning of Mr. Lozano, the confusion, of the people scrambling under tables and benches for shelter.

"Joe Mendosa opened the windows of the building, then everything was quiet . . . very quiet, everybody braced for the thing to hit," she recalled. Once the storm had gone, she, uninjured, took out her children, also relatively unharmed, along with her husband, limping and aided by Ricky Montes. She also assisted Lucas Carrillo's girls to extricate themselves.

Her thoughts turned to going home, getting out of the miseries of the rain and cold. Although her home was directly across the highway, she could not see it.

"My house wasn't there anymore . . ." She and her family

made their way to a neighbor's home, Maria Briceño's, next door to their own. "She is ninety-seven years old and blind. She was safe with her granddaughter in a closet . . . but her house was so badly damaged, its adobe walls so cracked, that it was dangerous and was later condemned and bulldozed away."

Mrs. Apodaca and her family went first to Gallegos's Chevron, then to Rosendo Carrasco's store, and finally to the Spanish Inn Hotel in Balmorhea, where Mrs. Lee, the manager, furnished the family with two free rooms.

"Around two o'clock in the morning, my daughter, Merelene Roman, came in from El Paso, where she and her baby had been visiting," she said. "My niece and nephew, Irma and Javier Martinez, brought her back after they heard the news. They had no idea where we were, and they searched all night, deeply concerned after the priest, Father Barringer, misidentified a body as me, and I had been reported dead! Imagine everyone's relief when they checked at the hotel and learned from Mrs. Lee that we were all there and safe. I heard Merelene crying, then she came running to me."

The Apodaca family were taken to the Pecos Hospital the following morning, checked over, and released. What a joy to discover her family — twelve or fifteen people in all — waiting for them in the hospital emergency room.

"All my sisters and my brother came . . . They were so beautiful, so wonderful, so supportive of us."

I asked Mary Lou how she came to be associated with Project CARE, and she told how the project was organized a little over a year before when the tornado destroyed a part of Sweetwater in April of 1986.

> **Mary Lou Apodaca:** The problems that follow the emotional stress and strain, sorrow and complications of readjustment are terrible beyond words for some people. The lives of multitudes of people are wrenched out of their sockets, and total changes suddenly sweep them off their feet. Overloaded emotions, lost properties, and personal treasures accumulated for a lifetime, never to be replaced, are not easy matters to handle. Project CARE was organized as a rehabilitative effort to assist such people in coping where the need for mental and emotional health services following any disaster occurs.
>
> A special grant, provided by the State of Texas, Department of Mental Health and Mental Retardation, underwrites the program. It is administered through the Big Spring State Hospital's

> Non-Residential Services, of Big Spring, Texas. The local outreach center is the Reeves County Mental Health Center, designated the mental health authority for this county, according to the Texas Mental Health Code of 1983. The director of the center is Teresa Gonzales, who is the coordinator/director for Project CARE during the present crisis.

Mrs. Apodaca then introduced me to Joanna Rodriguez, secretary, and Hector Tito Roman, counselor, and indicated that she herself was serving as a counselor. "I was a tornado victim myself . . . my family and I. We needed help, and we were helped, but our needs were small compared to those of many of our neighbors and friends . . . I owed God a great debt of gratitude, and I owed my fellow man all the service that I could give. So it was that I joined Project CARE."

I was moved deeply. All too few local people came in to volunteer their services, and we were forced to make public pleas for help. We had some wonderful responses from some people here, including several high school students, but more assistance came from out of town. I worked with people who came in from San Angelo, Fort Worth, Houston, Sherman, Midland, Toya, Barstow, Fort Davis, Alpine — all over. They drove long miles at their own expense, then donated their precious time. A carpenter came from Santa Fe, New Mexico, to work at Saragosa. A man came through from Tennessee, stopped and stayed on to pitch in and help for a week before he went home. I told the CARE office crew about these people, concluding, "Truly, it is more blessed to give than to receive."

* * *

Born and raised in Balmorhea, Rosendo Carrasco has long been a successful merchant in nearby Brogado. He is the present owner of Carrasco's Grocery Store, which has been in his family for at least fifty years. He acquired the store from his mother after his father's death.

As the longtime store owner, and lately justice of the peace, Judge Carrasco knew "just about everybody," which was a great help to him in identifying the dead that night at Saragosa.

Rosendo went earlier with his friend Robert Hinosos to the Head Start program to photograph the children, and during a period of time when a microphone problem delayed the program, he went outside to watch the weather. He saw two clouds "behaving strangely, one swirling from left to right, the other whirling in the opposite direction, each going around in a circle." He took several pictures, and finally took one of the actual tornado just after it came down about a mile south of town. He chatted with Javier Lozano just before the latter became alarmed and ran inside to sound his warning and rescue his little boy.

Carrasco called to his friend Robert, and with some persuasion, convinced him that they had better flee. They did. He had one last look at Sylvestra Sanchez, his secretary, and "was struck by the fright in her face" as he and Hinosos took off.

The two men fled through hail, blackness, driving rain, and windswept roads to an ineffective shelter north of town near the old Hamilton house, where debris was seen flying around. They drove north, fleeing the blast behind them, finally outdistancing it, and returning by another way to Balmorhea. They were wholly ignorant of the devastation that had descended upon the little town they had just left behind.

Carrasco found his store closed, blacked out; his wife Ercela and his sons Ray and Sammy were gone. In perplexity he was about to launch a search for them when Sammy pulled in beside him under the awning and blurted out the bad news about the tornado. Sammy climbed into his dad's car to go with him when Danny Dutchover drove up to tell Rosendo that there was an urgent need for him in Saragosa — a lot of dead people, buildings demolished.

After Rosendo located his family, who were with Hector and Elva Rodriguez (his daughter and her husband), he rushed with Sammy and Hector to Saragosa. The first person he met in the midst of the devastated Center was Orlando Sanchez, who wept out the news that his brother Omero, and Sylvestra, his wife and Carrasco's secretary, were both dead.

The justice of the peace set to work, with helpers, identifying and tagging the bodies of the dead. Haltingly, he told me, "The first person I uncovered . . . the first one was Sylvestra, my secretary . . . and the second was, I believe, Mr. Jose Madrid, a customer of mine for years. Then his wife . . . It was just one right after another that we identified."

They were not without their problems that night, and the task was a most difficult and ghoulish one. Some bodies defied identification and had to be reexamined later. A border patrolman from Pecos, off-duty at the time, assisted. Carrasco never knew his name.

Checking later with the Border Patrol station in Pecos, I learned that the man was Joe Mancha, and that one other patrolman, Lee Hatchell, also assisted at Saragosa.

Carrasco was troubled that he was unable to identify one woman and her baby. He drove with his son-in-law to Pecos the next morning and had another look at them at Bill Calloway's funeral home. Calloway thought the woman was Joey Herrera's wife Elsa, but could not be certain. Rosendo said that Elsa's mother had to come and identify her.

His voice raced on and on with rapid-fire details, most of them already recorded in this narrative. He told of being out there until 4:00 or 5:00 in the morning, then going home to find Kathy Escovedo's mother and father there, his wife working at helping them cope with stark tragedy. Then he heard Sammy, whom he had never heard weep before, out in the patio crying. Rosendo walked to him and they embraced, holding onto each other and mingling their tears.

Rosendo Carrasco never finished. His voice broke down then, and his eyes brimmed wet with tears at the tragic memory he had brought down through the months to that solemn moment there in his office.

* * *

Leonor Armendariz, a petite lady, lovely, compassionate, and talkative, is the mother of one of my student friends, Alex. Her husband Juan, a ranch hand, and daughters Leticia, twelve, and Edna, eleven, make up a lovely family both liked and respected in these parts. Their home was located about dead center and directly below the rotation cloud where the great tornado was spawned.

Warm brown eyes aglow, Leonor Armendariz related her story of a pleasant evening when she came home from work, ready for a nap. Alex later awakened her with loud banging at her door. He asked her where the camera was. He had sighted a tornado "over toward Saragosa" and wanted to photograph it. Groggy, his mother scolded him for playing practical jokes.

While the family ate dinner shortly afterward, Leonor noticed that her husband was anxious. A tornado was on his mind following his and Alex's sighting the funnel, and the man suddenly dropped everything and left for Saragosa. He was not gone very long before returning, when he slumped speechless on the front steps. He finally found his voice: "Saragosa has been wiped out by a tornado. The place where you were supposed to attend that graduation tonight is gone!"

After some discussion, the family drove to Saragosa, where Alex joined a search party, the same one in which I was involved. The family returned home around 2:30 A.M. and after a few hours of sleep, Alex went to the school shelter in Balmorhea and pitched in as a disaster volunteer.

> **Leonor Armendariz:** Sylvia Roman had kept the little Balderas girls who lost their mother that night in the storm. Elie Estrada had brought them in and left them in the gym that night. After Sylvia later took them, Mrs. Avalos, Socorro Balderas's mother, called me to go and pick up her grandchildren, Maria de la Luz and Ampara, so that I might keep them at my home until after their mother's funeral. The girls were here when Alex came home that evening, and he was troubled that they were dressed in boys' clothes.
>
> We decided to drive to the Salvation Army clothing center in Balmorhea for clothes for the children. The people there were most helpful. Robbie and Elaine Clanton assisted us in gathering a number of little dresses from the donated clothing there. We brought them home, and I washed, starched, and ironed them, and they fit the children perfectly! While all this activity was taking place, the phone rang, and Fernando Balderas, the girls' father, was the caller. He wanted me to take the girls over to their grandparents' place so that he could be with them.
>
> Upon our arrival there, Mr. Balderas tenderly hugged his girls, then he went inside. Moments later he came out with a cake, of all things, a yellow, heart-shaped cake! It was the cake his deceased wife had made for her family's celebration at home after the graduation — a celebration none of them ever would have, and it was the last thing Socorro Balderas, in her love for her humble family, would ever bake in this world, I suppose.

She did not wish to take the cake, but Balderas insisted. Leonor took it home with her and photographed the cake and the children together. When she later took the girls home to their grief-stricken father, Mrs. Armendariz returned the cake as well.

I was eager to clear up a matter that Raquel and I had been told, and I asked Leonor about it. We were told that Mr. Balderas would not stay at his home for several weeks after the tornado killed his wife but that he went there each evening and turned on the house lights. Mrs. Armendariz affirmed that the report was true.

"He went to their cottage every evening and lit up the place, then returned again early each morning and turned off all the lights."

We all wondered why the bereaved man did such a thing — perhaps we will never know. But he and the girls are once more settled in their home near the interstate, and since the recent fire at the girls' grandparents' home, the Avalos family has moved into the house too.

* * *

Larry Turnbough, trim but powerfully built, stands well over six feet tall, and is a no-nonsense native of Balmorhea — "born and raised here," as he says in his smooth West Texas drawl. Modest, businesslike, but casual, Larry will tell you that he has farmed "mostly around here from Toyavale and Balmorhea to Saragosa." As a consequence, he knows everybody, and everybody knows and respects Larry. So the tragedy left in the wake of the May 22 tornado "hit pretty close to home."

He is a very human and caring man and was particularly touched by the death of Socorro Balderas, whose husband works for the Turnboughs. Larry later purchased a mobile home and lot in Balmorhea as a residence in a quiet neighborhood for Fernando Balderas and his two motherless little girls. Now they live within walking distance of school.

Larry Turnbough had gone home from his farm about 7:30 P.M., and en route noticed Joe Gallegos standing outside and looking at the weather. Passing on through Brogado and Balmorhea, he likewise noticed people outdoors watching the gathering storm. He was then looking up himself, but having been on a tractor all afternoon, he had heard no weather reports.

Arriving home, Larry called Crennie Crenshaw, a fellow member of the fire department and of the local weather-spotter training program that he and Larry had designed. Crenshaw was outside watching the clouds and did not answer the call. Things happened fast after that. His wife Mary urged him to take her to his dad's home because of the ominous-looking weather. "We were just leaving," Larry said, "when I heard a lot of roaring down there . . . I listened and could tell it was going away from us, toward Saragosa. We were hearing the tornado then."

The phone rang, and Gina Garlick told them that James had just called from the truck stop and reported a tornado near the interstate. Larry agreed to pick Gina up and see what had happened.

At the Garlick home the Turnboughs found Kim Perrin, wife of Greg Perrin of the water district, there. Craig Huelster and his wife were just arriving in a very messed-up pickup. Windows were smashed, the windshield full of mud, and the Huelsters drenched with water. They had just driven in from their farm, where they had dived into an irrigation ditch near the place where the tornado came down. En route to Balmorhea, Craig had stopped and inquired of a highway patrolman "parked right near the Fina Station" and learned that the tornado had gone on through Saragosa. The officer was talking on his radio but hesitated long enough to report that Floyd was already there, that the Community Center was down, and a lot of people were trapped in the rubble.

"I remembered then about the graduation," Larry said.

He rushed to the fire station in Balmorhea and moved out the truck that was equipped with an electric winch. Pecos Cook, a local trucker and cattleman, showed up and went with Larry to Saragosa, "where we came upon a scene of unbelievable devastation. It would be about thirty hours before I would leave there!" Larry exclaimed.

They grabbed jacks out of pickups and pitched in, working around people who were already dead to look for others who were trapped. Local survivors of the storm — those physically able — rushed to the scene and plunged into the rubble, "along with people from Balmorhea, and eventually, from everywhere."

Larry Turnbough became interested in the plight of the people who had assumed the position usually taught for protection from a tornado. "You know," he said, "to flex your ankles to your knees on the floor with your body sloped over your thighs to protect your vital organs. That is the way you're taught . . . up against the wall. Most of the people in that position were the ones that were killed! The kids who were smaller, and the few adults who fell flat onto the floor, were the ones who survived."

He went on to explain that those people who assumed the fetal position sat up higher on the floor, and the large numbers of them, even though dead, supported the weight of the cement wall sufficiently to protect those who were lower, lying prone on the floor. He pointed out Lucas Carrillo, one of those people in the fetal position, sitting in that posture about ten or twelve feet out from the edge of the wall — "a fairly large man with definitely a lot of weight on him . . . dead." He could not be moved immediately, as his wife Rosie urged that the men do, "because he was supporting a lot of weight and was actually protecting at least two more people who were trapped beneath that slab . . . and not crushed." Turnbough stated that Carrillo had no table over him, that the wall with all its weight was right on the man.

"Another thing about ways to escape or survive a tornado," Larry added, "a few people drove away, which is another practice the experts tell you not to do. Those people who took to their cars and fled survived it. Those who did what you are most often told to do did not survive! They didn't run away in a car; they got into what they considered a sound structure. But for them it didn't work, and they died!

"Of course, the structure wasn't sound. People thought it was. That old building had cement walls, but there was no way for anybody to know that it had no cement foundation under those walls. It had wooden floors inside, but there was no foundation to support those heavy walls; they were set upon dirt! *It was a death trap!* . . . a fact nobody knew until it fell," the big farmer sighed with resignation.

Larry believes that had all the people at the Center attempted to leave in cars, there would still have been as many killed, because he doubts "they could have gotten away orderly enough for very many to have made it." He described how the cars were blown and stacked three vehicles high in places, some of them as much as 200 yards from the places where they had been parked. He concluded that if people could have in some orderly manner filled a few cars to capacity, more might have made it, "but there was so little time!"

Considering the possibility of people having taken refuge in the irrigation ditch that runs parallel to the highway on its east side all the way to Toya Creek, Larry said, "Most of that ditch was filled with two-by-fours and tin after the storm, and all the weeds were stripped out of it! I do not think you could have survived in that ditch, either!" He suggested that a ditch that was crossways to the path of the funnel might have provided some safety as the tornado swept over. But the ditch that was there ran parallel to the path of the tornado, "and a person could never have survived that. It is sad that a lot of people were killed as it was, but it easily could have been much worse. The hundred and thirty who were listed as injured could easily have represented the death count!"

Turnbough was impressed, as the night wore on, by the throng of volunteer workers who rushed in to help. "I don't see how you could ever again have a disaster of that magnitude anywhere with the likelihood of such a great army of rescue people who were able to do all of that work largely with bare hands, crowbars, those high-lift jacks . . . and with a lot of adrenalin! As night went on and all of this sophisticated equipment showed up . . . it was good, but most of it came too late . . . The Brookshire SWAT team did arrive early enough to be of great help, especially with their air bags and compressors. Those few who were further under and harder to reach we were able to employ Mr. Brookshire's air bags for their rescue."

I asked Larry whether he thought many people simply suffocated underneath the rubble. He had heard several theories on how a lot of them died. "Wes Elliot was there . . . he's an engineer, and he explained that their plight was similar to people being in a trench when dirt caves in around them. They actually suffocate because they cannot breathe due to the pressure around their bodies, particularly their chest cavities."

Larry agreed with that theory somewhat, but thought most had a tremendous amount of internal injuries. "Those bodies we saw up here at the school gave evidence of internal injuries by their black and blue tissue. This came from a tremendous amount of internal bleeding." He wondered what else could have caused the tremendous amount of discoloration.

We asked Larry Turnbough about his farm worker, Fernando Balderas, who had impressed my wife and me. Larry explained that Balderas had worked for him since August of 1980, and his wife's father had worked for the Turnboughs for over thirty years.

"Maria del Socorro had been in this country seven or eight years when the tornado killed her. She had come over here, then returned to Mexico within a year. Then they were married, and he came over illegally and worked for us ever since. After he'd been here awhile, he obtained a permit to work, but he couldn't go home . . . I've taken Fernando to El Paso about four times since the tragedy, and he now has a resident alien card; after eighteen months he will be eligible for citizenship," Turnbough informed us.

The big farmer told how the wife of Fernando Balderas took care of him and his children. "He neither reads nor writes English or Spanish, and she was a sort of go-between for him and the world," Turnbough said. "He has these two little girls, five and six years old, and Socorro really kept them clean and neat. She dressed them nicely too. They were just a simple little family getting started."

Even though Fernando had lost his wife, and another of Turnbough's workmen, Mike Sanchez, had lost his son Omero, both of them still stayed at the site of destruction and helped. Larry said,

"I had to go and identify Fernando's wife. Then I carried her out of the back of a pickup and put her in the bus loaded with bodies. I wanted to go and try to console them . . . but I couldn't stop for that . . . It was amazing to me the strength people showed that night. You knew what was their extreme human loss . . . but they plunged in and worked anyway."

Larry told of a group of people from Fort Davis, "some cowboys, mainly," who went out in the late hours of the night and gathered livestock, being alert for people out there as they went. Volunteers combed the darkened areas about town on the offhand chance that humans might have been blown out there.

With gas lines ripped apart all over Saragosa, there was a danger of fires. Q. A. Crenshaw and Larry stayed out there all night and the next day to man the firetruck in case fires did break out.

People kept urging Larry Turnbough to take a break, to go home for some sleep and rest, but he said, "Whenever I'd get still, or sit down, my mind was racing ninety miles per hour. I couldn't relax or rest . . . You know, seeing men, women, and kids lying there dead, and our knowing we couldn't save them — well, you just kept doing what you had to do. It hurt to see all those dead, especially the children, so you worked on in all your sense of urgency, but bearing the load of pain as well. I just hope that the Saragosa tornado will be the only one I will ever again be close to.

* * *

Joe Ortega is a neat little guy who was just finishing the tenth grade in May when the tornado came. Joe shared the same classes at school as Elvira Casias and Kathy Escovedo, whose lives were snuffed out by the storm. He was one of the first people to arrive on the scene as he and his brother Gilbert rode in "on the back edge of the tornado" as it made its sinister call upon Saragosa. Joe feels a lot of pain at the loss of two of his dearest friends, along with others, and he keeps asking himself: why?

Joe was at home watching TV with his mother and Gilbert as the violently rotating clouds did their dance just above the little mountain that lies immediately adjacent to Brogado on its south edge. Joe and his mother joined his father and watched the cloud formation hovering almost directly overhead.

Joe and Gilbert decided to drive around and watch the weather, driving first to Balmorhea, then on to Saragosa. Passing Ham's Exxon, they saw a cluster of cars, and Joe opened a window and learned that the twister had hit Saragosa. Nervous and frightened, the young men raced toward Saragosa, the wind tugging violently at their car as they went. At times the wind actually pushed them forward, "a really weird sensation," Joe said. "Apparently we were on the edge of the back side of the tornado, which we could not see for the curtain of rain. We were following it along, getting a bit too close for comfort!" In four or five minutes we drove in on the Saragosa scene and saw everything flattened out. It was scary — very scary. The whole town was wrecked — houses, trees — everything appeared to be gone!"

Joe and his brother decided to pitch in and help. "We were at the place where the kids' program was held, and I saw it all . . . the whole structure tumbled down to earth. People were crying for help for themselves and saying that a lot of other people needed help down below.

"After a bit I must have become overwhelmed with shock and while just standing there horrified, I spotted Delilah Alvarez standing huddled with her family. I went to her and hugged her, trying to comfort her as she stood crying for her lost sister Sylvestra. I realized that my gesture was a small thing in the presence of her crushing tragedy, but at least it was something, and I hope it helped."

After that Joe helped at running errands, asking for tools and other things the rescue workers needed. He saw dead bodies everywhere.

Joe stayed with his brother and worked several hours until it was quite late and their bodies were worn out and nearly in shock. I recalled that Joe was with our group when we found his friend Kathy, and he remembered too.

"Later, I was all shook up, and we came on home," he said. "I was in deep, troubled thought. I couldn't get over the loss of Kathy and Elvira — best friends of mine. My classmates. Why? Why them?"

"Joe, did you ever, down deep in your heart and soul, find a satisfactory answer to those questions?" I asked.

"No, sir. Not really. I suppose I'll never get an answer to that."

For Joe Ortega life goes right on in Brogado, the small Mexican-American *communidad* east of Balmorhea as one goes toward Saragosa. He has lived there all seventeen years of his life. Joe will go right on playing his favorite sport, which is basketball, at the Balmorhea High School. But classes, sports, school, and his private life will never be the same again.

[10]

Students Who Cared

Paul Matta, a handsome youth of quiet dignity, modest manner, and exalted purpose in life, is a young man wholly at peace with himself, with his fellows, and with God. I enjoyed the six years I taught Paul in English classes, and can state unequivocally that I never had one disagreeable moment or disciplinary matter to mar our accord. Paul won the valedictorian honor as a graduating senior. But Paul Matta, while academically superior, never was more interested in grades than in growth, and he achieved both — remarkably.

Paul watched the gathering tempest that day, saw one of the tornados, and raced home with some fright and concern. Word came of the disaster, and he went with his family to the stricken town, taking some blankets in case they were needed. With him were his father and mother, Alfredo and Lila Matta, and his brothers Jesus and Peter. Paul and Alfredo did what they could, inspecting the rubble-strewn area along Highway 17.

In his journal Paul later wrote: "I saw bodies wrapped and on the ground . . . shrouded because they were dead. I saw bodies carried up to the bus, identified, some of them, and then placed in the bus . . . Then somebody yelled that help was needed."

He joined the hordes and hurried off to join a search party. His brother Peter was in the group, a comfort to Paul out in the blackness of the unknown, death all around, in a night "that was deathly dark and quiet except for our weak voices." He wrote, "Home seemed too far away, and I was here, and I didn't want to leave. I wanted to help in some further way." He did help in days to come.

In his valedictorian address, Paul spoke of time having run out for public school days for him and his classmates. Now it was time for the real world beyond the classrooms. He spoke eloquently and the audience was moved to tears: "We have marched for almost an eternity to the beat of the drums of the school system, but after tonight . . . we'll be marching to the rhythm and beat of the drums of our own choosing!" He quoted Henry David Thoreau, "If one does not keep pace with his companions, perhaps it is because he hears a different drummer; let him step to the music which he hears, however measured or far away."

Would his class march to the drummer of pleasure? Of wealth? Of power? "Or, will we seek a walk with God? The Scriptures raise a frightening question in Mark 8:36, where the Lord Jesus Christ asked, 'What does a man profit if he gains the whole world but loses his soul?' "

Paul went on, his audience attentive. "How our hearts have been touched and broken because several of our friends and loved ones perished in last month's disastrous tornado! The magnitude of this sad loss of human life and human injury was immeasurably lessened when some of us remembered this one or that one who gave evidence of marching behind Christ as his chosen Drummer . . ."

* * *

Josie Rhyne, a sophomore at Balmorhea High School, was a classmate and close friend of both Kathy Escovedo and Elvira Casias. Josie, a beautiful person, wears her golden locks done up attractively, framing her lovely face. Her personality might be described as sparkling, exuberant, reflecting, as it does, a heart of gold, a soul of compassion and Christian love.

Incredulous and grief-stricken over the Saragosa tragedy, Josie joined the adult volunteers and pushed herself as if driven by a desperation which neither the long, arduous hours nor the dead-tired body could slow down or deter from pressing on.

Josie related her account of the tragedy to me with never a word of the selfless service she had rendered to help survivors. Had I not observed her "in the trenches," I never would have known that she did an ounce of work.

She and Glenn Humphries's band met for rehearsal of some songs they were to sing at the senior graduating party. Glenn was out monitoring the weather while the musicians waited, then became aware of the gathering storm and began watching it too. By 8:00 P.M. the group decided to give up their waiting and go home. Josie drove home in the family pickup, aware of a tornado warning, but ignorant that one had just destroyed a part of her life forever.

Upon reaching home at the Balmorhea State Park in Toyavale, Josie found the electricity off, the world about her in darkness. Only her sister Tammi and her kid brother Zane were there, and when Josie inquired as to the whereabouts of their parents, Tammi sobbed out the shocking story of Saragosa. They prayed, they cried, then they called to Saragosa. The phone lines were dead. Josie went outside for a momentary tryst with the sky and found it frowning, black and frightening as ever.

Frustration and even anger consumed her for an unmeasured time until a car pulled into the driveway. "It was my mother," Josie said. "She came on the run, dashing into the house; she was just in from Saragosa. Tammi and I threw a barrage of questions at her, but Mom was not sure about so many people we asked about. Kathy Escovedo was gone, she told us . . . That couldn't be! I did not want to believe what I was hearing, but it was true . . . incredibly true!"

Two of Josie's friends, Kathy Escovedo and Elvira Casias, were dead. "As her coffin was being placed in the ground, it seemed to me that she was screaming to get out! I can't describe my feelings at that time, but it seemed that some monstrous hand grasped a spear and hurled it right into my heart! I tried to think of happier moments — like that very day in history class when we all were laughing in a fit of merriment. Mr. Broadfoot, our teacher, allowed us to make predictions for ourselves . . . where we would be in ten years. I was to become the only doctor our class would produce, specializing in hair permanents! Kathy was going to become president of the United States by 1997. She would, of course, vote for herself."

For Josie and the others the tears still flow after the many months that have passed. The kids have stuck together, lending emotional support to each other, recognizing the significance of our need for each other.

"We're all going through this veil of tears together," Josie wrote me. "Shouldn't we all plan to be together in the end? My prayers and hopes are to see all of my friends again some day, but until that time arrives, I'd like to see all human hearts set free from fear, and happy . . . even with the sad memories we share sometimes looming in the way. We all need to rest in a hope that overrides the bitter memories, guiding us forward in a deathless faith that a day of resurrection awaits all who believe unto salvation."

* * *

A tall, slender, beautiful member of the junior class at Balmorhea High School in May of 1987, Adrienne Chance was the first person Tommy Ward and I met as we made our cautious way down into the demolished town of Saragosa on the night of May 22. A sweet girl with a bottomless well of tenderness and compassion inside her, she blurted out the names of some student friends who had just perished in the tornado less than an hour before.

For Adrienne, the day had been a happy one. She had been awarded her senior jacket at the Awards Assembly that morning. Also, it had been her first day at work at the great swimming pool at the state park. Another joy, her grandmother had arrived from Dallas to visit her family for a few days. People in West Texas generally always welcome rain, and the weather had been hot and dry. "As I reported for work at 4:00 P.M., the appearance of the weather promised rain, and I was glad as I sat in the hot sun doing lifeguard duty," she said.

The promise of rain turned into threats of storms by 7:30, and people were leaving early. "The day grew unusually dark, too, for that early hour. The pool closed at 8:00, and I hitched a ride home with Paul Miller on his motorcycle. Hail arrived at home with me!"

Her family almost followed her in, bursting through the door with the electrifying news that Saragosa was gone. This all but unhinged Adrienne's mind as a second, penetrating thought exploded in her brain: "HILDA! Hilda Castillo! Oh, no . . . she can't be . . .!" Adrienne joined her family in snatching up blankets and dashing off down a raindrenched highway into Saragosa. Except for a tiny cluster of emergency lights, not a light shone anywhere. And Hilda, her friend, was out there in the blight of that destruction, possibly dead.

"We arrived, me with my fears, and the truth confronting us was tough . . . harsh . . . no word for it . . . Here we stood, semi-dazed; we, the living few, walking among corpses! I looked about . . . afraid almost to see . . . then suddenly, I saw her . . . HILDA WAS THERE! ALIVE! Thank God forever! We stood, she and I, and we held each other in a trembling embrace, and cried together with mingled joy and sorrow in a world of death and carnage!"

Somewhat composed after their reunion, Adrienne and Hilda went out to bring in flashlights. "On our way we met you, Mr. Lane, with Mr. Ward." She and Hilda Castillo were the first people we had met after we arrived.

Adrienne later returned and helped in the wreckage of the town until around 1:00 in the morning.

"My heart broke into a million pieces out there, for, you know, Saragosa was my home too — that is, the home of those I'd loved and lost. And a part of me died out there with them that night!" she said.

I thought of something beautiful, written by Alexander Pope in "The Universal Prayer":

> Teach me to feel another's woe, To hide the fault I see;
> The mercy I to others show, That mercy show to me.

* * *

She is petite, alive with enthusiasm, holding a zest for life that could be the secret of her beauty. In junior high she volunteered year after year to work as my "class secretary." And she did a bang-up job, being a living dynamo of practical helpfulness. There is something of eternity in the beauty of expression in her eyes — eyes that reflect the inner tranquility of a heart given over to God forever.

Sandra's father, Ismael Dutchover, is the Reeves County commissioner for Precinct 3. He fought in Vietnam, and he is into the raising of livestock as an avocation. His daughters Lisa, Sandra, Cynthia, Tammy, Frances, and Brenda have gained much practical experience in animal husbandry during their formative years while helping to care for the flocks and broods.

Dutchover rushed into the chaos of caregiving at Saragosa right after the sudden assault of the killer tornado. Plastered on front pages of newspapers across America was an action photo of this nobly caring man hauling a fellow human being out of the rubble of the downed Community Center. That photo was awarded the number-one news photo in 1987 by the Associated Press.

Dutchover had endured enough of trauma and public visibility, and he did not wish to relive and relate his experiences at Saragosa. He preferred to retire from further confrontation with the grim facts. Thus it was that Sandra told me some of the details of her own experiences and others picked up from both her parents.

"Although months have passed," Sandra began, "still that day burns in my memory as a glowing ember . . . as if it happened yesterday."

Dutchover was outside working when the hail began rattling down. At the same time, Juan Castillo, Sandra's boyfriend, called, wanting to come over. Sandra invited him. Her sister Lisa came in after a while with the news that a tornado had struck Saragosa. When Juan arrived and learned the news, he dashed back over to Saragosa to check on his family. He found them safe, but the windows had blown out of their home. Juan rushed off to help at the Community Center, where he pulled bodies of neighbors from the rubble, and finally joined the search party with Floyd Estrada and me later that night.

The Dutchover family waited at home, engaging in much worry and speculation, but as the long, tedious hours wore on, they learned nothing. With phone lines dead, a darkened dungeon for a house, and an all-too silent world outside, the little family waited.

Sandra eventually slept. She said, "What time it was I had no way of knowing. The hour must have grown late when we heard a sound outside, sensed a movement, and in Dad came, looking as much a wreck as Saragosa! It was 4:00, we were all instantly awake, and were eager for some news. Dad tried to talk, began to name some of the dead, then lost all emotional control . . . I suppose the color drained from my face, and the blood felt frozen in my veins at his halting report."

Dutchover was devastated over the sudden loss of numbers of his day-to-day friends and associates. Sandra said, "He was soaked to the skin, and the grime he wore gave eloquent testimony that he had been helping to haul bodies up out of the debris of destruction in his great, strong arms. He showered and slept, but only for an hour. It was 6:00 A.M. Saturday morning, and in short order he was off again, and he did not come home at all except to eat during the following day. And that day following the storm was peaceful, calm, and still, almost as if Nature wore a mantle of guilt, sensing she had done something horribly wrong!"

* * *

When eleventh-grade student Prissy Gray returned to my English class in the fall of 1987, she wrote beautifully and with deep feeling for Elvira Casias and Kathy Escovedo. They were classmates, and Prissy expressed the prevailing feelings of other members of her class and other students as well. It would be almost impossible to record them all, and for that reason, a sampling of quotations and sentiments from Priscilla Gray's personal journal is representative here.

She writes of how she misses them, of the difficulty of starting school without her friends, saying, "I could only see them sitting in the classroom laughing and talking . . . They're still in my heart, but not in my classes at school. I guess I keep thinking that they simply haven't checked in yet, that they will check in . . . later."

Young Miss Gray expressed her belief that they are in "a far better world," and told of Kathy speaking to her in a dream, "We're living in heaven, and you're living in hell down on earth . . . be happy for us."

In a contemplative mood, Prissy once wrote, "I Wonder," a paper in which she wondered about many things that people usually take for granted. "I wonder what it would be like if I didn't have my parents . . ." She found out, in part, when her father, C. T. Gray, one of the members of the Balmorhea Volunteer Fire Department who gave unselfishly of himself at Saragosa, died suddenly of a heart attack on November 10. That was just under six weeks after his only daughter *wondered*. Now, Prissy, brokenhearted once again, writes, "Take every day as if it were the last day of your life."

That is true wisdom, coming from any age, but is significantly wise coming from a very popular seventeen-year-old high school cheerleader. Of particular concern to Prissy is not families dispossessed of earthly goods, but the "unfortunate kids who haven't any love in their lives." She expresses the wish somehow to go up to them and "give them all the love they need."

Of her lost classmate and friend, Elvira Casias, Prissy wrote on December 18, 1987, in anticipation of Elvira's birthday on January 25, "I never saw anything in Elvira but just beauty." What a tribute! Then she concluded, "I really do miss her, especially her smile . . . I love you, Elvira. Thanks always for being such a beautiful friend to me."

* * *

Connie Orozco is a blush of innocent charm that wears an ever-smiling face. Perhaps she is a little spoiled (and this may be the secret of her attraction), but she is modest, and most spoiled girls are anything but that. Her modesty and genuineness capture one's heart.

She lives in a not-very-famous little community called Alamo, which is not exactly located in a cow-pasture, although it is close to one. It does sit beside a few tumbleweeds in a chaparral-infested section of the great Chihuahuan Desert in Southwest Texas. Excitement runs close races with rumors in little places like Alamo, and the word was out that the tornado was going to smash Alamo to smithereens that afternoon when Saragosa sustained its fatal blow instead.

Everyone but Connie believed the dire word. Though scared, she did not regard the worsening weather as a serious threat to her community. Fears heightened later on when she saw ambulances on the main highway running back and forth toward Pecos during the evening hours.

It was only natural that Elvira Casias, who loved everybody, and Connie Orozco, who also loved everybody, should be great friends. Connie remembers being with Elvira at school that last day. In the morning they pre-enrolled in the gym for next year's classes and discussed taking my art class. "I wanted to enroll in that class for next year. That was the last time I spoke to her, for she died that same afternoon," Connie remembered.

Like so many others, little Connie Orozco has been concerned for the people victimized at Saragosa. In one of her journal entries, she described the neighboring town as appearing to have been "bombed out of existence" and that "bodies laid out on the shoulder of Highway 17." She mentioned a man reportedly taken to the Pecos hospital "in a truck with broken windows and full of mud." She was concerned that some people were "stealing from the helpless victims," and was glad to see the rebuilding of the town. With mature foresight, she hoped they would "install a city alarm warning system." She is happy that the surviving people in the area "are more closely drawn to each other now," and "that the Candelas store is to be rebuilt."

Angelica Casias, Elvira's beautiful younger sister, told Connie about an excited exodus from the trailers at Saragosa one night "because there was lightning, and the electricity went out just like before the tornado." Those people are understandably jumpy when the weather sheds its sunshine and clothes itself in somber clouds, muttering dire threats in their thunder punctuated with the exclamation marks of blinding lightning. Moods change with the weather, from serene in the sunshine to out of humor and desperate as the wind keeps pace with an overcast of sullen, menacing clouds.

Connie Orozco vows that "none of us will ever be the same again — especially the citizens of Saragosa."

PART IV
The Role of Communication

[11]

Communications Diary

Glenn Humphries is a quiet, modest man who is entirely innocent of sham or bluff. His career experiences include some years in radio dispatching communications with the Texas Department of Public Safety. His young wife Janie is employed by the Reeves County Sheriff's office in Pecos, making them a "law enforcement family."

Glenn has served as band director and computer instructor for the Balmorhea schools for a number of years. One might correctly surmise that he is an unpretentious man of many and varied talents.

In the late afternoon of the Saragosa tragedy, Glenn was doing a sky watch as he accompanied deputy sheriff Floyd Estrada in his patrol car. With Floyd, he was one of the first to burst in upon the scene of annihilation at Saragosa. Being a stickler for detail, Glenn logged his movement and activities for that afternoon, and his log is abbreviated and reproduced here in part as he put it down for the records.

> **3:30 P.M.** Driving school bus route out towards Saragosa. Dark cloud formations noted to the north and northeast. I carried my two-meter Handie-Talkie (H.T.), and hand-held radio transceiver on my bus run. Had forgotten my external speaker, and could not hear over the engine noises of the bus. I relied upon my eyes to monitor the clouds, and did not hear W5QGG, the club call signal for the Ham Radio Sky Warn Network quartered at the National Weather Service office in the tower at Midland Regional Air Terminal.

[Glenn explained that there are more than thirty or forty hams in the area trained as spotters and ready to go when needed. They all communicate with W5QGG, using a communications link called the "West Texas Connection" in the two-meter radio band, the 144-megahertz band. He wondered if W5QGG would activate the net that day, and kept monitoring his HT as he drove around his bus route.]

4:00 P.M. Finished route. Grandfather met me and gave me a ride home. With busy evening ahead, glad for the lift.

[Glenn was to practice with his country band at 7:00 P.M. in preparation for a senior dance in honor of their graduation on the 29th. Josie Rhyne, a sophomore, was to practice some songs she planned to sing as a tribute to her graduating friends.]

4:00 P.M. Suddenly, W5QGG activated the weather net. I checked in on my HT, offering my assistance, even though the storms were not yet in our area.

4:14 P.M. Athletic director Mike Barrandy came by and invited me to accompany him to Balmorhea Lake for some fishing. I went along, taking my HT, and continued monitoring W5QGG out there.

4:25 P.M. Fishing near the store, just north of old dock. With HT ready I watched the massing clouds and explained to Mike about the weather net; told him they might call me and ask that I move to specified places if needed. He said, "Okay."

4:34 P.M. Mike commented, "The fish will never bite today; the air feels too heavy." Wind very still on the ground, but clouds boiling above us to the north and northwest. Midland Weather Service advised that most of the activity was "way north of us and moving northeast," indicating no problem here.

5:00 P.M. Gave up fishing, went home, kept watching sky while wife prepared supper.

5:15 P.M. Nervous, restless, couldn't eat when supper was ready. Drove north to intersection of IH 10 and FM 2903, about two miles north of Balmorhea. Tornado watch on screen of TV just before I left home. I learned Reeves County included in watch area. Clouds seen earlier now had moved off to northeast, but new ones building up to north and northwest of me in the area of the junction of I-10 and I-20, some twenty miles west of town toward the north end of the Davis Mountains.

5:30 P.M. Observed the cloud moving northeast or east-northeast, but building to the west and southwest faster than the main cloud could move off. Left car to gain better view, and continued to offer comments on the cloud to W5QGG. A couple in a brown car took the eastbound off-ramp and stopped at FM 2903 watching me as I reported on the clouds.

After about five minutes they approached me for directions to Pecos and where they might buy gasoline. I gave them directions and warned them in Spanish that there is a tornado watch issued and there is possibility of tornados and hail in the area through which they would be passing. They thanked me and departed.

6:00 P.M. Clouds grown worse-looking. Boiling; scud moving quickly west, southwest, or south at different times. Dark swirling masses of clouds developed and began to mature over the area of the I-10 and I-20 junction some fifteen miles to the west of my position. Other spotters watching and reporting, but ours getting some real attention now. Even worse activity than ours seems to be developing in the vicinity of Hobbs, and around Jal, New Mexico, a hundred or so miles to the north. Yet another in the vicinity of Crane, Texas, to the east.

George Douglas, Radio N5ENY, Barstow, watching the cloud on the northeast side. George Toone, Radio WB5FBJ, was mobile, traveling from Seminole en route to his parents' home in Saragosa. At the time (6:00 P.M.) George near Pecos.

6:15 P.M. I rushed home and ate a quick bite to avoid hunger during our planned band practice, but had this gut feeling that I really ought to cancel our rehearsal in order to help watch and report on the clouds. Kept interrupting my meal to go outside and look at the sky. Nothing new to report . . .

6:30 P.M. Time to get the equipment ready for the band practice, but couldn't find the other members. Told wife I was going back to my weather watching, and I drove back to I-10 and FM 2903.

7:00 P.M. Returned to band hall. Only Josie Rhyne there. I asked her to wait while I went to search for the others . . . Larry, my brother, and the Matta brothers, Peter and Chewy. No success in locating them. I kept driving around watching the sky which looked ominous: clouds moving differing directions at different altitudes. Reported this information to W5QGG. Sky now looked wicked and full of energy, but at ground level the air was deathly still. Cloud building and building without moving off . . . appeared very restless.

7:30 P.M. Everyone now at band hall, preparing to proceed with practice. I described the clouds to the group and explained to them the W5QGG weather network. W5QGG called, said that the storm cell was a level 6 with top at 62,000 feet. I explained the significance of that and kept monitoring the net as the band readied their instruments.

7:40 P.M. Larry needed cigarettes. I told the group that I am the only spotter on the back side of the storm, and I wanted to watch the clouds some more. Larry and I left together, he expressing his feelings that I was exaggerating the potentiality of the cloud as well as my own importance. Back at my car we found that I had locked my keys inside! My spare battery and coat were inside, and, as well, I had left my cap in the bandhall.

Five minutes later, Larry and I were driving north to Main Street in his pickup, while I watched the sky. It looked bad just northwest of the Balmorhea city limits. Told Larry to forget the cigarettes . . . I needed to see this cloud better.

8:00 P.M. We were parked just west of town on Texas 17. A little rain coming down. Violent action in clouds moving southeast, over us. Reeves County Deputy Sheriff Floyd Estrada approached from the west at this moment, circled around behind us, motioned us to get in with him. He had been watching the cloud for some time too. Really raining hard now. Floyd and I agreed that we were directly under a wall cloud!

Charles Towry, Radio W4LCC, Balmorhea, was coming back to town from Fort Stockton. Reporting, as he passed Carrasco's Mercantile one mile east of Balmorhea, "pea-sized . . . no, marble-sized . . . no, golf-ball-sized hail!" Hail stopped rapidly, and Towry reports to W5QGG that he is seeing rotation above. I could not see it from my spot, but we listened as he made his report to Midland Weather Service.

Larry left in pickup for his cigarettes. I stayed with Floyd.

8:05 P.M. W5QGG told us that a tornado warning for Reeves County had been issued. Floyd said, "Let's go to the Jeff Davis County line so we can get out from under this thing and see it better." We drove west, then southwest into the foothills of the Davis Mountain Range. Meantime, Towry is driving out to Balmorhea Lake to spot weather out there. Now he tells us over W5QGG that he is definitely seeing rotation in the clouds. We instantly whirled around and raced toward town at a high rate of speed. Floyd called and asked the sheriff's office to call Balmorhea State Park Superintendent Darrel Rhyne on his radio hook-up, and to call the Balmorhea Fire Department. On the county radio we overheard Texas Department of Public Safety Highway Patrol Trooper Rob Bourland saying he saw a funnel crossing the interstate [I-10] near Milepost 210 [four miles east of Balmorhea].

We were almost on the interstate by then, just past the Tarin home on Texas 17. I reported to W5QGG the visual contact Bourland had with the tornado near Milepost 210. A long five minutes passed.

8:10 P.M. We had screamed through Balmorhea, heading for Saragosa, lights flashing. Passing the old experiment station farm [near Milepost 210], we saw a large green highway information sign which had been blown over. Floyd had just pointed this out to me when I indicated to him the milepost signs at Mile 211: they were twisting around at 360° both ways as fast as they could turn. Days later I was to see how warped that wind had left them!

8:12 P.M. Talked with George Toone, Radio WB5FBJ, asked him to phone my wife and have her unlock my car and ask Larry to take it to the I-10 Chevron as soon as possible. George was now home on the east edge of Saragosa. I would need another battery soon, and my jacket as well.

Did not know how fast we were traveling, but it was unbelievable! Floyd wrestling with car to keep it on road in the gusty wind. Saw eight or ten cars under the I-10/Hwy. 17 overpass as we headed north on Texas 17. Some electric company truck equipped with cherry pickers parked there on both sides of the road as we sped by. Faces of the people beside the road were grim, awestruck, and frightened.

8:15 P.M. Power lines down everywhere. We should be seeing buildings and houses by now. Floyd pauses at a downed power line stretching across the highway. He asks whether I think it safe to cross. I suggest we try crossing at its lowest point. It doesn't look hot, but still we worry. Too much adrenaline pumping through our bodies for either of us to be frightened. We drove on!

8:16 or thereabouts . . . We stopped on the west side of the road. Why? We were not there yet . . . but, then, are we? WE ARE! We both bound out of the car, Floyd pointing at the remains of the Community Center! Dismayed with unbelief, I scan the upheaval before me. No other buildings in sight . . . wind whipping gritty-feeling mist into our faces. Cold . . . we are soaked already! A woman is pushing small children into Floyd's car! Then I realized she was his wife Elie! She and those children had been inside that building lying now in total ruin! We had arrived but seconds behind a monster tornado!

[Floyd Estrada and Glenn Humphries quickly surveyed the scene, sized up the futility of rescuing people like Joey Herrera pinned under a wall, his wife and child dead beside him — the futility of any feeble efforts on their part . . .]

Glenn: We went for our radio and called for wreckers to help lift sections of the wall. I asked George to relay that we will need *lots* of ambulances, and that there will be a lot of bodies to carry to the morgue.

Someone had alerted the Red Cross and the Salvation Army, both of which needed authorization to activate their units. We took the liberty in our emergency to use Floyd's name for authorization of both organizations.

Time became lost, confused. Others were arriving now — Sharon and Larry Lippe, followed by Darrel Rhyne and Park Ranger Mike Henderson, Highway Patrol Trooper Bourland . . . and others. Very soon I found myself communicating on two meters [ham radio] steadily, then intermittently using Floyd's county radio and the radio in the patrol car. We were desperate to remove the injured to hospitals, and I kept calling for ambulances, but people on the other end of radio communication simply could not conceive of the gravity of our situation out there.

Earlier, I had called Mr. Towry [W4LCC] to have him bring in a school bus, asking that he also contact Mr. Clanton, the school superintendent, and ask that he open the school for use as a shelter. I foresaw that we would need that later.

It rained off and on, and the wind was blowing from the east-northeast, pelting us with a rain that still seemed gritty. I now used the highway patrol radio to contact B&B Wrecker in Pecos to have them bring their air bags for lifting the walls. I then radioed the Fort Stockton Highway Patrol unit to direct them on to the scene.

Larry arrived with my windbreaker, which soaked through in no time at all. Then I opened my car door to obtain the spare battery for my radio, and as I did so, a loud resounding clap of thunder smashed down. I had my left hand on the car door and my right hand on the roof of the car at the moment the lightning crashed down. Electricity traveled through my body somehow, shaking me up pretty badly. A few minutes later one of my students, Roman Muñiz, ran up to me and breathlessly explained that he saw a man struck by that bolt of lightning. The man couldn't move above his waist. The first firetruck from Pecos was driving up, and I sent them off with Roman to find the man who was about two blocks away to the northwest somewhere out there in the night.

Many hams were helping now. The weather net was forgotten as we had been the center of communications since we had arrived on the scene. George, WB5FBJ, arrived with his father and controlled communications from within Reeves County Chief Deputy Gary Ingram's car. The BBARC (Big Bend Amateur Radio Club) had an emergency command post on the way with Dave Cockrum N5DO, Bob McDaniels, WO5K, Bill Brooks, KE5OG, and others coming along to assist.

They set up before 10:30 P.M. near the location of the wrecked Saragosa Community Center. A command post was also established in Charles Towry's classroom at the Balmorhea High School. There, Mr. Towry kept a shortwave [HF — High Frequency] rig on hand with an all-band vertical antenna mounted on the roof. They used a generator left there by the BBARC van on its way through to Saragosa.

While I was running here to get this thing, running there to get that thing, a young mother, Lorena Avalos, wife of Richard Avalos, came to me and asked what she could do for her son who was between one and three years old and had blood rushing out of both ears. No available ambulances were on the scene yet, and there was no place of refuge from the rain and cold. I told Mrs. Avalos to keep him as warm as possible by holding him close to her inside a battered car nearby. We would get him into an ambulance as soon as one arrived. Soon the ambulances began coming in from towns all around, and I went back to find her, but she was gone. I later learned that the Avalos child survived and is recovered now.

More and more bodies were pulled from the rubble at the Center and lay stretched out in mud and water beside one another. I passed by them time and again, but tried not to see their faces, keeping my mind and eyes on my errands so that I could survive this monstrous ordeal myself. Then, right in the middle of all this horror, a boy [Jacob Sanchez] who has been one of my students ran up to me, hugging me, shaking me apart, blurting out that both his mother and father are dead. He was in shock, and I urged him to "hang tough" as I tried to get him into the bus and out of the weather.

I was suddenly arrested by the fact that my radio had shorted out with rainwater and no longer transmits. The receiver on it comes and goes. When Bob McDaniels, WO5K, of Alpine arrived, he loaned me one of his spare radios.

By that time it was nearly dark and difficult to see well. Someone found a natural gas leak over near the place where the man was struck by lightning. W5QGG told us about this time that another funnel was directly *over* us! We just kept on working. This *has* to be *worse* than any war zone I've ever heard about!

One of my band students, a senior girl, came up and hugged me, crying from the depths of her heart: her older sister was killed by covering her up with her own body to save her life. The girl, Delilah Alvarez, had survived with little more than scratches and a skinned leg, horrific fright, and a broken heart.

It went on like this all night until I was too tired to go on. The hour was 4:00 A.M. when we realized that there were no more people alive under those walls. A lot of help had arrived, and I could leave. I decided to go home, try to sleep, and come back around 7:00 A.M. I might just as well have stayed there and worked. The adrenaline pumping in my veins and the visions of what I had seen would never allow me any sleep for days and nights to come.

— Glenn Humphries

[12]

West Texas Connection

Some years before the explosive events that opened the veins of the nations of the world and bled them to death in World War II, Charles Towry was born in Fayetteville, Tennessee. Beyond high school, young Towry became a navy man and served his country as a petty officer during the war and for some years afterward until his eventual retirement from military service.

While Chief Towry was on one tour of duty at Guantanamo Bay, Cuba, a friend introduced him to a ham radio operator there. This fellow proved to be an obliging individual who patched in telephone communications via radio to Mrs. Towry, who was then living in Jacksonville, Florida. This favor of no small significance for Charles and Nancy Towry was a vast improvement over the snails-pace mail that required two weeks for a letter home and an answer in return. By then, news from Nancy was ancient history, and now, with regular radio calls patched through to her thrice weekly, they could keep current with each other.

Towry became so intrigued with the possibilities of amateur radio that he began studying radio for the purpose of becoming an amateur radio operator himself. With his background in electronics, Charles found the science of radio easy enough for him to grasp and master, and in time he received his operator's license.

Earlier, somewhere along the line, Petty Officer Towry, on furlough, had paid a visit to an aunt in Fayetteville, Tennessee, the town of his birth. On a blind date he met an interesting young lady by the name of Nancy Foster. In time love grew, and in time they were married. Together they did their share of globe-trotting, seeing the world both during the navy enlistment and since retiring. In their R.V. they still travel far and wide during vacations from their duties at school.

The Towrys came to Balmorhea in 1972 after teaching for two years at Weslaco, in the Lower Rio Grande Valley of Texas. He has taught in the high school at Balmorhea since that time, and Nancy has been employed as a teaching aide in the special education department of the school.

When asked his philosophy of life, Charles answered, "Keep a good positive outlook on life. Don't get ulcers . . . don't sweat it." That probably accounts for his, and others of us, living and working out in the wide-open spaces of far West Texas, where life is a bit slower-paced and relatively uncomplicated for those of us who wish it that way.

On Friday, May 22, the Towrys had gone to Fort Stockton to replace Charles's glasses, which had been broken that morning on his bus run. Eating dinner at K-Bob's Steak House that evening, they met Raquel Lane and Betty Hopper, who were dining there too. Charles and Nancy finished eating first and left about 6:30 P.M. for home.

On the way to Balmorhea, they observed a big wall of clouds to the north "about twenty miles in length." Towering straight up, the clouds left no blue in the skies. Towry switched on his radio to learn whether any tornados or rainstorms were indicated. He said that the people at the Midland Weather Service had already activated the amateur station W5QGG there, involving the West Texas Connection. This organization is made up of amateur radio repeaters scattered over the western part of Texas. It is not a commercial radio system. All input and output comes and goes over the ham short-wave HT sets that the members carry with them when out in the field.

When Charles Towry checked in, W5QGG had already activated the net, and amateurs were already reporting in from all over the Permian Basin, describing what they each saw of bad weather.

Charles Towry: Well, I continued making observations and reports for about twenty miles, bringing us within about eight miles of Balmorhea. By then, the clouds looked much worse. While I was reporting to Midland, Glenn was also making his reports, and I noticed that none of our reported sightings jibed with each other.

Nancy and I proceeded on toward Balmorhea, and I stopped on the way two or three times and got out of the car to observe the cloud formations more clearly. The last time I stopped was about a mile this side of where Curtis Logston used to live — about two miles east of Balmorhea. To the north I could see this very large, ominous-looking cloud up there with whirlwinds underneath it. There was agitated twisting and turning of the clouds above, seeming to indicate something sinister.

Just about a mile back we had run into a small amount of rain, then hail: first, pea-sized, then marble-sized, and then, golf-ball-sized. When I stopped again, I saw these clouds bearing down on us, straight out of the north. They were between us and, I'd say, Interstate 20. I made my weather report and stood there observing the strange weather phenomena for a few minutes. I would estimate the time at about 8:15 P.M., possibly a few minutes earlier.

We drove on to the Balmorhea Lake rather than going straight home. I wished to report on the storm from out there. To the northeast I could see the twisting and turning of more of those agitated clouds, only about 700 feet high at their base.

Now, I hear Midland report a tornado had crossed Interstate 10 and Highway 17. I had just come from there, less than ten miles back! We immediately returned home, unloaded our groceries. Two neighborhood boys, Greg Borland and Taylor Woodruff came along, excited and happy that a tornado might be coming through here — kid talk, you know.

To the northeast were swirling clouds, and observing them, I said, "Boys, would you like to go and do a little cloud chasing?" They climbed in with me, and we were soon on the frontage road racing out toward the I-10 and Texas 17 intersection. We noticed a tree blown down out there by the old experiment station . . . about where Midland Radio had placed the tornado that crossed the interstate. By the time we reached the intersection, the boys had sobered remarkably, having seen a little reality and become scared of what tornados can do. I had made my point that they are something to fear and nothing to be happy about. While turning around, we could see the flashing emergency lights three miles to the north, where the storm had struck Saragosa. Being curious, we reversed directions and drove up there. A few emergency vehicles were already on the scene by that time.

I contacted some people at the scene of destruction by radio and learned that they needed transportation to haul people out of there to hospitals. I wheeled around and brought Nancy and the boys back here, put them out, and climbed into a school bus and hightailed it back to Saragosa. It was dark when I arrived, and the big job of searching for victims was under way. I stood by the bus, ready to go when needed, standing there for about three hours. Most of the bodies were hauled away by emergency vehicles. I simply waited and kept my radio going. I learned that the Big Bend Radio Club, which is located in Alpine, had left about an hour and a half earlier, and they soon arrived with their emergency van and antennas to set up disaster communication since all power was out in the area. The only contact with the outside world was via ham, and the sheriff's department, radios.

While the BBRC fellows set their antennas up and established communications there in Saragosa, two of their members were in Balmorhea setting up a radio station in the school. These men were Banks Campbell, AE5J, and Doug Otapal, N5HYD. Then, George Toone, WB5FBJ, a blind amateur, helped by his father and brother, monitored the weather from his father's farm about a mile east of Saragosa, feeding input, along with others of us, into the Skywarn system at Midland.

The tornado came hurtling into Saragosa at 8:16 P.M., just twenty-one minutes after the initial warning was sounded by W5QGG, but there was no local warning system except word-of-mouth out there.

Using the West Texas Connection, Toone began describing the disaster. The news was flashed instantly throughout the vast network sprawled all over the West Texas area. Manager of the Big Bend Emergency Net Bob Ward, WA5ROE, immediately activated the net from his home in Alpine. Listening in on the 2M, Rick Sohl, WB5MPX, got busy loading supplies — gasoline, water, and other needs — and moved them to Ward's home. James Cook, K5FD, arrived at the Ward place about that time, and he assisted Rick in operating the West Texas Connection over WA5ROE. Cook also contacted Bill Brooks, KE5OG, and Dave Cockrum, N5DO, and told them to get the Big Bend ARC's emergency van on the road to Saragosa. Those men, along with Jim Thomas, N5JOE, arrived at the scene of destruction in Saragosa that evening around 10:50 P.M. They lost no time in setting up their generator, a wire dipole, and putting their station on the air.

In the meantime, we learned that the school over here at Balmorhea was going to be base camp for all the sleeping shelters, the Red Cross, Salvation Army, and other emergency and governmental agencies. Our school being the only usable large buildings within thirty-five miles of Saragosa made it the only practical place for use in this terrible emergency.

Once I learned I would not be needed in Saragosa, I drove the school bus back here. Before leaving Saragosa, I stopped by the communications van and borrowed an emergency power supply and brought it on over to the school to set up the radio gear there.

Within an hour after I came back here, we had the communications going right in my classroom. We had the HF rig, and we had the VHF rig going — the two-meter band. The UHF is strictly short-haul communications, and the VHF is the long-haul service. This second one enabled me to run communications to Dallas, and we began running emergency messages for the people of the two towns here who were cut off from the outside world.

With our telephones out, and after the initial newscast that both Balmorhea and Saragosa had been wiped out, there were a lot of anxious people from all over the country who were frantic for news, and we were happy to help with communication. We continued throughout that night with this work of relaying messages for people who came in and requested it.

One of the guys who helped — I'd say he was only about eighteen years old — stayed with us roughly twenty-four hours, manning the radio. He took a nap now and then when nothing was coming in or going out, but he stayed right on, never leaving his post. His name was Ken Clouse, licensed at that time only a couple of weeks. He did a great job! I stayed up all night, too, and Ken's manning the radio freed me up for a lot of miscellaneous tasks — matters I needed to handle, some of it being interviews by news reporters, furnishing important information to them.

About sixty messages went out by radio that night, and an undetermined number came in — one of them from somewhere in Old Mexico inquiring about Ramon Meneses. I think it was his uncle over there. Another came in from Houston, from his sister Rita, I believe.

Through the West Texas Connection, which is the two-meter amateur radio that connects the Permian Basin, we all kept in touch. In another sense some of us . . . were a vital information link with the outside world. During that never-ending night, reporters came in from everywhere . . . They were sometimes a bother, but I always felt that the people out there . . . were desperately eager for news which they deserved to hear.

When the BBARC came to Saragosa, they stayed on for about two days and maintained communications during that time. Once they felt that all the action could be transferred to Balmorhea, they took down their antennas, folded their gear, and returned to Alpine with the parting word to us here that if we needed them, they were as close as a radio set. In the meantime, we continued to use their emergency 80m/40 meter dipole antenna, which we strung up and used for the balance of the week.

All of the radio equipment used in our communications center here at Balmorhea was my own. I already had radio equipment set up in my classroom, gear with which I had tried, during the school year, to get some junior high students involved. This was older, tube-type gear, about twenty-five years old. Since the power was all off, we came over to my own radio shack at home and picked up a battery-powered rig. It is compatible with both battery and 110-volt power. I had fully charged batteries, and so we used it for our long-haul emergency operations . . .

Most people do not know the benefit of amateur radio — what it can do in a pinch. It is generally considered to be a hobby, nothing more, but if you check on disasters, you will find that the amateurs always come in and render invaluable aid.

Let me explain a bit about the network out here known as the West Texas Connection. It is approximately thirteen repeaters set up on some high mountain peaks — thousand-foot radio antennas — any place where they can gain some height. These repeaters cover the Permian Basin as far south as Lajitas, as far west as Sierra Blanca, as far as Lubbock to the north, and as far east as Big Spring, an area of about 60,000 square miles. It is hoped that the connection will connect with San Angelo in the near future.

The whole thought is on with the Station K5QMJ in Odessa, a station operated by . . . Jim Jeffers. Most of the stuff is his personally — set up with his personal gear, no money coming in, except his own personal outlays . . . or, money from anybody who desires to donate to the effort.

Jim Jeffers and several other amateurs who own these repeaters all together make up the West Texas Connection. This WTC is connected to the weather station at Midland Terminal in Odessa in the event of bad weather. When the amateurs in Odessa feel like it is necessary to man it, they bring the station on the air, and those people who report their findings from it are usually from the Sky Warn.

So, the WTC is the brain child of Jim Jeffers, W5QMJ . . . a man with an enormous investment in personal equipment, a man who is dedicated to amateur radio and to communication with his fellow citizens, not merely as a friendship hobby, but as a far-flung communications network ready for instant mobilization the minute disaster strikes anywhere in the region. Health, human welfare, and personal communication are possible during emergencies when other facilities and power are out in such situations as we experienced in Saragosa.

Once our emergency was finally over here, there were some two-hundred and thirty-six messages that had passed through the HF net, not to mention countless hundreds more that passed via the two-meter band. Jim Jeffers' foresight and investment was a real godsend for Saragosa, and he is due a great deal of thanks and appreciation, as are the numberless men and women out there who did their part, unsung and without heroics to draw attention to themselves. I only wish it were possible to list all of those wonderful radio amateurs who assisted us in both the weather watch and the disaster as they manned their sets and assisted with both net control and relays. The West Texas Connection is a priceless asset to the entire West Texas region, because it is ever ready to swing into action whenever any situation anywhere calls for its services. Had WTC not existed, the local communications, so essential after the storm, could not have taken place between such places as Balmorhea, Saragosa, Pecos, and many other places. The WTC coordinated their efforts and matched them to the needs.

Speaking of coordination . . . the other day lightning went in on one of Jim Jeffers's repeaters in Odessa and burned the thing out, and it was a half an hour or longer, possibly an hour, before he could get this thing back on the air again. He did it, though, because he knew how vital that the WTC is to communications there at Weather Central at the Midland Terminal.

Survival in an uncertain world is the name of the game. Like insurance, if you don't have it when you need it, it is impossible to get it. We are both veterans of World War II, and we know the value of survival preparedness.

[I pointed out that the school systems should cut into athletics enough to incorporate nationwide survival training into the curriculum of our public schools. We all stand in certain peril if we don't.]

Let me lay one on you: in case of atomic attack, the old tube-type radio with batteries, which we have cast aside in our society, would continue to operate, whereas, our new sophisticated electronic gadgets with transistors in radio communication would go by the wayside! There will be an electromagnetic excitement — an average of voltage beyond human comprehension! We now have surge black boxes in our computers these days, but these are but small defenses for our electronic equipment, small things too puny to match the monstrous thing that could happen . . .

Your old battery radio rig like I've got back there on the

shelf — take it and your old emergency generator that powers with a standby can of gasoline, and you're still in business when all other communications systems are smashed out. I guess that's the main reason I won't get rid of my old tube equipment . . .

A few of us are ready to roll with our old rigs and batteries and gasoline and emergency generators. We only hope there is someone out there in the net with whom we can talk!

We are going to have to come up with a sensibly realistic plan that embodies both communication and cooperation. And I'm holding my Army MARS back here . . . you know, Military Amateur Radio System. A very good example of cooperative effort in communication is Military Amateur Radio, its primary purpose being its use in cases of emergency. We relay messages for military personnel to their families in time of need or during holiday seasons.

Each Sunday morning at 8:30 A.M. we check in to a network of ham stations, using the special frequency 3922 kilohertz — the Big Bend Emergency Network. This radio net covers New Mexico, Arizona, Texas — as far east as Dallas — and then a portion of Oklahoma. This network pretty well serves the Southwest where about fifty amateurs are involved, and it is growing . . .

When these people saw the need in Saragosa, they stepped in and filled the bill for communications to a significant extent. Alpine was alerted down there, and in short order all of the members got into the act. Whatever any one of us said through the system of eighteen or twenty repeaters situated up there on the McElroy Ranch in the Davis Mountains was broadcast out over about 6,000 square miles of the Permian Basin, and beyond.

The repeater mounted in high places on two antennae repeats everything that is broadcast into it. It relays the messages on, and is picked up and repeated in an ever-expanding geographical circumference, giving greatly expanded coverage to any broadcast. This equipment and our own portable sets give us tremendous flexibility. We carry hand-held sets out in the field — the HTs I mentioned earlier, otherwise termed "Handie-Talkies"; they are the counterpart of our old World War II Walkie-Talkies . . .

So, as you can see, amateur radio is a vital link with scores of uses and applications. We hope there will never be another Saragosa tragedy again . . . anywhere, but we know that, in our weather, war, and violence-prone world, future contingencies will arise, and we stand ready and available for instant mobilization to confront the need, whatever it may be, and wherever it may arise.

— Charles Towry

[Epilogue]

The New Saragosa: A Sitting Duck?

The little town is building back, thanks to the selfless help and contributions of the American people and their government. One watches with mixed delight and misgivings as now the new Saragosa, like the Phoenix, is slowly emerging from the ash heap of her own destruction, spawning out there in a desert of fond dreams dashed on the desolate rocks of trauma.

Crushed but courageous folks seem now less afraid, and yet most live in fear. Wrapped up in a compelling aura of friendship in the new awakening dream of hope, they bud now, hoping to blossom later in the recognition of caring fellow human beings. A great half-conquered unhappiness and pain lies back of their elation as new houses for homeless families push upward. Elation is contagious, and one moves about among the town builders at Saragosa these days feeling a great deal of joy and personal pride for them. Seeming to stand higher than the Sierra Nevada, these modest cottages rise from the desolate sands.

Realistically, however, there are misgivings voiced here and there. Some say a tornado will never strike here again, while others voice fears that it just might. "I don't think I could ever sleep soundly out there any time the weather seemed unsettled . . . I'm afraid of it." Some who were heard making such negative statements in the early weeks following the storm are now accepting houses built for them. One man, however, moved his house away.

One wonders what misgivings go through their minds. "Definitely not! We're moving on. No more Saragosa for me and mine," some vowed before departing the town.

These are the voices of the people, and mine is but one other voice in the debate, virtually the voice of a bystander adding further dissonance to the disharmonious chorus. I do not see myself as a prophet of doom, but, realist that I am, I cannot avoid wondering whether the town, the new Saragosa now in the making, is a sitting duck for another killer tornado. Are people at risk out there more than elsewhere?

As a nine-year resident of nearby Balmorhea, and somewhat of a weather watcher all of my life, I have observed a characteristic wind-flow pattern that affects the weather about these sister towns with almost predictable consistency.

Weather develops and flexes its muscle in, or near, the Davis Mountain range to the south and west of us here. The foothills encroach almost to the doorsteps of Balmorhea on nearly all sides. There are resident volcanic upthrusts and mounds at the community of Brogado, to the east one mile where a line of hills leads off the land features at Brogado, toward Balmorhea Lake a distance of two miles south. To the southwest and west, the basin is dotted with hills and low mountain scarps ascending to the shoulders of the mountains themselves. More hills are sprinkled to the north of our town two or three miles distant. While all of these land features create picturesque views for the tourist, the local nature lover, and the camera bug, they do, as well, act as partial diversionary wind-flow barriers that seem greatly to influence local weather.

Like islands in a bay influencing the flow patterns of ocean currents, the hills that dot our scene affect the wind flowing over them, causing the tendency to skirt around and between them in definite currents — bringing them to bear on Saragosa rather than on Balmorhea.

Ours is a desert country where powerful clashes occur between dry cool fronts and hot moisture-laden air masses as both migrate in here during the spring and summer seasons. Cool fronts out of the north and northwest bring in winds that square off with the warm, moist gulf air masses moving out of the south and southwest. Toward and upon the Davis Mountains, cloud columns mushroom and grow; they either ride the crests in a typical northerly direction or debouch downward, riding the ridges toward Balmorhea. As they drive straight toward us, their grim aspect betrays the anger of mass wind-tormented cloud formations about to vent their bitterness upon the entire basin. Down they come, racing across the rocky crust of the stony tablelands in bursts of invincible obstinancy, overspreading the skies with dust and dirty weather and leaving the foothills wallowing in cascades of beautiful rain.

On such rain-promising events, often when the land languishes, sear and thirsty, newcomers have heightened hopes that soon rains will relieve the trauma of man and beast and shrub.

Those who are accustomed to giving the wind-flow patterns a bit of serious attention are not fooled, however. Clouds out toward the mountains promise all, but seldom deliver a load of water to the town. Dark, moisture-laden thunderstorms, rapidly building up with promise of rain, soon form a solid wall to the west, south, and southwest, and move toward town. But our trees and flowers seldom delight in a thirst-quenching drink from that quarter. Neighboring farm and ranch houses melt from view behind a curtain of life-giving rain to the west of town, but one watches in vain as an uncanny thing nearly always occurs.

The promising clouds invariably choose one of several options: They split and freight their weight of water around the town to the south and to the north; or, they gather in a mass and move around us one way or the other, watering the lake and desert beyond the line of hills to the south and east; or the precipitation follows the line of Toya Creek to the north of town and to the north of it beyond the interstate, some two miles away.

The rainclouds, typically bypassing our town, tend to reconverge to the east and northeast, and then to bear directly in upon Saragosa. Thus the little town seems to lie, like nine pins in a bowling lane, right on target for the mainstream of weather activity to this basin country. Clouds that form in the flatlands to the northwest, near the head of the mountains, pose the greater threat. As they move down our way, they gain strength and follow a path parallel to the range that brings them due south, then move into a sweeping curve that swings them through a "J" pattern, hurling them east-northeast once more, right over Saragosa. The town has suffered tornado activity before, with funnels in the vicinity and three that have struck the town.

Jose Muñiz pointed to a few evidences of a long-gone structure just across from his home. "A cotton gin stood there for many years," he explained. "It was hit by a twister in 1977. The funnel was bearing directly upon our house here, but it veered off and missed us just like this last one did! It came from exactly the same direction," he concluded, pointing from his yard on the southwestern edge of Saragosa, the edge of town missed by the recent tornado. His finger, aimed like a rifle, was oriented toward the southwest, in the direction of Balmorhea. "It came straight at us from out there, then it banked into a turn right about the spot where this recent one turned and zeroed in on the town."

Pat Brijalba told me of watching a funnel cloud that bore down upon the town in 1975. Richard Contreras later confirmed his account as to the year. It wheeled aside from its course, missing Saragosa and damaging a barn just south of town. This twister followed the same path as our recent one, according to Brijalba.

He related another incident that occurred when he was a boy. A vicious storm which he thought was a tornado struck and partially wiped out "old" Saragosa, which was then located about two miles to the north, northeast of the present site of the town. That incident occurred in the 1930s.

A descrepancy appears between dates and labels regarding the "old" Saragosa to which Brijalba alludes, and the "new" Saragosa. Jay Oates, a longtime resident in Balmorhea, refers to the now-abandoned "old" Saragosa as "new" Saragosa, with the following explanation:

> A long time ago, it seems, some farmer allowed a Mexican laborer to build a small house out there where Saragosa now is. As time went by, other workers came and added a shed room onto the original shack, and thus the community had its start. This small village grew into what is now known as Saragosa. This was the original, or "old" Saragosa. In time a site was chosen about a mile north, and settlers built there.
>
> During the 1920s it had become quite a town, the "new" Saragosa. It boasted a bank, a hotel, a grocery store, and a railroad station across from the spot where the Hamilton house still stands. A small gasoline-driven streetcar-type trolley which became known locally as "The Toonerville Trolley" made a daily run out from Pecos and back. It brought in the mail and some small freight, and it hauled passengers.
>
> Along about 1928 or '29 the Saragosa school, which was located in "old" Saragosa, and which I attended, was consolidated with the Pecos schools, thirty miles away. The people who had set-

> tled in New Saragosa were very unhappy about this school consolidation, because they did not wish their kids to ride the sixty-mile round trip each day. My dad moved his family to Balmorhea, and eventually all of the other families left New Saragosa, most of them moving to Balmorhea to send their children to school here. This is how the "new" Saragosa died. A few of the families moved to "old" Saragosa, but most of them came to Balmorhea.
>
> When all of the residents abandoned the new town, it quite naturally died. The business enterprises closed down, and the trolley ceased operations after a while. "Old" Saragosa grew some from the move, but never did amount to much as to growth, and remained static until the tornado wiped it out this year.

Beary Woods related a story of one tornado that came down in the mountains to the west. "That tornado hit the top of a high mountain, and then sheered off at least a half a mile of timber along a path 200 yards wide! That happened back about 1935, according to my dad. He has been up there and seen the scars inflicted years ago. He ranched in that region for a long time, and remembers it very well."

The longtime farm operator Larry Turnbough was in his fields near Saragosa when the 1977 tornado developed nearby.

> I watched a small ropelike tornado ten years ago when we were told that tornados were possible but not probable out here, particularly the big, killer types — don't worry about them!
>
> But I watched that thing from the very start until it quit. Greg Perrin and I were running tractors in that field where our barn was hit this time . . .
>
> We were on our tractors, side-by-side, heading to the south. The sun was out — no clouds over us, but there was a big, heavy thunderstorm that stretched from right north of Balmorhea on toward Toya, to the north. The line of thunderstorms must have been twenty miles long. South of IH-10 it was clear and dry.
>
> I glanced up and saw this cloud to the west, its underside shaped like a point. Greg was raised in Hamlin, Texas, in tornado country, and recognized the thing for what it was. We found a safe place, taking refuge in the edge of a dirt tank, and watched the long, thin funnel hit the ground spinning and stirring up a tremendous dirt cloud, growing larger and larger at the base, but remaining a small funnel high above. As it bore down on the Cuban's house to the west of us, we thought we would see it disintegrate, but the dust storm blocked our view, and when it cleared the house was still standing.

> The funnel was a weird thing, dangling and snaking around from ground to cloud base, part of it at times suspended directly over our heads, but tilted at such an angle that it would be in contact with the ground at least half a mile away. Dangling ropelike, it traveled about 150 yards behind that two-story house, then moved slowly on in a northeasterly path toward Saragosa. Once it was beyond us, we followed it in our pickup and watched it turn from its path, moving east, playing around in those fields just south of town, then heading due east toward Mr. Rowe's house, the one Bob Walker owns now . . . or did before this last storm. Once again the funnel changed directions, heading a little bit southeast, crossing highway 17 where the gin yard is located right across from Dale Toone's barn. It played havoc with corrugated tin sections and other objects there at the gin, then moved on and played out just after crossing the road to the north of our house a bit east of Saragosa.

Larry Turnbough hesitated, his mind ten years behind us. "So, the Cuban house has had a tornado pass only 150 yards on each side of it. One I saw, the other crossed my fields, leaving its unmistakable trail."

Turnbough summed up his beliefs on local patterns of dangerous weather:

> The weather we have to watch here comes from the northwest. Weather from the mountains doesn't pack much of a punch, but those wall clouds and thunderstorms that develop out in those flats to the north and west of us are the ones to watch for really dangerous weather. Both of these tornados circled in from the northwest and curved in, bearing right down on Saragosa. That is where our potential for really bad weather lies.
>
> I observed that every building that went down out in Saragosa showed the worst damage on the east and north sides. The tornadic winds move in a counter-clockwise direction. As that thing approached from the south or southwest, the direction of its wind curling around each building at unbelievable speeds and force smashed into the east and north sides, doing the greatest damage there. I noticed at the Community Center, where Pat and Corina Brijalba were on the south side near the southwest corner, that part of the wall and corner were still partially standing. The same was true of the Walker home and the Adventist bakery. Everything left standing at Saragosa was on the south side of the buildings — usually the southeast and southwest corners and some of the south walls. So, it appears that one is safest

> lying flat against the wall on the same side from which the tornado is approaching a building. If there was any consistent pattern observable at all in the rubble and remains of Saragosa, that was it. But you can't outguess a tornado! My best thought is that if you see one, and have time to drive away, do so! I'll take my chances in a car, if possible, driving at a right angle to the path of the funnel. I feel a person's best chance is in intelligent flight.

Others have reported these natural troublemakers associated with weather in this area. Pete Vasquez described a tornado that he once witnessed in a most unlikely place. It was up in the Davis Mountains to the west of Balmorhea and Saragosa. "It came down in the mountains away up near Madiera Canyon," Pete said, adding, "That twister went down a steep mountain slope and off into an arroyo. Then it came out on the other side and just kept lifting itself until it disappeared right on back into the cloud above."

Alfredo Matta described a similar incident when he saw a tornado thrashing its way up in the canyon and mountain wilds of the Davis range. "It was on the Lasco Ranch, up in the mountains a ways, and it came down out of a storm cloud. It ran along the ground, zig-zagging like a snake for some distance, then went back up again."

On a recent trip to my home in the Colorado Rockies, I was discussing with friends Bill Mormon and Susan Marshall the Saragosa story when they told of a vicious tornado that had but a few days previously hit in the high country of the Rockies, "mowing down a wide swath of trees in a heavily timbered area." This incredible story reminded me of another surprise call made by a tornado not far from Jasper, Texas, deep in the East Texas timberlands where I lived in the mid-1970s. The twister cut a path of destruction through thick timber just to the north of the small town of Colmsneil. I drove over for a look and was amazed at the unbelievable destruction done to the timber.

In my knowledge and experience prior to that, the most common ground for twisters had been out in the flatlands where they strike with surprising swiftness and strength and with little surface resistance as they sweep along. With my kid brother, I stood once on the front porch of a house in Central Texas and watched as a twister tore past us, not a hundred yards away, leaving a flood of water three feet deep in the yard. I never forgot the date: May 25, 1935. On another occasion I stood with my kids in a cornfield on the banks of the Washita River in Oklahoma as we interrupted our collecting of arrowheads a minute to watch a tornado drive by in all its frenzy; then we returned to the greater fascination of our hobby. Again, I watched from the levee of the Trinity River in Dallas, Texas, on April 4, 1957, as people fled in headlong desperation before a tornado tore through Oak Cliff, crossed the Trinity bottoms, then went ripping up Harry Hines Boulevard.

I suppose my first tornado sighting occurred when I was a very young boy and watched with my family from the door to our storm cellar one dark night as a tornado blew away Frost, Texas, killing a reported twenty-two persons. I visited the devastated sites following the tornados at Waco, Wichita Falls, Lubbock, and Sweetwater, Texas, learning what I could of the nature of such storms and, having learned a little, wishing I might learn far more. My hope is that science might learn far more for the education and benefit of mankind as a whole. As I respect but do not fear electricity and rattlesnakes, so I respect but do not fear tornados. The ability to cope with natural dangers stems from knowledge and understanding, the first requisites for survival.

We understand better the behavior of electricity than we do tornados. Perhaps more study of tornados should be done with a view toward understanding how to predict and cope with them and thus to be competent in knowing how to sidestep their malicious onslaught. They surely follow some well-defined natural laws of physics, of motion, direction, and intensity. We need to convert our general understanding of their predictability and behavior into in-depth and specific comprehension of these phenomena of nature that, like the rattlesnake, can be both beautiful and destructive at the same moment.

On a recent visit with some friends in Saragosa, we were discussing the usual topic of conversation, tornados. Their homes, being on the western periphery of the town, were spared by both the 1977 and the 1987 tornados. Offhandedly, I hinted that it might not be a bad idea if they dug a storm cellar on the southwest part of their property, so situated as to prevent their house being blown on top of the cellar and blocking the exit. There were some very positive responses to the suggestion. "A very good idea! We had even thought of building something like that. And this whole community needs something . . ."

We discussed the feasibility of four large underground shelters, one in each quadrant of the town, large enough to hold thirty or forty persons

— if and when. But people, in their quest for creature comforts, are often too short-sighted to be survival-minded, or so it seems to me.

We learn terrible lessons from wars, floods, fires, famines, tornados, and hurricanes, but the hard-won lessons are all-too-soon forgotten, and we become sitting ducks all over again. One can only hope that the Saragosa tragedy is never repeated, or that, if another tornado comes, the town will not be trapped and ill-prepared to survive. The new All-Purpose Community Building, now begun by the Meadows Foundation, has a huge storm cellar designed for its basement, along with a warning siren mounted high upon a tower.

Is Saragosa a sitting duck, awaiting another tornado? I certainly do not profess to know, but I have noted here indications worthy of consideration by everyone concerned. Time will tell.

We cannot touch tomorrow any more than we can touch and dissuade a tornado. When tomorrow comes, bringing whatever it will, we must and shall touch it then. Today, we can only anticipate it and prepare ourselves a little better for its eventualities. Edmund Burke once wrote, "You can never plan the future by the past." Perhaps not, but cannot we, in some large or small measure, prepare for it by learning some sober lessons from past mistakes and pains?

Those of us who endured the Saragosa tornado wish you "absit omen" — may there be no ill omen. But, should one come in the wake of a wall cloud, or in any other form, may we suggest, with Dante, "The arrow seen before cometh less rudely." Be alert to its coming, and step aside.

Storm-Tossed Passage

(Written in memory of
Kathy Escovedo and Elvira Casias)

A songbird to my garden daily came
Year after year, summer, winter, and spring,
And her sweet melodies sung to me there
Were songs of youth to lasting love and care.
That lilting voice now silenced, mute and still,
Has quit my world to quiet; my empty hill
Is lonely now, and ever deep within
My heart sustains a hurt too large for time to mend.

My garden suffers, too, a vacant space
Where grew a special flower with upturned face
Reflecting sunshine, it blossomed there for me,
But took leave with the bird from nearby tree.

Both symbolized some sweet perpetual spring
Of youth, of hope that urged the heart to sing.
But these receded early far away,
Forsaking very life as it began its day.

What brutal mystery this wanton waste?
What painful cup of dregs the soul must taste!
The human heart, like heaven and earth, is stilled,
Breathless and numb, with pain and sorrow filled.
Hushed all, as well, from starry hosts nearby.
Brief, brave, and gracious grew their short career,
Abridged youth's precious promises down here.

Tears now unmeasured flow besides my own:
Enough to fill an ocean full are flown . . .
In one benumbing moment, can it be?
They left us to wander Eternity!
And in a fleeting moment plunged our years
To grief, and turned our blood to endless tears.
When I last saw their sweet brown eyes, they smiled
In parting then . . . so unlike now! Oh, Child!

In retrospect I cry and contemplate
How sudden stormy winds can seal one's fate
And hurl sweet life into a headlong flight,
Paled out and gone . . . blended with hues of night,
Their tender touch lent charm to each caress,
Enduring time in memory now to bless;
Like lovely lilies, given once to me,
That time would wither, fade, and free
Of further pleasant charm to human touch
I never can again reject as such!

Let pleasant memory live, though they be gone . . .
The sweet and silent spell live on and on!
One's lilting voice of charm, one's fragrance fair
Wrung now to wounds time never can repair . . .
Which lack the power to kill, but cannot heal,
Yet, in my heart and on my harp I feel
Both instruments have lost a precious string . . .
So, I to grief and gladness both shall cling,
Blend of sweet memory with poignant pain,
And what, to some, may seem a dreary strain
Of no forgetfulness shall ever seem
To me a grand tribute and glorious theme:
Of Nature hushed, intense for you, Dear Ones alone,
Stunned out of sense at your momentous going Home!

One moment in the swirl of storm that night,
Torn from life's moorings your sweet souls took flight,
Leaving two ghastly gaps behind down here
Where broken heart and bitter scalding tear
Fell earthbound, mute by battlement, wind-torn,
While dying day winked out, where wind and storm
Obscured the light of sun while day departs,
To give place to a night of broken hearts.

Broken, a mirror still will multiply,
Cast images at angles, all awry:
The sweet mirror of Life of blows will break,
The more to reflect sorrow in its wake . . .
To Thee, Sweet Kathy, one final Adieu,
And to our Dear Elvira, Goodbye, too . . .
To each of you whose dust was once on fire,
Aflame with all life's true modest desire.

These words, for you, now woven into song,
Voice but a sigh of sorrow stretching long . . .
Children of Love, tho' born in bitterness,
Countless the hearts that you both warmed and blessed;
And tho' your graves have closed between us now,
In God's own Time, we'll meet again, I vow . . .
Parted for time, but 'ere long it may be
We'll embrace once again in Fair Eternity.

Derwood Lane
June 15, 1987

Kathy Escovedo and Elvira Casias

Eddie Lopez

A scene of devastation at Saragosa the morning after the tornado.

Saragosa — second day after the storm.

Saragosa reduced to rubble.

A portion of Saragosa that was not blown away, seen on the southwestern edge of town looking toward the Davis Mountains.

Destruction in the wake of the Saragosa storm.

Toya Creek and Saragosa, after the removal of much of the rubble.

Lower foreground: Gallegos Bar and residence where some took refuge.

Raul Lopez's red Camaro after it had been righted following the storm.

Second from left: Ted Galindo, section foreman, Texas Highway Department, Pecos, Texas, directs clean-up operations following Saragosa disaster.

Aerial photos of Saragosa after the tornado.

Gary Boagas, left, and Jim Brown of Pecos, volunteers in clearing rubble following the tornado at Saragosa.

An unidentified worker, thought to be from Carlsbad, New Mexico, assists in cleanup operations following the storm.

After the tornado at the Bob Walker home.

Kiki's automobile.

Charles Towry

Glenn Humphries

Retired Baptist men from Iowa Park, Texas. (Rear, from left) Joe Singer, Virgil Woodfin; (front) Terrell Silvers, Joe Ward, Russell Guyette, Bill Curry, Charles Heacock. Others not shown: Glen Miller, Jack Railsback, Clyde Patterson, Wayne Williams, John and Peggy Miller, Garrett Marshall (Wichita Falls), and Wesley Prougre (Monahans). These men built another home for Tomas Lopez.

[Ra]chel Carrillo was flung [th]rough the air and around [th]e building with her mother [du]ring the tornado.

Delia Rodriguez

Ramon (Kiki) Meneses

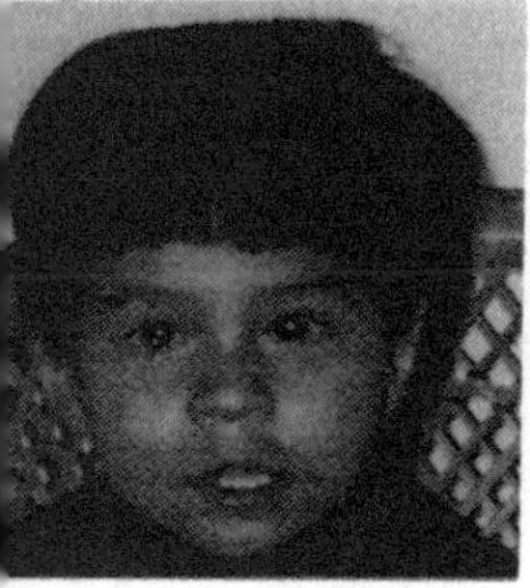

Andrew Morales

Armando Morales lost his parents and baby brother.

Dorothy Berdan died with her husband Herbert.

Herbert Berdan

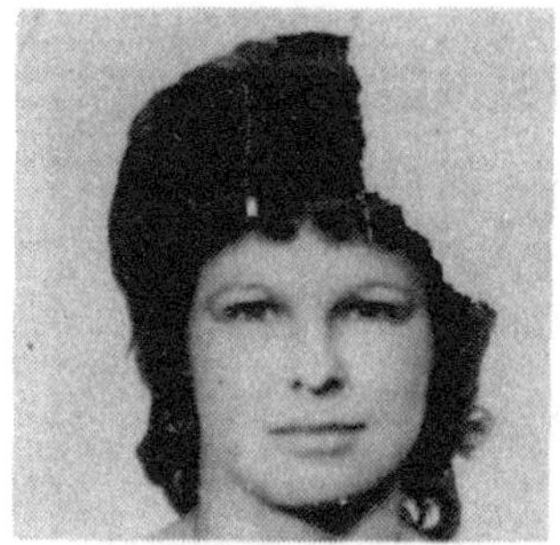

Juanita Casias

Albino Casias

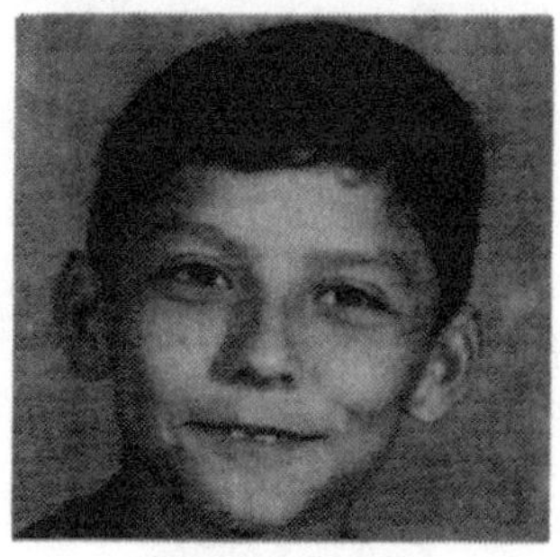

Adrian Casias

Antonia Madrid

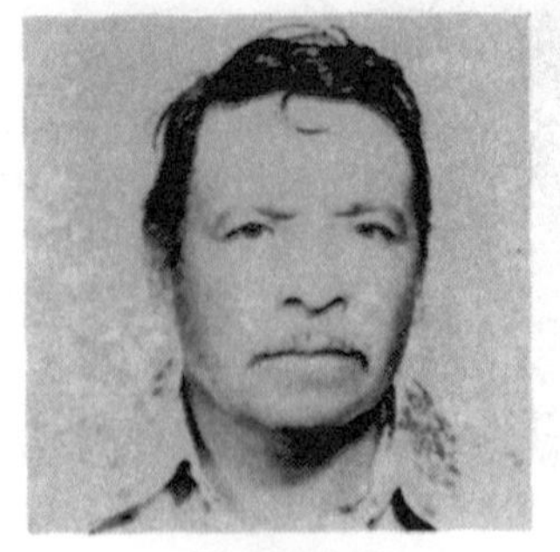

Jose Madrid

Irma Garza

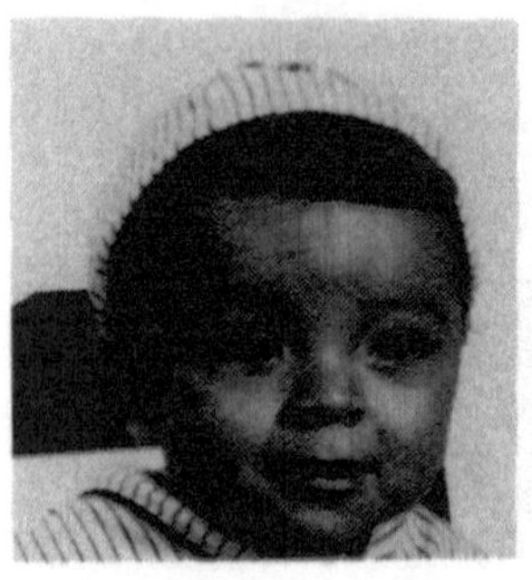

Joe Lionel Garza, Jr.

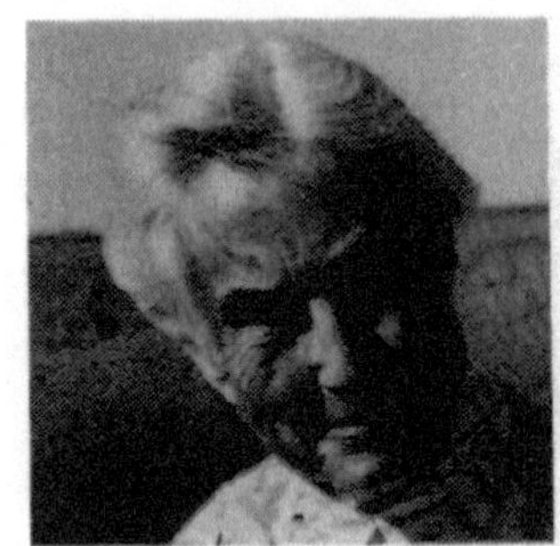

Esther Lansberry, eighty-seventh birthday.

Jose Candelas made forty cement blocks a day to rebuild his store.

Billy Joe Lozano

Aidee Muniz

Lucas Carrillo saved others' lives but lost his own.

Corina Morales

ge Martinez and daughter xanne.

Socorro Rodriguez

Liberty Ray Wofford, grandson of Pete and Socorro Vasquez.

gelica Casias, saved when ıds rolled her up in a rug ke a cigarette."

Dora Vasquez, saved by a suitcase.

Lucia Lozano

Paul Matta

Joel Muniz

Jose Muniz

Maria del Socorro Balderas

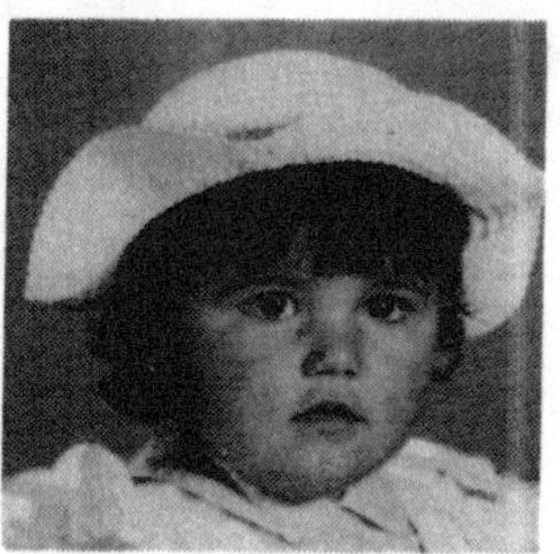

Amber Briceño

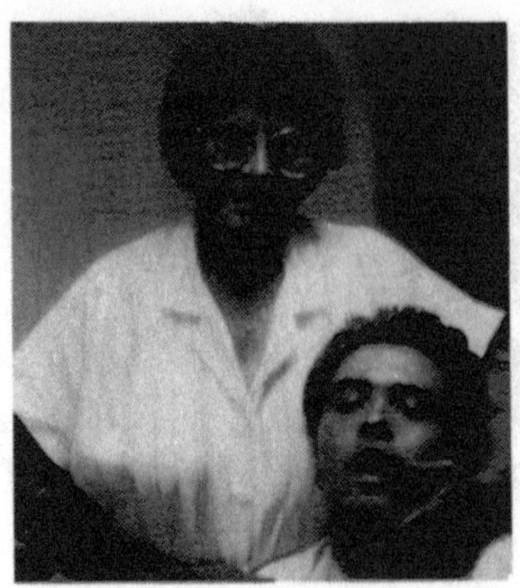

Mrs. Lydia Meneses and her invalid son Ramon (Kiki), a year after the storm.

Fernando Balderas, who lost his wife Socorro, is shown with daughters Maria de la Luz and Ampara.

Olga and Joe Mendosa with Joe Derrick, their son, who was in the ill-fated Head Start graduation at Saragosa, and Robbie Dwayne, the younger child.

Lionel Garza, his wife Irma and daughters Abigail and Joanna.

(From left) Orlando Contreras, his sister Olga in wedding dress, Olivia Contreras (her mother, killed in tornado), Jacob Mendoza. Boy in front of Orlando is Gerald Contreras.

Bob and Peggy Walker

Corina and Anastacio Morales, parents of Andrew. All three lost their lives at the Head Start graduation.

Delilah Alvarez

Omero and Sylvestra Sanchez, who died in the Community Center. With them, top to bottom, are their children: Jacob, Alexa, and Debra.

Joe and Amparo Gallegos hid under the Toya Creek bridge.

(From left, clockwise) Ricky, Jerediah, Elda, and Kevin Montes.

Pedro and Eva Meras, who died in the tornado, shown with grandchildren.

(From left) Tomas Lopez, wife Maria de Jesus, daughter Elizabeth and son Raul.

Pat and Corina Brijalba.

(From left, top down) Marlene, Eddie, Hector, Linda, and Amber Briceño.

(From left) Martin, Matthew, Becky, and Orlando Sanchez.

Astolfo and Norma Carrasco and baby Jose.

Ninfa Ontiveras

Miriam Mondragon and Octavio Muñiz.

Jimmy Gallegos and wife Regina with their daughter, Jo Gina Lee.

The Wendt family. (From left, back row) Bill, Kara and Mara; (center) Hazel; (front row) Billy, Jr., Willina.

Teresa Quintana (third from left, top row).

Jose and Pas Candelas after their store was rebuilt by Catholic Charities.

Matilde Prieto

Linda, Javier, and son Billy Joe Lozano.

(From left) Amelia Carrillo, Danny Carrillo, Corina and Pat Brijalba.

Pete and Socorro Vasquez.

Rose Mary and Rose Lynn, twin daughters of Mary Lou and Joe Apodaca.

Rene, Alex, Natividad, and Frank Ramirez, whose home was blown away while part of the family was inside.

Elie and Floyd Estrada

Eddie and Debbie Lopez and their parents rode out the storm in a car.

Israel and Victor Mondragon.

(From left) Jason, Isela, Ernesto Bordayo, and daughter.

Photograph Contributors

Derwood Lane
Tomas Lopez
J. F. Gassett
George Arranda
Jesus Matta
Kelly Perryman
Saragosa Mission, Inc.
Miriam Mondragon
Bob and Peggy Walker
Joe and Pas Candelas
Joel Muniz
Lisa Carrillo
Delia Rodriguez
Olga Barrera
Genora Prewit, Pecos Museum
Maribel Morales Ortega
Delilah Alvarez
Joe and Amparo Gallegos
Elda Montes
G. Cruz Casias
Lorena Avalos
Norma Carrasco
Lydia Machuca
Jimmy Gallegos
Linda Briceño
Linda and Javier Lozano
Aidee Muniz
Corina Brijalba
Belen Rodriguez
Pete Vasquez
Orlando and Becky Sanchez
Ernesto Bordajo
Brenda Lopez
Estrada Family
Paul Matta
Charles Towry
Donnie Hall

Index

About the Author

For eight and a half years, Derwood Lane served as a high school English teacher in the Balmorhea, Texas, public schools.

Reared on a Central Texas cotton farm near Corsicana, he earned a bachelor's degree in English and Bible from John Brown University in Siloam Springs, Arkansas, and a master's degree in vocational-technical education from North Texas State University.

He pursued graduate studies in anthropology, education, psychology, music, art, and English at the University of Oklahoma (Norman), Central State College (Edmond, Oklahoma), the University of California at Riverside, Northern Arizona University (Flagstaff), and Texas A&M University.

His sixteen-year teaching career included work with the Bureau of Indian Affairs on the Navajo Reservation, as well as positions in Texas public schools.

Lane's varied career has also included ownership of an antiques business and a natural history museum, as well as service as president of a food industry company. He has additionally worked as an archaeologist at Mesa Verde National Park in Colorado. During World War II, he served in the U.S. Army from 1942 to 1943.

He and his wife, Raquel, retired to Salida, Colorado.

www.ingramcontent.com/pod-product-compliance
Lightning Source LLC
LaVergne TN
LVHW091125080826
845145LV00008B/2047

* 9 7 8 1 6 8 1 7 9 3 9 7 9 *